Lotus 1-2-3 Self-Taught on the IBM PC

Note to Authors

Do you have a manuscript or software program related to personal computers? Do you have an idea for developing such a project? If so, we would like to hear from you. Brady produces a complete range of books and applications software for the personal computer market. We invite you to write to the Editorial Dept., Brady Books, Prentice Hall Press, One Gulf+Western Plaza, New York, NY 10023.

Limits of Liability and Disclaimer of Warranty

LOTUS™ 1 2 3™

Self-Taught on the IBM PC

Ira Krakow

A BRADY BOOK
Published by Prentice Hall Press
New York, NY 10023

A Brady Book
Published by Prentice Hall Press
A Division of Simon & Schuster, Inc.
Gulf + Western Building
One Gulf + Western Plaza
New York, NY 10023

Library of Congress Cataloging in Publication Data
Krakow, Ira H.
Lotus 1-2-3 self-taught on the IBM PC

Includes index.
1. Lotus 1-2-3 (Computer program) 2. IBM Personal Computer—Programming.
3. Business—Data processing. I. Title. II. Title: Lotus one-two-three self-taught
on the IBM PC
HF5548.4.L67K73 1984 650'.028'5425 84-21612

ISBN 0-89303-628-5

Printed in the United States of America

5 6 7 8 9 10

To Laura and Sam

Acknowledgments

Many people encouraged me to write this book. Particularly, I would like to thank Douglas Cobb, author of several 1-2-3 books and former editor-in-chief of *Absolute Reference: The Journal for 1-2-3 Users*, for publishing a 1-2-3 model of mine in an early edition of the magazine. His confidence in my technical knowledge of 1-2-3 and of my writing ability gave me the impetus to start writing this book.

I also discussed this project with several people at Lotus Development Corporation, who were very helpful and supportive. I would like to thank Ezra Gottheil, who made many suggestions in the early stages of this project, and Steve Miller and Chris Morgan, who encouraged me to push on.

The people at Brady were also helpful and supportive. My editor, Sue Love, and her assistant, Christi Mangold, guided the project to completion skillfully, every step of the way. Barbara Werner did a masterful job getting the book through the production process. I would also like to thank Dave Culverwell for seeing the merit in this kind of book.

Marie Sullivan took the time and had the patience to use a draft version of this book to learn 1-2-3. Her perceptive comments were invaluable.

The reviewers for this book were superb. In particular, the comments of Cynthia Harriman, Eric Weiss, and Dick Ridington were detailed and accurate. If this book is well organized and accurate, a large part of the credit must go to them. Any errors, of course, are mine.

Finally, I would like to thank my wife, Sandra, for her understanding and patience. She has always supported my efforts and encouraged me to try new ventures.

Contents

About This Book

This book is 1) an overview of the IBM PC, and 2) a comprehensive tutorial for Version 1A of Lotus Development Corporation's 1-2-3 software package as it functions on the IBM PC and an IBM PC compatible computers which use the IBM PC keyboard design. The aim of this book is to provide, in one place, the information necessary to operate the IBM PC and to be proficient in 1-2-3.

Almost from the first day of its availability, Lotus 1-2-3 has become the most popular software package available for the PC. In spite of fierce competition, it has remained at the top.

Why such staying power? Because 1-2-3 is easy to use, powerful, and versatile. 1-2-3 is unlike most IBM PC software, in that it wasn't designed for a specific use, such as accounting, word processing, or database management. Rather, 1-2-3 was designed to help you become more productive. Its popularity is due to the enormous variety of applications for which it can be used.

Even though it's powerful, 1-2-3 is easy to learn. If you have never used a program before, you'll quickly feel comfortable with it. If you have used other programs, with complicated command syntax, you'll wish they were designed like 1-2-3.

Lotus Development Corporation understands the need for making 1-2-3 easy to learn. 1-2-3 was one of the first software packages which had an accompanying tutorial diskette. The tutorial is fun to use and introduces you to the basic capabilities of 1-2-3. While you're in 1-2-3, you can press the HELP key [F1]; 1-2-3 tells you what options are available. And the reference manual is comprehensive.

So why *Lotus 1-2-3 Self-Taught?*. This book is not a substitute for 1-2-3's tutorial disk, help screens, or reference manual. Rather, it is a supplement to them. This book is a logical presentation of all 1-2-3 topics in easy-to-grasp chapters. The chapters cover 1-2-3's worksheet (the **1** of **1-2-3**), graphics (the **2**), and information management (the **3**). The advanced worksheet commands and 1-2-3's macro capabilities, are also discussed.

I have more than 10 years of experience in programming, technical writing, and training with a wide variety of computer systems. In September 1983, I started teaching Lotus 1-2-3 classes to all kinds of users, from computer novices to experienced programming professionals. I have also developed many 1-2-3 models, and I have used a number of handy techniques for making model development more efficient. I want to share these techniques with you. Through my teaching and model development experiences, I also have found a number of common pitfalls into which many beginning, and some advanced, users fall. I want to share these pitfalls with you as well.

Organization of the Book

This book is divided into seven parts. The organization is modular, so that if you are familiar with a particular topic, you can skip over it, and start with the unfamiliar topics. On the other hand, even if you have never used a computer before, you can start from the beginning and gradually build up your computer confidence.

Part I (Chapters 1 through 4) introduces the 1-2-3 program, the IBM PC, and the PC-DOS operating system. Chapter 1 introduces a sample 1-2-3 application, a year-end revenue comparison. Even though the example is quite comprehensive, it illustrates only a small part of the many capabilities of 1-2-3. The aim is to demonstrate the avenues of creativity open to you by learning how to use 1-2-3 effectively. If you are unaware of the tremendous potential of 1-2-3, you should read this chapter.

Chapter 2 provides guidelines for configuring the IBM PC hardware memory, disk storage, display monitors, and printers, for efficient use with 1-2-3. Since your hardware configuration affects the types of 1-2-3 applications you can develop, you need to understand these options. At the end of the chapter are three possible PC configurations geared to different levels of use of 1-2-3. If you understand the hardware options available for the PC, you can skip this chapter, although you should read the section on suggested hardware configurations for 1-2-3. If you are confused about hardware options, reading Chapter 2 should help.

Chapter 3 introduces the PC-DOS operating system. Although you don't have to be an expert on all the details of PC-DOS, you do need to know how to use the basic commands: how to run a program, format a disk, copy files, display the directory, and so on. 1-2-3 uses the PC-DOS operating system. To be comfortable using 1-2-3, you must also be comfortable with PC-DOS. A comprehensive PC-DOS exercise, aimed at giving you familiarity with the needed commands, is included. If you have never used PC-DOS before, do the exercise. On the other hand, if you are an old hand at PC-DOS, you can skip this chapter.

Chapter 4, describing the configuration process for 1-2-3, is a must. You cannot use 1-2-3 unless you configure it for the PC hardware and the PC-DOS operating system. Mercifully, the configuration is done infrequently. In fact, if you never change hardware or operating system versions, you do it once. *However, you must do it before you can use 1-2-3.* In addition to describing the configuration process for 1-2-3, the other parts of the Lotus 1-2-3 package are described.

Part II (Chapters 5 and 6) introduces the supporting cast—the Lotus Access System and the 1-2-3 tutorial disk. Along with the 1-2-3 program, Lotus Development Corporation has supplied a set of programs to make using 1-2-3 easier. The Lotus Access System lets you run these programs easily—without you having to remember the names of the programs or on what disk they are found. Using the Lotus Access System, with its user-friendly menu structure, and its extensive help information, is the subject of Chapter 5.

In addition to the Lotus Access System, Lotus includes a tutorial disk, to help get you started in 1-2-3. Chapter 6 describes the tutorial disk. The lessons on the tutorial disk are a good introduction to the capabilities of 1-2-3.

Part III (Chapters 7 through 16) is a thorough grounding in basic 1-2-3 worksheet skills. You must understand the worksheet operations of 1-2-3 because they are the basis of the product. You cannot understand how to use any of the advanced capabilities such as graphics or database management, until you understand how the worksheet is put together.

Chapter 7 discusses how to enter 1-2-3, how 1-2-3 displays the worksheet, how to get help, how to move around the worksheet using the pointer movement keys and the function keys, how to enter simple labels and values into the worksheet, and how to exit 1-2-3. That's quite a bit, but it's absolutely necessary!

Chapter 8 introduces the main 1-2-3 menu and the process of saving a worksheet file on the disk. Chapter 8 also discusses the other disk file management commands you can use in 1-2-3 without having to use PC-DOS. Here's where your understanding of the basic PC-DOS commands is essential, because unless you grasp the discussion of PC-DOS in Chapter 3, you will not understand how 1-2-3 manages the PC-DOS environment.

Chapter 9 is about formulas: how you enter them, and what they mean. The ability to define formulas tells 1-2-3 how to recalculate the worksheet when you change a number. You can make "what-if" changes to your worksheet and have 1-2-3 display the changed worksheet in a flash. Chapter 9 also introduces the concept of functions, which makes formula writing even easier.

Chapter 10 shows you how to use cell ranges—how to define rectangular groups of cells for more efficient 1-2-3 operations. The ability to manipulate groups of cells is one of the keys to unleashing the power of 1-2-3. If you understand how to use cell ranges, you can make 1-2-3 do cartwheels.

Chapters 11 and 12 are concerned with making the worksheet look professional. Chapter 11 shows you how to define numeric formats, to make your numbers display with dollar signs, commas, percent signs, and the like. Chapter 12 discusses creating windows, freezing titles, and protecting and unprotecting cells. With the information contained in these two chapters, you should be able to make 1-2-3 display the worksheet just the way you want it.

Chapter 13 discusses copying and moving cell ranges from one part of the worksheet to another. There are many subtleties involved in copying and moving; the BEWAREs and HOW TOs in Chapter 13 point out the pitfalls and make suggestions for circumventing them.

Chapter 14 discusses inserting and deleting rows and columns. By mastering these commands, you can expand or contract the contents of your worksheet.

Chapter 15 discusses recalculating the worksheet and describes subtle problems you might encounter, such as forward references and circular references, and gives you tips on how to troubleshoot these problems.

Sooner or later, you'll want a printout of your worksheet. With 1-2-3, you can enter a few simple commands and get a printout almost immediately. Or, you can add all sorts of options, such as headers, footers, and border columns. If you are using the IBM PC dot matrix printer, Chapter 16 shows you how to use setup strings to create italic, boldface, and compressed print, and even how to set your own line spacing!

Part IV (Chapters 17 through 19) deals with advanced worksheet capabilities. After mastering these chapters, you should be able to write even the most complex worksheets using these advanced capabilities, which are not as widely known as they should be. Chapter 17 deals with advanced formulas and functions. It also covers writing complicated formulas using logical expressions, as well as using all of the 1-2-3 functions, except the database statistical functions which are discussed with databases. The section on list and table lookup functions shows you several alternatives for calculating the number of days in a particular month, taking into account whether the year is a leap year or not.

Chapter 18 shows you how to incorporate data in other 1-2-3 worksheet files into your worksheet, and how to allow other 1-2-3 worksheets to use all or part of the data in your worksheet. Applications such as budget consolidation and production of meaningful income statements can use these techniques. In Chapter 18, you are shown how to import data files from sources other than 1-2-3, such as mainframe databases, accounting systems, other PC programs such as VisiCalc, programs which support the DIF format, dBASEII, and word processing programs. In this way, you can use 1-2-3 as part of a network of other programs, thus increasing your productivity.

Chapter 19 is a discussion of 1-2-3 commands which are not as widely used as they should be. The /Data Table command lets you automate the "what-if" process by creating a table of changed values or formulas based on different values in one or two cells. You can produce, for example, a table displaying monthly loan payments based on different interest rates and terms. /Data Fill is a handy shortcut for entering an arithmetic series of numbers. /Data Distribution helps in statistical analysis of a group of numbers, such as sales results for a group of salespeople, by creating a frequency distribution. /Range Justify lets you create a simple memorandum or letter from 1-2-3 labels.

Part V (Chapters 20 and 21) is about graphs. Chapter 20 discusses how you display them; Chapter 21 discusses how you print them. Since you are graphing directly from information in the worksheet, graphing is a snap. As with printing, you can produce a graph by entering a few simple commands. Or, you can produce a fancy graph, complete with titles, legends, data labels, and scales for the X-axis and the Y-axis that you define. You can add grid lines to improve the clarity of the graph. If your display monitor permits, you can display graphs in color or black-and-white.

Depending on your printer or plotter, you have additional options when you print your graph. You can add even more color, specify fonts for the text, control the positioning of the graph on the paper, and print as many graphs as you want at a time. The discussion in Chapter 21 of PrintGraph, the program that lets you do all this, should thus prove immensely valuable.

Part VI (Chapters 22 and 23) is about database management. You can organize virtually any information you are keeping with pencil and paper into a 1-2-3 database. Once you do that, the possibilities are mind-boggling. You can sort the list into another order. You can ask virtually any question imaginable about the information in your list by specifying a few simple query commands. You can develop database statistics using the database statistical functions. Chapter 22 discusses sorting; Chapter 23 discusses the other database capabilities.

Finally, Part VII (Chapter 24) is an introduction to keyboard macros and writing 1-2-3 programs. You can use macros to automate the operation of 1-2-3. Instead of typing in a long series of keystrokes, you can create a macro, and then you can get 1-2-3 to do the work by pressing two keys. You can write menus in 1-2-3, so that all your worksheets are linked together. You can write programs, complete with subroutines and if statements, to control even further 1-2-3's operation. Chapter 24 is intended only as a beginning. Use it as a base to expand your creativity.

Who Can Use This Book?

This book can be used by 1-2-3 novices and experts alike. If you are an experienced 1-2-3 user, you will gain valuable insights. Perhaps you have developed some simple 1-2-3 worksheets and you want to enhance your skills. You might want a better understanding of how to combine worksheets to do consolidations. Or you might want to import files from programs such as WordStar and dBASEII, or from the corporate general ledger. This book provides such examples.

Perhaps you understand the 1-2-3 worksheet and would like to become more comfortable with the advanced and sophisticated features of 1-2-3, such as information management and keyboard macros. This book is for you as well. Skip the chapters with which you are familiar and proceed to the chapters that interest you.

If you are new to both computers and spreadsheets, you can become comfortable with the PC and with 1-2-3 by reading this book from beginning to end. Do the exercise at the end of Chapter 3. The exercise is designed to familiarize you with operating the IBM PC using PC-DOS. You'll be surprised at how easy it is. After you have become comfortable with the PC and PC-DOS, read Chapter 4 to configure 1-2-3 for your PC hardware. After 1-2-3 is properly installed, you are ready to start learning the capabilities of 1-2-3 and its supporting programs.

How To Get The Most From Each Chapter

1. Read the chapter with the computer off. Each chapter introduces a related set of 1-2-3 skills, such as producing a simple graph or creating a simple database. Most 1-2-3 skills are surprisingly easy to learn.

After you understand the basics, you can become more comfortable with complex situations. Each chapter is designed to help you master not only the basic skills, but the complex ones as well. As you become confident, you can use 1-2-3 better to increase your productivity.

My aim is to help you achieve this goal. In addition to familiarizing you with 1-2-3 skills, there are suggestions, or HOW TOs, based on ideas that have worked in models I have developed. The HOW TOs are techniques, which you can incorporate into your 1-2-3 models, to make them easier to understand and easier and/or faster to change. Read the HOW TOs and think about how to use them in your 1-2-3 models.

1-2-3 is a powerful and sophisticated program. If you understand its rules, you can develop applications you never thought were possible. Although, for the most part, the rules are simple, there are some situations where what you might expect to happen may not correspond with what 1-2-3 does. Entering a few keystrokes at the right time could save you many hours of work reentering your worksheet. If you are aware of these situations beforehand, you can confidently tell 1-2-3 exactly what you want it to do. These potentially troublesome situations are called BEWAREs. BEWAREs are like CAUTION signs—you are free to continue, but first slow down and make sure the road is clear.

2. Read the chapter with the computer on and follow along by doing. The examples reinforce the discussion. There is no substitute for learning by doing.

Try the HOW TOs and the BEWAREs. Mastering the HOW TOs should help you design your worksheet efficiently. You may have a need which fits the HOW TO. Experiment! You may find a better solution. 1-2-3 is a program which reinforces your creativity. So enjoy!

Mastering the BEWAREs is just as important. The more you understand how 1-2-3 acts, the more comfortable you feel using it. Like an old friend, 1-2-3 has some quirks and idiosyncracies. Once you understand them, however, you start to see them as part of 1-2-3's personality. You'll come to enjoy both its many powerful features and its few quirks.

Conventions

For clarity and consistency, this book uses some simple conventions to show the commands or keys to press.

1. What you are to enter is shown in computer type. For most situations in 1-2-3, you select from a list, or menu, of options. You can tell 1-2-3 which option to perform either by pointing at it using the arrow keys, or by typing its first letter. Instead of typing the entire command word, you type its first letter.

For example, the command sequence to print a worksheet is /Print Printer Go. You need simply type **/PPG** to invoke the command. In the text, the command is shown as follows:

/**P**rint **P**rinter **G**o

The idea is that you can both see the entire command sequence, and what you type, at once.

2. *Prompts* are shown in underscored computer typeface. In this way, you can separate what the computer is asking you to do from what your response should be. *Messages* produced by the computer are also shown in this way.

3. Special key names are enclosed with brackets [ ] as well as shown in computer type. The IBM PC keyboard contains many keys with special names. For example, the key to the right of the space bar is labeled "Caps Lock". This is a special key which reverses the entry of upper and lower case letters. To press the "Caps Lock" key, you don't enter the words "Caps Lock"—you simply press the key. To show a key you simply press, for the most part the key label is used. Thus [CAPS LOCK] is used to indicate pressing the "Caps Lock" key.

Certain keys, those with arrows on their keycaps, indicate movement. Instead of using the arrow graphic, a one-word description of the type of movement is used. For example, instead of using the right arrow graphic [->] to indicate the special key for moving to the right, this key is indicated as [RIGHT].

Finally, some special cases. The Enter key is indicated as [ENTER]. The space bar, while part of the typewriter keys, acts as a special key in some circumstances. When this occurs, the space bar is indicated as [SPACE]. The Shift key is indicated as [SHIFT]. The Scroll Lock or Break key is indicated either as [SCROLL LOCK] or [BREAK], depending on the situation in which it is used. The period is sometimes indicated by [PERIOD] to avoid confusion.

4. Keys with special meaning in 1-2-3 are shown with both the key label and the 1-2-3 meaning. The function keys, [F1] through [F10], have special meaning in 1-2-3. For example, when you want additional help from 1-2-3, you press [F1]. Since [F1] means Help in 1-2-3, both meanings are used when indicating that this key is to be entered. Thus [F1] is indicated by [F1/HELP]. This should remind you that the key has a double meaning—one for the IBM PC generally, and another for 1-2-3 specifically.

5. A hyphen is used to indicate two keys pressed simultaneously. There are times when you must press more than one key simultaneously to invoke a particular action. For example, to stop printing your worksheet, you must hold down both [CTRL] and [BREAK] at the same time. To indicate this simultaneous use of more than one key, they are separated by hyphens. Simultaneously pressing [CTRL] and [BREAK] is indicated as: [CTRL]-[BREAK]

The Optional Accompanying Diskette

You can purchase, separately, a tutorial diskette which supplements this book. The diskette contains 1-2-3 worksheets which explain the operation of 1-2-3 commands. The purpose of the diskette is to guide you through the steps in using the various 1-2-3 commands. For example, you may forget the meaning of all the options of /Data Table, or your options in selecting a pie chart. By running the examples in the tutorial diskette, you can review the steps. The contents of the diskette and loading instructions are described in the appendix to this book.

The tutorial diskette also describes adding the more complicated options, such as print borders or graph legends, once you have mastered the basic commands. Altogether, it's intended to be a mini refresher-course.

Use On Other Computers

Although this book is for the IBM PC, you can also use it for any computer which runs Version 1A of 1-2-3. Not all of these computers use the IBM PC keyboard. Even if they don't use the PC keyboard, there are equivalents for each of the 1-2-3 commands. For example, if your computer calls the [ALT] key the [2ND] key, you should be able to do the examples if everywhere [ALT] is indicated you press [2ND]. Refer to the 1-2-3 manual for your computer.

PART I

Introducing 1-2-3, the IBM PC, and PC-DOS

CHAPTER 1

A Sample 1-2-3 Application

This chapter introduces a sample 1-2-3 application. The objective is not to teach you 1-2-3 but rather to give you an idea of its versatility. This is a simple, yet typical, application. By no means does this example exhaust all the powerful features of 1-2-3. Rather, the aim is to give you a hint of its power. You will develop this application in 1-2-3 as the relevant concepts are introduced.

A YEAR-END REVENUE COMPARISON

Acme Widget Corporation is a national corporation with field offices in Atlanta, Boston, New York, Chicago, Los Angeles, and Miami. The Home Office sets target revenue goals for each field office at the beginning of the year. The target revenues are as follows:

Atlanta	$440,000
Boston	$600,000
New York	$350,000
Chicago	$230,000
Los Angeles	$540,000
Miami	$308,000

The year has ended, and the field offices have reported their actual revenues. These are as follows:

Atlanta	$385,000
Boston	$685,000
New York	$300,000
Chicago	$250,000
Los Angeles	$600,000
Miami	$250,000

Acme's president would like to produce the following:

- A report showing target sales, actual sales, and percent of target achieved for each field office. The report will also show the total target sales, actual sales, and percent of target achieved for the entire company.
- Believing that a picture is worth a thousand words, the president would like to see this information reflected in a bar graph. For each field office, a bar representing target sales and a bar representing actual sales, is to be printed.
- S/he would also like to see a pie chart which analyzes revenue by field office. The chart will be used to show the Board of Directors how each office contributes to the company's revenues.
- The president would like to know which offices are the winners and which need more help. Therefore, s/he would like a report ranking each field office by percent of target achieved. The field office with the highest percent

should print out first, followed by the field office with the next highest percent, and so on. The top field office gets a prize. We will not speculate on the fate of the bottom field office.

- To see whether to beef up the Boston sales staff, the president would like a table showing the effect of a change in actual Boston office revenue on total corporate revenue, from 500 to 700, in steps of 50. The results should also be graphed.
- Finally, the president would like to send a short memorandum to the field office managers. The field office ranking report is to be included in the memo.

HOW 1-2-3 CAN HELP

1-2-3 contains a unique combination of capabilities. In fact, it's hard to categorize 1-2-3 because it combines several seemingly unrelated features. Lotus Development Corporation calls the product 1-2-3 because it combines the following three features:

Automated Spreadsheet 1-2-3 is, at its base, an automated spreadsheet. Automated spreadsheets display information in the form of entries in a two dimensional table. This table displays in the form of rows and columns, and looks like a paper spreadsheet used by accountants. Figure 1.1 is a simple 1-2-3 spreadsheet comparing Acme Widget's target and actual revenues.

	A	B	C	D	E
1			ACME WIDGET CORPORATION		
2			YEAR-END REVENUE COMPARISON BY FIELD OFFICE		
3			(in 000s)		
4					
5	OFFICE	TARGET	ACTUAL	% OF TARGET	
6	Atl	440	385	87.5%	
7	Bos	600	685	114.2%	
8	NY	350	300	85.7%	
9	Chi	230	250	108.7%	
10	LA	540	600	111.1%	
11	Mia	308	250	81.2%	
12		-----	-----	-----	
13	TOTAL	2468	2470	100.1%	
14					
15					

Figure 1.1 A Simple Spreadsheet

In 1-2-3, the columns are indicated by *letters* A, B, C, and so on, and the rows are indicated by *numbers* 1, 2, 3, and so on. You can enter the following types of information into a spreadsheet:

- Labels. The titles, column headings, office names, and the word TOTAL are entered as labels. Labels are sometimes called *text* or *characters.* 1-2-3 labels are typically used to indicate the meaning of a row or a column. For example, the OFFICE label in Column A indicates that Column A will be used to list Acme's field offices; the Atl label in Row 6 indicates that Row 6 will be used to display data for the Atlanta office; and so on.

- Values. Each field office's target and actual revenue numbers are entered as values. A value is simply a number which you enter.
- Formulas. The percent of target and the totals are also numbers. However, you do not enter these numbers. Rather, you enter a formula which tells 1-2-3 how to calculate the number. For example, you tell 1-2-3 to calculate percent of target by specifying a formula that expresses the following relationship:

% of Target = Actual / Target

When you change a value, such as the new revenue for Atlanta, 1-2-3 *automatically* recalculates the entire spreadsheet. Without using a calculator, not only will Atlanta's percent of target change, but also the total revenue and total percent of target will also change. This recalculation seems to happen almost by magic! Indeed, once you have created the formulas, you can change values to your heart's content. You can try different "what if" scenarios. For example, you can see what happens if Los Angeles' actual revenues change from 600 to 700. Or you can change New York's target revenues. You can make more than one change and see the effects. Figure 1.2 illustrates how the spreadsheet changes when Miami's actual revenue increases from 250 to 350.

	A	B	C	D	E
1			ACME WIDGET CORPORATION		
2			YEAR-END REVENUE COMPARISON BY FIELD OFFICE		
3			(in 000s)		
4					
5	OFFICE	TARGET	ACTUAL	% OF TARGET	
6	Atl	440	385	87.5%	
7	Bos	600	685	114.2%	
8	NY	350	300	85.7%	
9	Chi	230	250	108.7%	
10	LA	540	600	111.1%	
11	Mia	308	350	113.6%	
12		-----	-----	-----	
13	TOTAL	2468	2570	104.1%	
14					
15					

Figure 1.2

With a spreadsheet, Acme's president can see at a glance how close the field offices are to meeting their targets.

Graphics With Lotus 1-2-3, once you have created the spreadsheet, you can display or print graphs. With the graph commands, you can create graphs directly from the spreadsheet information.

1-2-3 is sometimes called an *integrated spreadsheet*. This means that 1-2-3 has capabilities which go beyond simply recalculating formulas. Graphics is one of these capabilities.

With 1-2-3, you can easily fill Acme's president's request. Figure 1.3 is a bar chart, comparing target and actual revenue for each office, based on the original 1-2-3 spreadsheet. Figure 1.4 is a pie chart, showing what percentage of actual revenue was contributed by each office, produced by a few simple 1-2-3 commands.

What if Miami's actual revenue changes from $250,000 to $350,000? Not only does the spreadsheet automatically recalculate, but so do the graphs! The "what if" capability also changes the graphs. This automatic change feature means that graphics are integrated with the spreadsheet.

Figures 1-5 and 1-6 are the bar chart and the pie chart after the change to Miami's actual revenue was made.

Information Management 1-2-3 can do more than simply recalculate and graph from the spreadsheet. It can *reorganize* information as well. The original spreadsheet simply listed the offices with no logical order. The president, however, would like to list the offices from the highest to the lowest percent of target revenues achieved.

1-2-3 can produce such a sorted report easily. Figure 1.7 is a sorted report, ranking each office by percent of target revenue achieved, based on the original spreadsheet.

1-2-3 lets you reorganize spreadsheet information in many other ways. Figure 1.8 is a table, produced by 1-2-3 on the original spreadsheet, showing the effect on corporate revenue target percentage based on changes to Boston's actual revenue.

Figure 1.9 is a graph based on the "what if" table.

In addition to *spreadsheet*, *graphics*, and *information management*, 1-2-3 provides simple *word processing* capabilities. Figure 1.10 is the president's memo to all field offices, incorporating the year-end revenue results, printed from the 1-2-3 spreadsheet.

Altogether, you can answer all of the president's requests with 1-2-3. Although the capabilities shown in the example are quite impressive, they only scratch the surface. As you become increasingly adept with 1-2-3, you will doubtless discover other uses. 1-2-3 is so versatile that you are limited only by your imagination.

Now that you can see the potential of 1-2-3, you are ready for an introduction to the IBM PC. Chapter 2 discusses configuring the IBM PC hardware for 1-2-3; Chapter 3 introduces the PC-DOS operating system. If you understand PC hardware and PC-DOS and want to start learning about 1-2-3 and Lotus-supplied programs which support it, start with Chapter 4.

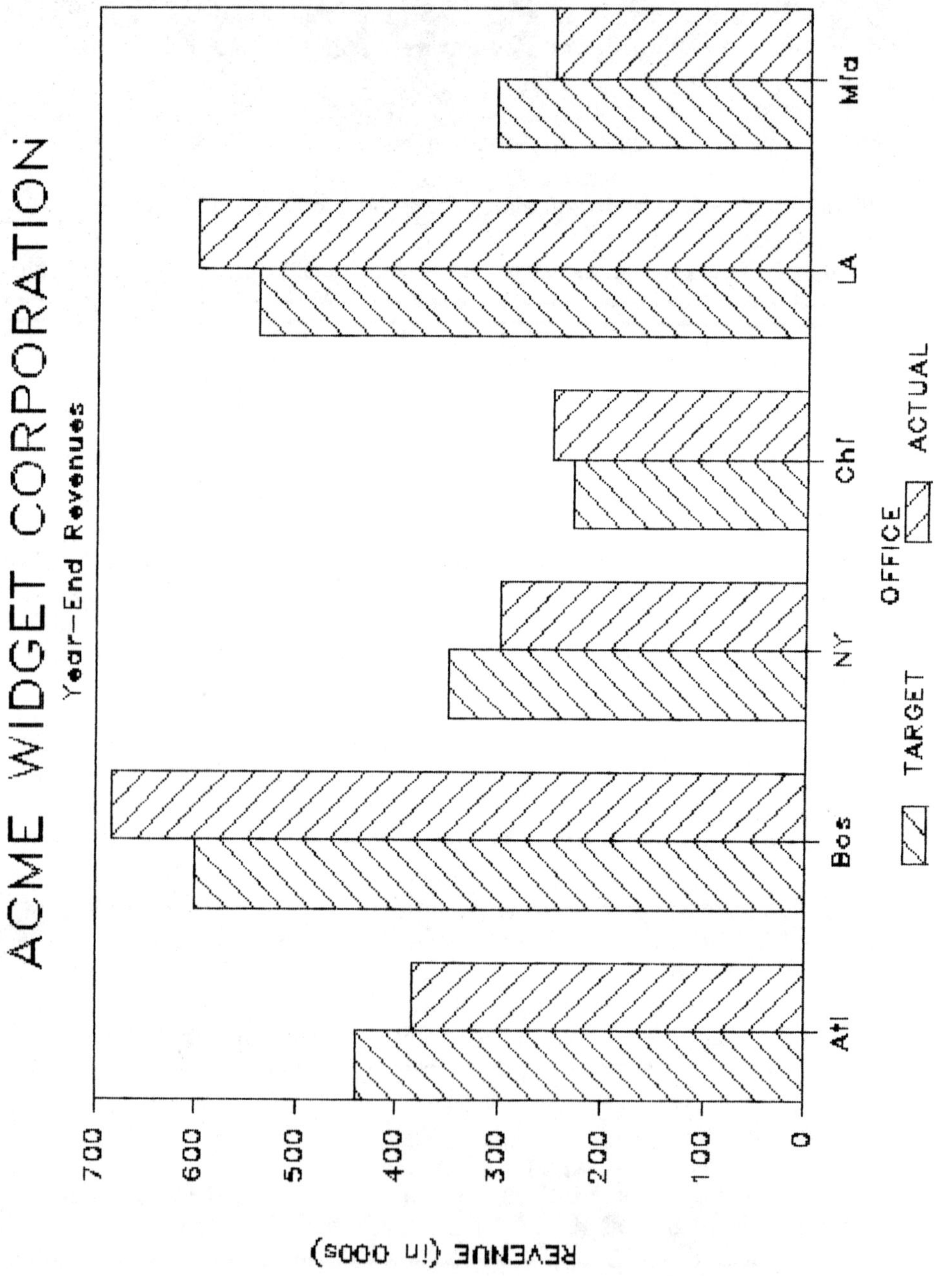
ACME WIDGET CORPORATION
Year-End Revenues
REVENUE (in 000s)
700
600
500
400
300
200
100
0
Atl
Bos
NY
Chi
LA
Mia
OFFICE
TARGET
ACTUAL

Figure 1.3

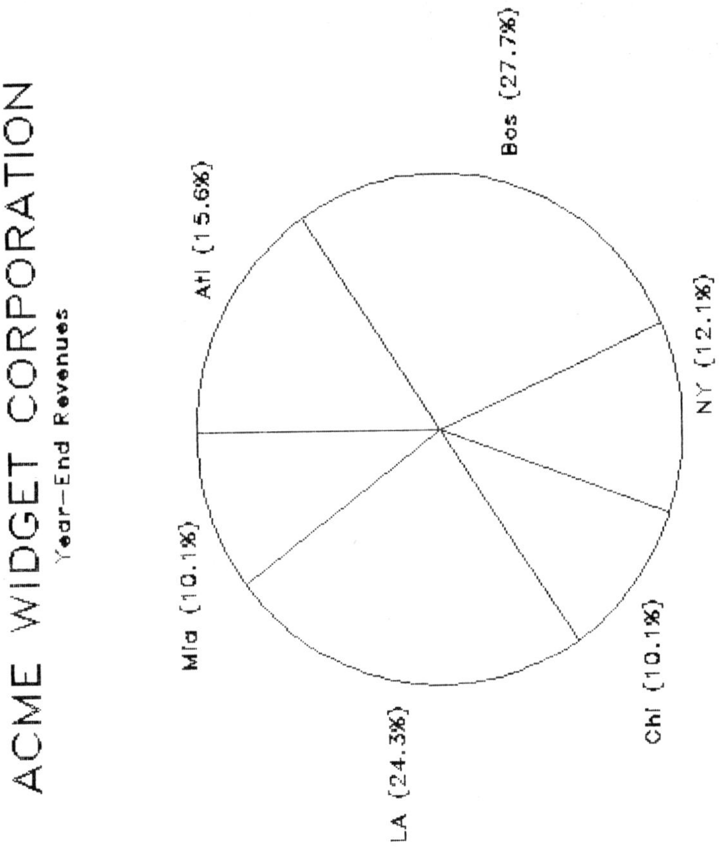
ACME WIDGET CORPORATION
Year-End Revenues
Bos (27.7%)
Atl (15.6%)
NY (12.1%)
Mia (10.1%)
Chi (10.1%)
LA (24.3%)

Figure 1.4

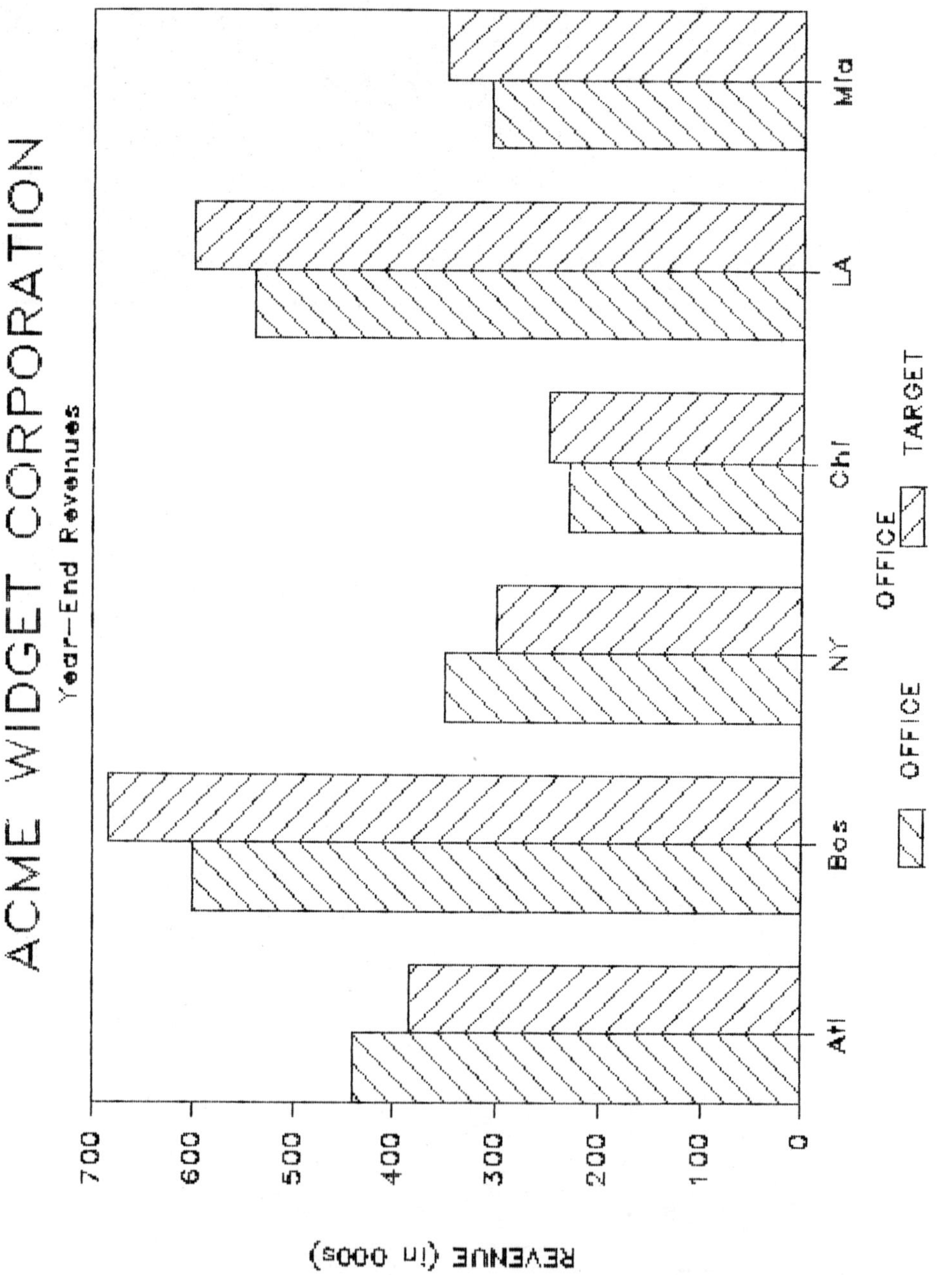
ACME WIDGET CORPORATION
Year-End Revenues
REVENUE (in 000s)
700
600
500
400
300
200
100
0
Atl
Bos
NY
Chi
LA
Mia
OFFICE
OFFICE TARGET

Figure 1.5

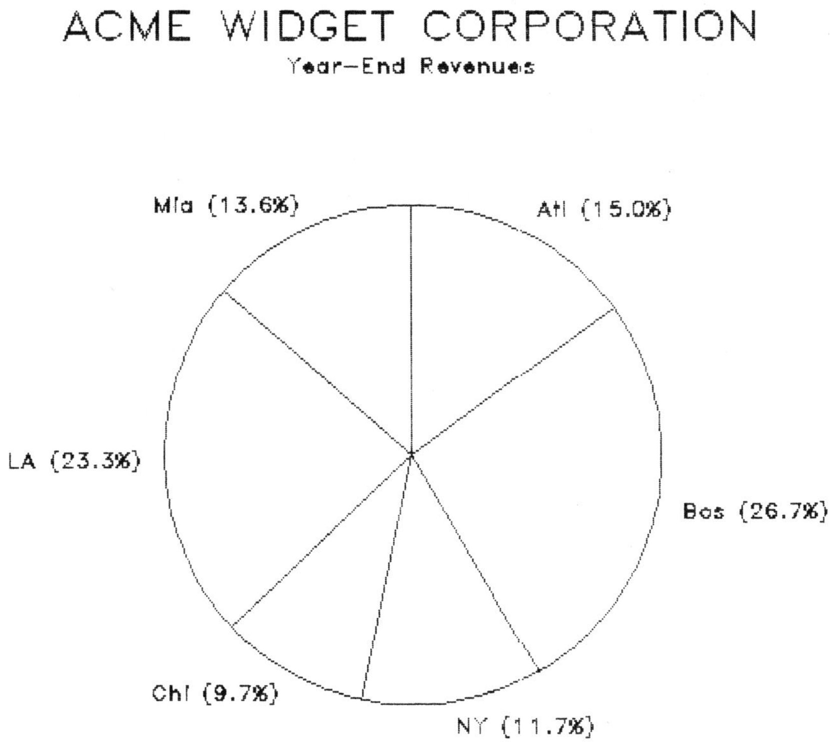
ACME WIDGET CORPORATION
Year-End Revenues
Mia (13.6%)
Atl (15.0%)
LA (23.3%)
Bos (26.7%)
Chi (9.7%)
NY (11.7%)

Figure 1.6

	A	B	C	D	E
1			ACME WIDGET CORPORATION		
2			YEAR-END REVENUE COMPARISON BY FIELD OFFICE		
3			(in 000s)		
4					
5	OFFICE	TARGET	ACTUAL	% OF TARGET	RANK
6	Bos	600	685	114.2%	1
7	LA	540	600	111.1%	2
8	Chi	230	250	108.7%	3
9	Atl	440	385	87.5%	4
10	NY	350	300	85.7%	5
11	Mia	308	250	81.2%	6
12		-----	-----	-----	
13	TOTAL	2468	2470	100.1%	
14					
15					

Figure 1.7

	A	B	C	D	E
21			ACME WIDGET CORPORATION		
22			EFFECT OF BOSTON REVENUE ON CORPORATE TARGET REVENUES		
23			(000s omitted)		
24					
25		BOSTON REVENUE	% OF COMPANY TARGET		
26					
27		500	92.6%		
28		550	94.6%		
29		600	96.6%		
30		650	98.7%		
31		700	100.7%		
32					

Figure 1.8 A "What If" Table

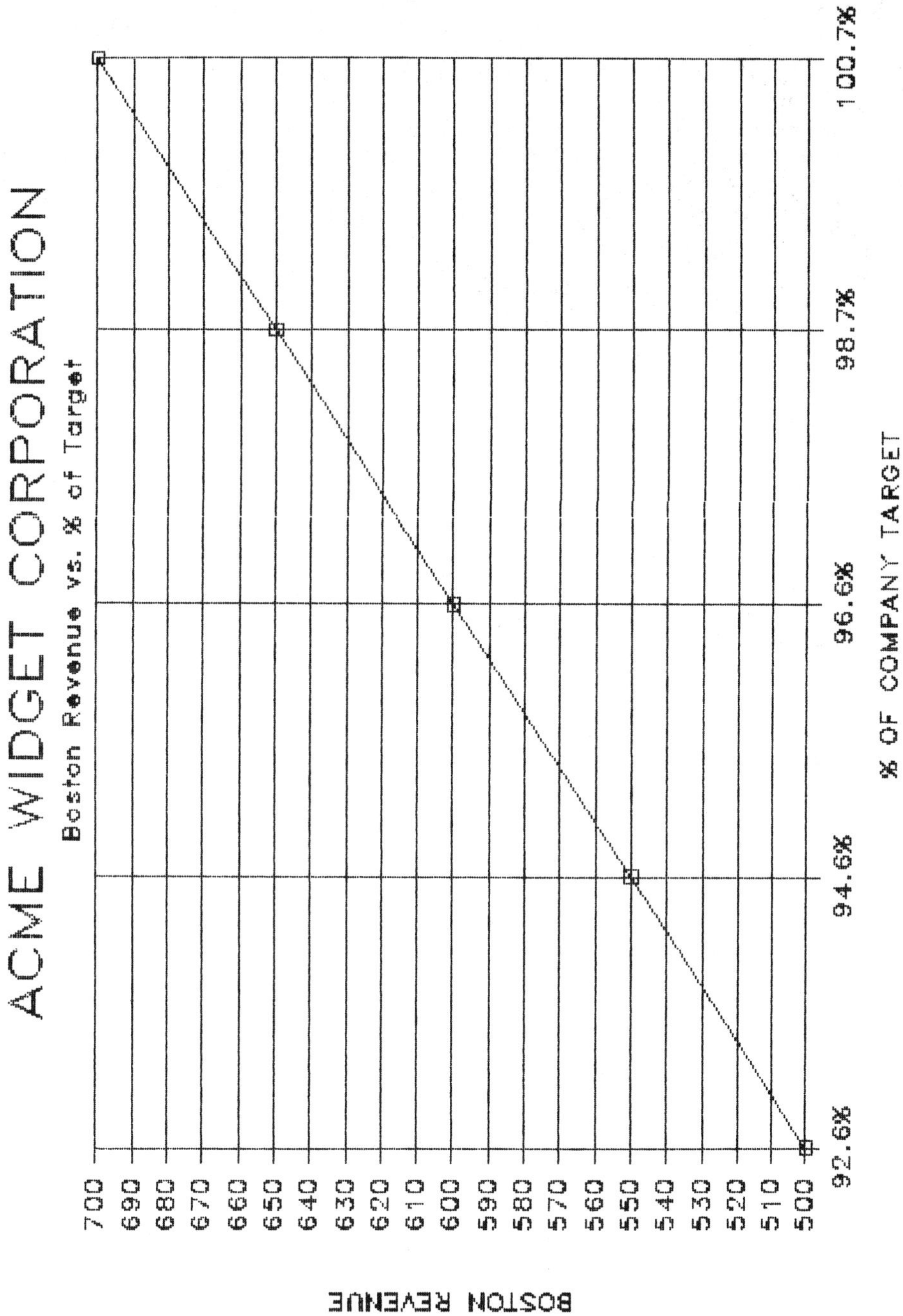
ACME WIDGET CORPORATION
Boston Revenue vs. % of Target
700
690
680
670
660
650
640
630
620
610
600
590
580
570
560
550
540
530
520
510
500
BOSTON REVENUE
92.6%
94.6%
96.6%
98.7%
100.7%
% OF COMPANY TARGET

Figure 1.9

TO: FIELD OFFICE MANAGERS
FROM: Dana Widget, President

Here are the year-end results. Congratulations to all on achieving our target. Special congratulations to the Boston Office for its superb showing! We look forward to even greater achievements for next year.

ACME WIDGET CORPORATION
YEAR-END REVENUE COMPARISON BY FIELD OFFICE
(in 000s)

OFFICE	TARGET	ACTUAL	% OF TARGET	RANK
Bos	600	685	114.2%	1
LA	540	600	111.1%	2
Chi	230	250	108.7%	3
Atl	440	385	87.5%	4
NY	350	300	85.7%	5
Mia	308	250	81.2%	6
	-----	-----	-----	
TOTAL	2468	2470	100.1%	

Figure 1.10

CHAPTER 2

Introducing the Hardware

CHOOSING THE BEST HARDWARE OPTIONS FOR RUNNING 1-2-3

This chapter is a nontechnical introduction to IBM PC hardware. It is intended for those who are considering purchasing the PC to run, among other applications, Lotus 1-2-3. 1-2-3 was designed to fit with the IBM PC, and it succeeds marvelously. There are many possible IBM PC configurations which can run 1-2-3. Three configurations are recommended at the end of this chapter, depending on the level of use of 1-2-3.

When buying a PC, you have a large, and possibly bewildering, variety of options to choose from. Do you need a color monitor, or will the monochrome monitor do? Should you use a hard disk, or can you live with two diskette drives? How much RAM should you buy? Don't worry if you don't understand these terms, since the purpose of this chapter is to give you the information to choose from these options. My aim is not to overwhelm you with buzzwords, but rather to give you a compass to guide you through the maze of options.

There is no best configuration for running 1-2-3. Your requirements differ from someone else's. Instead of thinking of what's best think of what fits. Think about how you want to use 1-2-3, what kinds of models you want to develop, and what other programs you want to run. Use this book to help your decision making. Then get the PC that suits you.

MEMORY REQUIREMENTS

You can think of temporary memory, or RAM, as a scratchpad on which you revise the worksheet until it is right. The amount of RAM available to you is measured by a letter you have probably heard—K. K is an abbreviation for the number 1,024. You have probably heard the letter in combination with a number, such as 64K or 256K.

Memory capacity is measured by the number of characters of information that can be contained in it. To calculate this number, say 64K, take the number before the K, the 64, and multiply it by 1,024 giving the result 65,536. The result is the number of characters of information contained in memory. Each letter in this book, if stored, would occupy one character of information.

You need a minimum of 192K of RAM to run 1-2-3. If you use 192K, however, you will probably find that the worksheet size is too small for your needs. Today, largely because of 1-2-3, a typical PC in a business environment has at least 256K of RAM. A PC with 256K of RAM will let you develop a wide variety of worksheets. If you find you need more RAM, 1-2-3 can use up to 544K.

DISK REQUIREMENTS

RAM is called *temporary memory* because it is erased when the IBM PC is turned off. The RAM scratchpad is thrown in the wastebasket; when you turn off the PC, the information in RAM is irretrievably lost. In other words, if your computer contained only RAM, you would have to keep it on all the time to keep your worksheet.

Even if you kept the computer on all the time, you would have another problem. You could use only one worksheet! If you developed one worksheet for your budget, another for your checkbook, and a third for your stock portfolio, you would need three computers!

What if you want to store your 1-2-3 models data in a more permanent form? Fortunately, there is a more practical solution—the use of disks for more permanent storage. You have developed your model and entered the data. You would like to save your model and turn off the PC. Perhaps tomorrow, you would like to modify the model. You can use disk storage to accomplish this, using the following steps:

Step 1. Save your 1-2-3 model to the disk. Models are saved on disks in the form of *files*. Files are discussed in more detail in the next chapter. These files are actually a copy of your worksheet in RAM.

Step 2. End the 1-2-3 session. When you end a 1-2-3 session, your worksheet in RAM is gone. You cannot retrieve it. However, the copy of your worksheet on disk is intact. In fact, you can even turn off the PC without changing the disk file. So you can turn off the PC with peace of mind.

Step 3. When you want to retrieve your work, reenter 1-2-3 and retrieve your file from the disk. Any time you want to retrieve your file, turn on the PC, run the 1-2-3 program, and issue the command to retrieve the file. You can then make changes.

The changes are made in RAM. Your disk file is not changed until you issue a 1-2-3 command to save the file. This feature is very handy. It means that you can make whatever changes you want to the worksheet, and see the results. You can change your sales unit numbers, for example, and see how the change affects net profit. You can analyze as many "what if" scenarios as you can imagine. If you want to save the changed worksheet, you can issue the 1-2-3 command to save it to a disk file. If, on the other hand, you don't want to save the changes, simply end the 1-2-3 session.

DISK STORAGE

Diskette-Based PCs

There are two common types of disk storage for the PC—diskettes and hard disks.

Introducing —

Software to Accompany Lotus 1-2-3 Self-Taught on the IBM PC

Ira Krakow

Makes Learning 1-2-3 Easy As A-B-C!

Because the program keyboarding has already been done for you. This companion tutorial contains a series of 1-2-3 worksheets (33 in all!) which explain - fully and clearly - the operation of 1-2-3 commands. You'll be able to see each of the steps that make up the various program commands.

And once you've mastered the basic commands, the diskette will show you how to add the more complex options. Including ***print borders . . . graph legends . . . file consolidations,*** and more.

Here's How To Order

Enclose a check or money order for $30.00, plus local sales tax, slip in this handy order envelope, and mail! No postage needed. Or charge it to your VISA or MasterCard.

Just complete the information below.

☐ **YES!** I want to enjoy 1-2-3 productivity with a minimum of hassle. Please rush me **Software to Accompany Lotus 1-2-3 Self-Taught on the IBM PC**/ D 6307-5. I've enclosed payment of $30.00 plus local sales tax. (Payable in U.S. dollars only.)

Name ______________________

Address ______________________

City ______________ State_____ Zip_____

Charge my Credit Card Instead

☐ VISA ☐ MasterCard

____
Account Number

____
Expiration Date

____
Signature as it appears on Card

Brady

BRADY
Published by Prentice Hall Press
New York, NY 10023

A typical IBM PC diskette-based system uses double-sided, double-density diskettes with a storage capacity of either 320K or 360K. The precise capacity depends on which version of the PC-DOS operating system you use—a topic to be discussed in the next chapter.

Almost all PC software is supplied on diskettes. The Lotus 1-2-3 package has *five* diskettes. There are so many features of Lotus 1-2-3 that Lotus Development Corporation could not fit them all on one diskette.

Diskettes are a bit like phonograph records. You can't play them unless you have the PC's equivalent of a record player: the diskette drive. After inserting the diskette into the diskette drive, you can transfer information either *from* the diskette *to* RAM (retrieving); or *to* the diskette *from* RAM (saving). After your valuable information has been recorded on the diskette, you can then remove the diskette from the drive and store it for safe keeping.

The PC System Unit has space for two diskette drives. Why two? Because, for efficient operation, you use one drive for the *program*, and the other for *data*. If your PC has 2 diskette drives, you use the diskette drive on your left, the A-drive, for the 1-2-3 program, and the drive on your right, the B-drive, for your data files.

If you use 1-2-3 with diskette drives only, Lotus requires that you have two double-sided, double-density drives. *Double-sided* means that the diskette drive can store information on both sides of the diskette; *double-density* means that the diskette can store twice as much information as earlier, single-density, diskettes. You insert one of the five 1-2-3 program diskettes into the A-drive. You store your data files—the models you develop while in 1-2-3—by inserting diskettes into the B-drive and issuing the appropriate 1-2-3 command.

Using a Hard Disk

You may run other applications, such as word processing or database management, with the PC. If you do, it is likely that you will quickly use many diskettes. One diskette may hold your word processing documents, another your customer list, another your 1-2-3 models, and so on. You might have trouble simply keeping track of what files are on all those diskettes.

One diskette simply doesn't contain enough room to hold all the various types of files you will probably create. Your normal workflow is disrupted if you must keep track of your diskettes. Your data may be scattered across as many as 50 different diskettes.

Is there a better way? Fortunately, yes! You can buy a *hard disk*, also known as a *Winchester disk* or *fixed disk*. Hard disk technology provides for high capacity disk storage without inserting and removing all those floppies. Data files are stored on the hard disk, with no need for removal of the diskette.

If you are considering using the PC for business use, you should seriously consider a hard disk. The hard disk has the following advantages:

- *Higher capacity*. The typical hard disk attached to the PC contains 10 *megabytes* (1 megabyte = 1,000K) of storage. You can store the equivalent of about 30 floppy diskettes on one 10 megabyte hard disk. You'll find it convenient to have the data you need available to you as soon as you turn on your PC. No need to insert and remove floppies to find the data you were working on last week.

- *Sealed environment.* The hard disk is a sealed, dust-free, and secure environment for your data, providing a more reliable environment than diskettes.
- *Faster data transfer rate.* Data transfer rate, the rate at which data is transferred from the disk into RAM, or from RAM to the disk, is approximately 10 times faster with the hard disk. This means that 1-2-3 will load faster, and your data files can be retrieved and saved faster, than with diskettes.
- *On-line access.* As soon as you turn on your PC, your data is on-line. You have access to it. You can make changes; if you make the program store the changes to the disk, the most current version of your data is stored. You can make decisions based on the most current information.

1-2-3 performs excellently with the hard disk. Since a 10 megabyte hard disk contains enough storage for the Manhattan phone book, you can save a large number of 1-2-3 models on it. You also have the benefit of having all of them available to you as soon as you start running 1-2-3!

THE KEYBOARD

Use of the Typewriter Keys

You use the typewriter keys to enter labels, such as column headings or labels for rows, into the 1-2-3 worksheet.

Certain typewriter keys have special meaning when you are in 1-2-3. These keys are:

[ENTER]	[ENTER] is located where the carriage return is on a typewriter. In 1-2-3, [ENTER] means "Computer, do what I've asked you to do!"
[ESC]	[ESC] is in the upper left corner of the typewriter keyboard. In 1-2-3 [ESC] means "I made a mistake; let's back up and do it over.".
[BACKSPACE]	[BACKSPACE] means "erase the last character before the cursor". The cursor is an indicator showing you where the next character will be displayed.
[ALT]	[ALT] is used, in conjunction with a letter, to invoke a keyboard macro. Instead of entering many keystrokes, you can write a macro which saves the keystroke entries. Instead of entering the keys, you use [ALT] to have 1-2-3 automatically enter the keys for you. Macros are a great time saver.
[CTRL]	1-2-3 uses [CTRL] sparingly. The most common use of [CTRL] when pressed simultaneously with [BREAK], is to

stop a process, such as printing a worksheet. [CTRL] is also used in conjunction with [RIGHT] and [LEFT] to tab through the worksheet.

[SHIFT]-[PRTSC] Pressing [SHIFT] and [PRTSC] simultaneously will print a copy of the screen display. This is useful for obtaining a quick printout of your worksheet as it displays.

Use of the Numeric Keypad

The numeric keypad was designed by IBM for both data entry and cursor movement. The state of [NUM LOCK] determines whether the numeric or cursor movement meaning is in force. Like [CAPS LOCK], [NUM LOCK] is a toggle which can be turned on and off. 1-2-3 displays an indicator when [CAPS LOCK] or [NUM LOCK] is toggled on. Depending on the state of [NUM LOCK], 1-2-3 defines the keys on the numeric keypad as follows;

KEY	WHEN [NUM LOCK] ON	WHEN [NUM LOCK] OFF
[7/HOME]	The number 7	[HOME] Go to the upper left corner of the worksheet
[8/UP]	The number 8	[UP] Go up one row
[9/PGUP]	The number 9	[PGUP] Go up twenty rows
[4/LEFT]	The number 4	[LEFT] Go left one column
5	The number 5	The number 5
[6/RIGHT]	The number 6	[RIGHT] Go right one column
[1/END]	The number 1	[END] Go to the end of a block of data
[2/DOWN]	The number 2	[DOWN] Go down one row
[3/PGDN]	The number 3	DN] Go down 20 rows

Lotus 1-2-3 exploits this dual capability of the numeric keypad to both scroll the display and enter numbers.

Use of the Function Keys

1-2-3 uses the function keys, [F1] through [F10], as shorthand for an elaborate series of commands. Lotus 1-2-3 was designed to exploit the capabilities of the IBM PC. One of the ways in which this is apparent is its use of the function keys. 1-2-3 uses each function key to stand for a commonly used set of commands. For example, if you press [F10], you are telling 1-2-3 to redisplay the graph; if you press [F8], you are telling 1-2-3 to recalculate the last "what-if" table.

1-2-3 uses all the function keys. The special meaning of each of these keys in 1-2-3 will be explained as they are introduced.

DISPLAY MONITORS

With the IBM PC, you have a choice of display monitors. A monitor is simply the type of screen on which the project will display. The most commonly used monitors are:

The IBM monochrome monitor. The monitor displays 25 rows by 80 columns of text. The text normally displays in light green, with a dark green background. There are 256 shapes or *characters* of text which can display. 1-2-3 uses the monochrome monitor to display the spreadsheet. However, the monochrome monitor cannot display 1-2-3 graphs.

The IBM monochrome monitor with a graphics adapter. With a graphics adapter, you can make the IBM monochrome monitor display 1-2-3 graphs as well as the spreadsheet. You cannot, however, display both the graph and the spreadsheet at the same time. Rather, you *toggle* between graph mode and spreadsheet mode using the [F10/GRAPH] key.

The color/graphics monitor. Rather than modifying the monochrome monitor to display graphs, you can use a separate color/graphics monitor. In addition to displaying 1-2-3 graphs, if the monitor supports color, 1-2-3 graphs can be displayed in color.

If you use a color/graphics monitor only, you toggle between graph mode and spreadsheet mode using [F10/GRAPH]. You can also operate 1-2-3 with *both* the monochrome *and* the graphics monitors. In this case, you get a bonus—you don't have to toggle between graph mode and spreadsheet mode. You can have both the spreadsheet and the graph display at the same time. This is useful, because if you make a change, you can see the changed spreadsheet and graph simultaneously.

Which to use? If you do not need to derive graphs from the spreadsheet, you can use the monochrome monitor alone. In that case, you cannot display 1-2-3 graphs. You can print them, however, by creating a *graph picture file* and using the PrintGraph commands. Since printing a graph is slower than displaying a graph, you lose however the flexibility of making quick changes to the spreadsheet and seeing it automatically reflected in the graph. To get the most from 1-2-3 graphics, get either a monochrome monitor with a graphics adapter, or a color/graphics monitor.

In addition to these monitors, Lotus Development Corporation supports the Hercules card, a hardware card which enables the IBM monochrome monitor to display 1-2-3 graphs, and the monitor for the COMPAQ computer, which can display spreadsheets and graphs. 1-2-3 must be *configured* for a particular monitor—a process discussed in Chapter 4.

PRINTERS

1-2-3 supports a wide variety of printers. As of August, 1983, the list of printers officially supported by Lotus Development Corporation for 1-2-3 was as follows:

Anadex 9620A Silent Scribe
Epson FX80, MX80, and MX 100 (single or double density)
IBM Graphics Printer
IDS Prism 80 and 132
NEC 8023
Okidata 82A, 83A, 84, 92, and 93

The following plotters are supported:

HP 7470A
Strobe 100
Sweet P

The list grows daily. Printer manufacturers, realizing the versatility of 1-2-3, are rushing to make their printers 1-2-3 compatible.

The performance of 1-2-3 will not be affected by your printer choice. If you are interested in just running the numbers, and print quality is a lesser concern, the IBM dot matrix printer will do just fine. If, however, you would like to generate presentation quality output, then you might consider a letter-quality printer, a color printer, or a plotter.

Not only is there a variety of printers, but you can also attach them to a variety of places. The places where you can attach external devices are called *ports*. There are two types of ports: a *parallel port* in which more than one bit of data can be transmitted simultaneously and a *serial port* in which each bit of data must be transmitted one at a time. You can attach a printer for 1-2-3 use at either the parallel or the serial port. In fact, if you have a second parallel or serial port, you can attach the printer there as well.

SUMMARY: RECOMMENDED HARDWARE CONFIGURATIONS

Depending on your needs, several possible configurations will fit. The following are three suggested configurations, which I call low-need, medium-need, and maximum-need.

The Low-Need Configuration

If you have no need for display graphs from the 1-2-3 spreadsheet, you can use the low-need configuration to develop many powerful applications. This configuration consists of:

- 256K RAM
- two double-sided, double-density diskette drives
- monochrome monitor
- IBM dot matrix printer With this configuration, you will have a fairly large spreadsheet. You can store your models on diskettes and access them when necessary. You have access to all 1-2-3 capabilities except displaying graphs. This is a common IBM PC configuration which will allow you to run many other applications, such as word processing and project management.

The Medium-Need Configuration

Perhaps you need to generate more formal reports and graphs. These might be used for high-level corporate meetings. Then, you would need a configuration which could generate such output quickly and efficiently. I recommend the following configuration to fit this need:

- 256K RAM
- two double-sided, double-density diskette drives
- color/graphics monitor
- IBM dot matrix printer
- letter-quality printer

In addition to developing models, you can now display graphs using the color/graphics monitor. Changes in the spreadsheet can be displayed almost immediately in the graph. Additionally, you can produce professional printouts with the letter-quality printer.

The High-Need Configuration

What if you are developing ultra-sophisticated models in 1-2-3? Perhaps you are developing a corporate consolidation model which depends on many subsidiary worksheet files. In that case, you need as much memory and disk space as you can get. You also want to have the spreadsheet and the graph available to you simultaneously. Therefore, for the high-need users of 1-2-3, I recommend the following configuration:

- 544K RAM
- one double-sided, double-density disk drive
- one 10 megabyte Winchester hard disk
- monochrome monitor
- color/graphics monitor
- IBM dot matrix printer
- letter-quality printer
- graphics plotter

With this configuration, you have access to all the RAM 1-2-3 can use, as well as virtually all the worksheet files you will ever create. You can see the spreadsheet on the monochrome monitor and the graph on the color/graphics monitor. You can produce rough copy with the IBM dot matrix printer, formal reports with the letter-quality printer, and high-quality graphs with the graphics plotter. You will be able to use 1-2-3 to the maximum.

Which is best? Obviously, everyone would love to have the high-need configuration. But it's really not necessary. Even with the low-need configuration, you'll discover that 1-2-3 is an incredibly powerful product. So figure out what you need and what you can spend. Use what fits.

CHAPTER 3

Introducing the PC-DOS Operating System

Chapter 2 discussed the PC's *hardware*—the parts of the computer that you can touch, connect to each other, and turn on and off. An operating system is something quite different: it's *software*. If you think of a phonograph as hardware, you can think of all the records you can play on it as software. Without the phonograph, you cannot use the records. The phonograph interprets the grooves on the records; so too the hardware interprets the magnetic imprints on the disk surface. With the right software and hardware, you can make beautiful music.

An operating system is software that has a special function: to make sure that the hardware components understand each other. The operating system provides a framework for all parts of the PC to work together. 1-2-3 uses the PC-DOS operating system. Virtually all major IBM PC application programs run with the PC-DOS operating system.

A PC-DOS PRIMER

This section introduces you to the PC-DOS commands you will need to know to use 1-2-3 effectively. You do not need to become a PC-DOS expert in order to use 1-2-3. This primer, in fact, does not cover all the PC-DOS commands. Nor does it explain every option of the PC-DOS commands covered. My goal is to introduce only those commands and options which you need in order to use 1-2-3 efficiently. For information on *all* of the PC-DOS commands, consult the IBM PC-DOS manual which is furnished with the PC-DOS diskette.

STARTING UP YOUR PC

The first use of PC-DOS is to initialize the PC, preparing the hardware for using 1-2-3. You cannot use 1-2-3 unless PC-DOS is operational.

IBM supplies PC-DOS on a diskette. You use this diskette to start PC operations. If the PC is off, the startup procedure is as follows:

1. Insert the PC-DOS diskette in the A-drive and close the drive door.
2. Turn on the monitor. If you use the IBM PC monochrome monitor, this step is not necessary, since the monochrome monitor's power supply is drawn from the PC.
3. If you have a printer attached to the PC, turn the printer on.
4. Turn on the PC. Set the red "on/off" switch to the "on" position.

Note: When you use PC-DOS Version 2 with the hard disk, the operating system is commonly installed on it. If this is the case, you do not need to insert the PC-DOS diskette in the A-drive. Simply turn on the monitor *if necessary*, the printer if attached to the PC, and the PC itself.

The PC should pause for several seconds. You will see the red "in use" light turn on. This indicates that the PC is accessing PC-DOS from the diskette in the A-drive. Part of PC-DOS is being loaded into RAM, preparing the PC for work.

Depending on the amount of RAM in your PC and whether or not you are using a hard disk, after about 15 seconds the following message displays:

```
Current date is Tue 1-01-1980
Enter new date: _
```

The PC is waiting for you to enter a date. The date is used to mark the creation of files. This is very useful. You can easily create many 1-2-3 data files, which store models you have created. If you create many files, it's easy to lose track of when they were created. PC-DOS will assist you by labeling the creation of a file using the date you enter.

If the displayed date is the current date, press [ENTER]. If the displayed date is incorrect, you can enter the date as a number. You do not have to enter the day of the week: PC-DOS calculates the day of the week from the date you supply. The number is in the form *mm/dd/yy* or *mm-dd-yy* where *mm* (the month number) is a one- or two-digit number from 1 to 12. You can enter a one-digit number with or without a leading zero—1 is equivalent to 01.

dd (the day number) is a one- or two-digit number from 1 to 31. As with the month, you can enter a one-digit number with or without a leading zero.

yy (the year number) is a two-digit number from 80 to 99, representing 1980 to 1999.

You can separate the month number, day number, and year number, with a slash (/) or a hyphen (-). The following are equivalent entries for April 1, 1984.

04-01-84
04/01/84
04/01-84

After you have typed in the date, press [ENTER]. The PC will then display the following:

```
Current time is 0:00:nn.mm
```

on your PC, the values of nn and mm may differ

```
Enter new time: _
```

The PC uses the time, as well as the date, for labeling files. If you create several worksheet files on the same day, you can use the time to sort out precisely when you created them.

The PC is a precise timekeeper. It keeps time to hundredths of a second—

indicated by the *mm* number. For labeling 1-2-3 files, you need be concerned with entering hours and minutes. To do this, enter the hour number, from 0 to 23, followed by a colon (:), followed by the minute number, from 0 to 59. PC-DOS uses international ilitary conventions—to represent p.m. time, add 12 to the a.m. time. Some examples of valid times are:

00:00	12 midnight
07:59	7:59 a.m.
8:30	8:30 a.m.—the first zero is not required
12	12 noon—PC-DOS assumes zero if minutes not entered
13:30	1:30 p.m.—add 12 to get p.m. time

After you have typed in the correct time, press **[ENTER]**. The PC-DOS copyright message should display, and you will get the following prompt:

```
A> _
```

The A-prompt indicates that PC-DOS has successfully started up the PC, and is ready for you to enter commands. You can use PC-DOS to change the date or time, for example, by entering a PC-DOS command. To change the date, type **DATE[ENTER]**; to change the time, type **TIME[ENTER]**. After you reset the date or time, PC-DOS uses the new value.

PC-DOS FILES

Using PC-DOS Version 1.1

The 1-2-3 program, and the worksheets and other data you will create in 1-2-3, are stored on the disk as *files*. To distinguish among files, you must name them. With PC-DOS 1.1, you name files as follows:
[disk-drive-specification]:[filename].[extension]

The following subsections examine naming files in more detail.

The Disk-Drive-Specification

The *disk-drive-specification* indicates which diskette drive contains the diskette in which the file is to be stored. With a two-diskette drive PC, you can enter **A** for the disk drive on your left, or **B** for the disk drive on your right.

PC-DOS does not require that you enter the disk-drive-specification. The A-prompt, which displays after successful startup, indicates that any files which are named without a disk-drive-specification will be stored on the A-drive. If you wish to store the file on the diskette in the A-drive, you can omit the disk-drive-specification. This prompt contains a *default value.* A default value is any value which the system assumes; a default value remains in effect until you change it.

What if you want to store files on the B-drive? You have two choices. You can either specify the disk-drive-specification as B; or you can change the default value of the PC-DOS prompt to point to the B-drive. To change the default, enter the following:

```
A>B:[ENTER]
```

You are telling PC-DOS to change the default value of the disk-drive-specification to the B-drive. PC-DOS responds with the following prompt:

```
B> _
```

If you do not specify the disk drive, the file will be stored on the diskette in the B-drive. Typically, when using 1-2-3, the *program* diskette files (the files of the 1-2-3 program itself) are accessed from the A-drive. The *data* diskette files (the models you create while in 1-2-3) are accessed from the B-drive. These are, in fact the assumptions made by 1-2-3. Since they are the 1-2-3 *defaults*, you typically do not have to enter the disk-drive-specification when storing a 1-2-3 data file to the disk.

The Filename

The filename is the most important in defining a 1-2-3 data file. The filename can have up to 8 characters. These characters should consist of letters of the alphabet, A through Z, and/or numbers, 0 through 9. Blanks are not allowed except at the end of the filename.

When you are in 1-2-3, you need only specify the filename. Use the following guidelines:

Make the name meaningful. If you are creating a 1-2-3 worksheet which monitors cash flow, name the worksheet CASHFLOW. Call a budget worksheet BUDGET. If you choose a filename which is not meaningful, such as naming the worksheet after your pet canary it's more difficult to keep track of it. Could you tell whether the CANARY worksheet contained cash flow or budget data?.

Don't make the name more than 8 characters. Although it would be desirable to name the 1983 budget worksheet file BUDGETFOR1983 and the 1984 budget worksheet file BUDGETFOR1984, PC-DOS won't permit it. PC-DOS only uses the first 8 characters of the filename. In this case, each file would be called BUDGETFO and you have a good chance of losing valuable data.

The Extension

The PC-DOS extension is a way of distinguishing types of files. Extensions are useful if your diskette contains data from different types of programs. You might, for instance, give your word processing documents the extension .DOC or your data base files the extension .DBF. When you specify a file, you can add an *extension* of up to 3 characters.

When using 1-2-3 to define data files, you need not specify an extension. 1-2-3 automatically provides it for you. In fact, 1-2-3 uses three extensions, depending on the type of file you are defining. These are:

.WKS worksheet files—your 1-2-3 models
.PIC graph picture files—pictures of graphs to be printed later
.PRN print files—copies of 1-2-3 reports on the disk

The Directory

The PC-DOS Version 1.1 directory consists of all the files on a diskette. You can display the files on a diskette by issuing the DIR command. The particular drive, A or B, for which the diskette directory displays depends on the PC-DOS prompt. If you issue the following command:

```
A>DIR[ENTER]
```

The filename, extension, size, creation date, and creation time for all files in the diskette in the A-drive will display. On the other hand, if you issue the command with PC-DOS pointing to the B-drive, as follows:

```
B>DIR[ENTER]
```

you get the directory for the diskette mounted on the B-drive.

You can also get the directory for the diskette mounted on the B-drive without changing the PC-DOS prompt, by issuing the following command:

```
A>DIR B:[ENTER]
```

This command displays the directory for the diskette in the B-drive, even though the PC-DOS prompt points to the A-drive.

USING DIRECTORIES WITH PC-DOS VERSION 2

In PC-DOS Version 1.1 the directory refers to files on the entire diskette. PC-DOS Version 2 was developed for the large-capacity hard disks. Because of its large capacity, the hard disk may store hundreds, or even thousands, of files. These files may be created by many programs. A directory listing thousands of files will quickly become confusing. You don't want to sift through 2,000 directory entries to find out when your BUDGET worksheet was created.

PC-DOS Version 2 was designed to avoid this situation. In Version 2, you can create multiple directories on the same disk. Directories can group files according to their use. You could, for example, place all your 1-2-3 worksheet files in one directory and all your word processing documents in another directory. Thus, all your data files are together.

The DIR command in Version 2 refers to this logical grouping of files, rather than to the entire disk. You can indicate to 1-2-3 which directory contains your 1-2-3 data files, and make 1-2-3 remember the default directory. 1-2-3 will access all your data files in that directory, as if the files in that directory were stored on a diskette-type directory.

PREPARING DISKS FOR USE BY PC-DOS

Before you can use a diskette to store your 1-2-3 data files, you must prepare it for PC-DOS. When you take a diskette which has never been used out of the box, it cannot be used by PC-DOS. PC-DOS requires that the diskette be prepared, or *formatted*, for its use. Different operating systems use different formats. This means that a diskette formatted by PC-DOS most likely cannot be used with another operating system. You cannot, for example, take a 1-2-3 diskette containing your models and use that diskette with Apple IIe VisiCalc. The Apple IIe and the PC-DOS operating systems do not use the same diskette formats.

With PC-DOS Version 1.1, use the following steps to format a data diskette, preparing it to be used to store data files you create in 1-2-3.

1. Insert the PC-DOS diskette in the A-drive and close the drive door. The PC-DOS diskette contains the program which formats the diskette.
2. Insert the new diskette in the B-drive and close the drive door.
3. Format the disk. Issue the following command:

`A>FORMAT B:[ENTER]` (Don't forget the B:)

You are instructing PC-DOS to format the disk which is in the B-drive. After the FORMAT command completes, the diskette is ready for storing your 1-2-3 data files.

BEWARE ***FORMAT Destroys All Diskette Data***

FORMAT destroys all data files on your diskette. All the information on the diskette is erased and is lost forever. So before you use the FORMAT command, make sure that the disk to be formatted either (a) is new and unformatted; or (b) contains no files that you wish to keep.

BEWARE ***Never FORMAT the 1-2-3 Program Diskettes***

Lotus Development Corporation supplies the 1-2-3 programs on diskettes which they have already formatted. If you format these diskettes, you erase some of the 1-2-3 programs. Then, you cannot use some or all of the 1-2-3 features. So don't do it! This BEWARE also applies to any other programs you use.

If you are using PC-DOS Version 1.1, you should keep at least one formatted diskette, a diskette with no data files stored on it, handy. The reason is that if you try to store a 1-2-3 data file on a diskette which does not contain enough space for your files, you may need to insert the blank diskette and store the file there. You will probably store your 1-2-3 data files on several diskettes if you use PC-DOS Version 1.1.

However, if you use PC-DOS Version 2 with a hard disk, you should use FORMAT with caution. Formatting the hard disk destroys all the data on it. With one command, you can wipe out 10 megabytes of data. Should you run out of space on the hard disk, consider copying or deleting unwanted files instead of formatting the entire disk.

MANAGING YOUR FILES

The DIR command lists all the files in your directory. You can also use the following commands to manage your files:

- COPY make duplicate copies of data files for backup purposes
- ERASE delete unwanted files to get additional disk space
- RENAME give a file another name

The Need for Duplicate Copies

You use the COPY command to make a duplicate copy of your files. Why should you do this? Disks and diskettes, while highly reliable, occasionally become damaged. A power failure could occur, for example, while you are accessing the disk file, causing invalid information to be stored on it. Although your original data file might be invalid, your work is not lost. You can simply use the copy of the file. Although power failures or PC hardware malfunctions are rare, when they occur the results can be catastrophic. Keeping duplicate copies of your valuable files is an ounce of prevention.

Another reason for keeping duplicate copies is for the times when you make extensive changes to your models. You might make the changes and save them in a file. Later, you or your boss might want to undo the changes because they were not needed. If you had a copy of the file, you could simply access it. If not, you would have to painstakingly remember what changes you had made, and then undo them. This can be a frustrating experience.

To copy a 1-2-3 worksheet file named BUDGET, assuming that the PC-DOS default drive is A and the diskette containing the BUDGET worksheet is in the B-drive, from the diskette in the B-drive to a formatted diskette in the A-drive, use the following command:

```
A>COPY B:BUDGET.WKS A:[ENTER]
```

You are instructing PC-DOS to copy the 1-2-3 worksheet file called BUDGET, which is on the B-drive, to the diskette on the A-drive. You could then remove the diskette from the A-drive, label it as a copy of the budget worksheet, and you would have created a copy for emergency purposes.

You may have created many worksheets on a diskette. Rather than requiring you to use a separate COPY command, PC-DOS provides a method for copying *all* the worksheet files at once. To copy all worksheet files (i.e., all files with the .WKS extension), from the diskette on the B-drive to the diskette on the A-drive, use the following command:

```
A>COPY B:*.WKS A:[ENTER]
```

The asterisk (*) means *match any filename*. In this case, the command tells PC-DOS to copy all files on the B-drive with the extension of .WKS, to the A-drive. As the command is executing, PC-DOS displays the names of the files being copied. The red "in use" light flickers on and off. You will hear the whir of the diskette drive. Wait until the in-use light is off, the whir has ended, and the A-prompt displays, before removing the diskettes.

Erasing Files

The ERASE command deletes files from the disk. The space formerly occupied by the file is available for other files. There are typically two reasons for erasing files. They are:

1. You don't need the file any more. Perhaps the worksheet file you created is no longer needed. You can erase it, making room for other files.

BEWARE *You Cannot Restore Erased Files with PC-DOS or 1-2-3*

You should be certain, however, that you never will need erased files again because an erased file cannot, using normal procedures, be restored to its original condition.

2. You need the space. If your diskette does not contain enough space to store a file, you can erase unwanted files to provide the space.

BEWARE *Use the Wild Card Character with Caution When Erasing Many Files*

As with COPY, you can use the asterisk to erase many files at once. For example, the following command:

```
A>ERASE B:*.WKS[ENTER]
```

erases all 1-2-3 worksheet files on the disk in the B-drive. If you want to erase all of these worksheet files, fine. You may inadvertently erase more files than you intended.

Renaming Files

The RENAME command lets you rename a disk file. Unlike COPY, RENAME does not create a copy. It simply renames the original file. You might want to use RENAME to rename a file without having to make a duplicate copy. For example, to rename the BUDGET worksheet file to ACMEBUD, for Acme's budget file, use the following command:

```
A>RENAME B:BUDGET.WKS B:ACMEBUD.WKS[ENTER]
```

MANAGING THE DISK

PC-DOS contains, in addition to commands designed to manage files, commands designed to manage the entire disk. These commands are:

- FORMAT prepare a disk or diskette for file storage
- CHKDSK check the status of the disk or diskette, reporting on available space and possible defects
- DISKCOPY copy the contents of an entire diskette
- DISKCOMP compare the contents of two diskettes

FORMAT has been discussed earlier in this chapter. The other commands are discussed below.

Checking the Disk Status

You can use CHKDSK to determine how much space in bytes remains for new files, and how much space in bytes is currently being used on the diskette or the hard disk. CHKDSK will also tell you how much RAM is installed in your PC. With CHKDSK, you can get a good idea of how many more data files you can fit on your diskette or hard disk.

CHKDSK has another valuable feature. It checks for bad sectors on the diskette or hard disk. If 1-2-3 cannot read one of your worksheet files, it is possible that the disk hardware is bad, or that the diskette or hard disk contains bad sectors. If you suspect this, use CHKDSK to check the integrity of the disk. If the disk has become corrupted, you are in good shape if you used COPY to produce a duplicate copy of your files. You can use the duplicate diskette. This is where the ounce of prevention idea comes into play.

Copying the Entire Diskette

A fast method of copying an entire diskette is to use the DISKCOPY command. Rather than copying one file at a time, as COPY does, DISKCOPY copies the entire diskette. DISKCOPY is a fast way of making a duplicate of an entire diskette. To copy the contents of the diskette on the B-drive to the diskette on the A-drive, issue the following command:

```
A>DISKCOPY B: A:[ENTER]
```

This command instructs PC-DOS to copy the entire contents of the diskette on the B-drive to the diskette on the A-drive. One interesting feature is that the diskette on the A-drive does not have to be formatted. DISKCOPY formats the diskette automatically before copying the contents of the diskette on the B-drive to it.

After you have performed the DISKCOPY, you should issue the DISKCOMP (compare diskettes) command. DISKCOMP checks to see whether the DISKCOPY copied the diskette contents successfully. It's a good idea to verify that the copy was successful, so that you know that the data is indeed a true copy. To compare the two diskettes, issue the following command:

```
A>DISKCOMP B: A:[ENTER]
```

Exercise (For Diskette-Based PC-Users)

For review and reinforcement, do the following exercise if you are using diskettes to store data files, and you are using PC-DOS Version 1.1. If you are using PC-DOS Version 2, and you are using diskettes to store your data files, the display will vary in several places from the book. For example, a blank, formatted diskette contains 360K rather than 320K of free space. The exercise assumes that you are storing your data files on diskettes in the B-drive. If you are using a hard disk to store data files, simply read the exercise.

First, perform the PC startup procedure, as follows:

1. Turn on your printer and monitor if you are not using the IBM PC monochrome monitor.
2. Insert the PC-DOS diskette into the A-drive. Close the drive door.
3. Turn on the PC. You should see the following display:

```
Current date is Tue 1-01-1980
Enter new date: _
```

Enter **04/01/84** for April 1, 1984, and press **[ENTER]**. Don't worry. You will enter the correct date later.

4. PC-DOS now prompts for the time, as shown below:

```
Current time is 0:00:nn.mm
Enter new time: _
```

Enter **8:30** for 8:30 a.m., and press **[ENTER]**. You'll also enter the correct time later.

5. The PC-DOS copyright message, and then the A-prompt, should display. PC-DOS is now ready to enter commands. Let's change the date to the actual date. Enter the following:

```
A>DATE[ENTER]
```

Note that PC-DOS figured out that April 4, 1984 was a Sunday. Enter the correct date.

6. You can also change the time. Enter the following:

```
A>TIME[ENTER]
```

The PC is now ready for action. Let's try some of the file manipulation commands. First, you need to format a diskette. Do the following:

7. Insert a diskette with no files you wish to keep, or a diskette fresh out of the box, into the B-drive and close the drive door.

8. Enter the following command:

```
A>FORMAT B:[ENTER]
```
(Don't forget the B:)

PC-DOS prompts you to insert the diskette to be formatted into the B-drive. Press **[ENTER]** to start formatting the diskette.

When the diskette has been formatted, PC-DOS informs you of the number of bytes available on the diskette. If you are using PC-DOS Version 1.1 you should have 322,560 bytes available. If parts of the diskette are damaged, PC-DOS informs you of that as well. When PC-DOS asks whether you want to format another diskette, answer **N** for no.

9. List the files on the PC-DOS diskette using the DIR command. Enter the following:

```
A>DIR[ENTER]
```

You should see a list of files on the diskette in the A-drive, starting with COMMAND.COM, display. To display the names of files on the diskette in the B-drive, enter the following:

```
A>DIR B:[ENTER]
```

PC-DOS displays the following message:

```
File not found
```

The diskette has been formatted successcully, although there are no files on it at present.

10. To copy the first file, COMMAND.COM, to the diskette in the B-drive, type the following:

```
A>COPY COMMAND.COM B:[ENTER]
```

When the file has been copied, PC-DOS displays the following message:

```
1 File(s) copied
```

Now, issue the directory command again for the diskette in the B-drive, as follows:

```
A>DIR B:[ENTER]
```

PC-DOS displays the entry for COMMAND.COM for the diskette in the B-drive. The entry displays the filename (COMMAND), its extension (COM), its size in bytes, and the date and time the original COMMAND.COM file was created.

11. Now let's get fancy. Issue the DIR command for the PC-DOS diskette. Note that there are many files with the .BAS extension. Use the following command to copy *all* files with the extension of .BAS to the diskette in the B-drive.

```
A>COPY *.BAS B:[ENTER]
```

PC-DOS displays the names of the files, starting with ART.BAS, as they are being copied. Wait for the A> prompt and issue the directory command for this diskette, as follows:

```
A>DIR B:[ENTER]
```

You should see an entry for COMMAND.COM and for each of the 12 files with the .BAS extension.

12. You can check the status of the diskette using CHKDSK. Issue the following command:

```
A>CHKDSK B:[ENTER]
```

The following information should display:

```
322560 bytes total disk space
51200 bytes in 13 user files
271360 bytes available on disk
nnnnnn bytes total memory
mmmmmm bytes free
```

CHKDSK indicates that the 13 copied files occupy 51,200 bytes of disk space, and that 271,360 bytes remain for additional file storage. In addition to calculating disk statistics, CHKDSK is the easiest way of finding how much RAM—nnnnnn bytes—is available.

13. Now that you have copied some files onto the B-disk you can practice renaming and erasing files. Files can be erased individually, or as a group. To erase the copied COMMAND.COM file, type the following command:

```
A>ERASE B:COMMAND.COM[ENTER]
```

Then, use the DIR command to verify that COMMAND.COM is erased from the B-disk.

Let's rename the file ART.BAS on the B-disk to CRAFT.BAS. Enter the following command:

```
A>RENAME B:ART.BAS B:CRAFT.BAS[ENTER]
```

Issue the DIR command for the diskette in the B-drive to verify that the file was renamed.

Now, let's erase a group of files. Let's erase all files on the B-disk with an extension of .BAS. Enter the following command:

```
A>ERASE B:*.BAS[ENTER]
```

The DIR command for the diskette in the B-drive should produce the same `File not found` message as for a newly formatted diskette.

14. Finally, to copy the entire PC-DOS diskette to the diskette in the B-drive, use DISKCOPY. Type the following command:

```
A>DISKCOPY A: B:[ENTER]
```

The entire contents of the PC-DOS diskette will be copied to the diskette in the B-drive. The *source diskette* is the diskette in the A-drive, containing PC-DOS; the *target diskette* is the diskette in the B-drive. DISKCOPY, like FORMAT, erases all data on the target diskette before copying the source diskette information to the target diskette.

After DISKCOPY completes, answer **N** to the `Copy another? (Y/N)?` prompt.

To verify that the diskettes copied correctly, use DISKCOMP. Enter the following command:

```
A>DISKCOMP A: B:[ENTER]
```

If the message `Diskettes compare ok` displays, the diskettes contain identical information. Any other message indicates a problem with the DISKCOPY process.

After DISKCOMP completes, answer **N** to the `Compare more diskettes?` prompt.

HOW TO: Restart the IBM PC without Turning the PC Off

If you want to restart the IBM PC without turning it off, press the following keys at the same time. Be sure that the PC-DOS diskette is in the A-drive.

```
[CTL]-[ALT]-[DEL]
```

Pressing these three keys starts the *rebooting* process. PC-DOS starts up the PC again, prompting you for the date.

BEWARE ***Rebooting Destroys the Contents of RAM***

You should only reboot the PC in emergency situations, such as a power failure. Rebooting is also used when you switch from one operating system to another. Normally, when you are using 1-2-3, you should never reboot the system.

CONCLUSION

In the last two chapters, you have been introduced to the IBM PC hardware and the PC-DOS operating system software. You should now understand your hardware configuration options for using the PC with 1-2-3. You should also feel comfortable operating the IBM PC with PC-DOS.

Many of these PC-DOS commands can be used from within 1-2-3 itself. In fact, it is possible to remain in the 1-2-3 program and never use PC-DOS commands directly. Lotus Development Corporation has made many of the PC-DOS commands easier to use by allowing you to run them from the Lotus Access System. The Lotus Access System uses the COPY, ERASE, RENAME, and DIR commands to manage files; and the FORMAT, DISKCOMP, DISKCOPY, and CHKDSK commands to manage the disk. In Chapter 5, you will see that these commands are actually easier to use from the Lotus Access System than from PC-DOS.

It's time now to install 1-2-3 on your PC. Turn to Chapter 4 to find out how.

CHAPTER 4

Configuring 1-2-3 for the PC

The 1-2-3 diskettes, supplied in the package by Lotus Development Corporation, are not ready to be used on the PC. Before you can use 1-2-3 and its associated programs, you must install, or *configure* them to match your PC hardware and version of PC-DOS.

BEWARE ***When You Must Configure 1-2-3***

In addition to configuring 1-2-3 when you receive the 1-2-3 diskettes from Lotus, you must configure 1-2-3 again if you make any of the following changes:

1. You change the type or the number of monitors.
2. You change the amount of RAM in your PC from 320K or less to more than 320K and you are using PC-DOS Version 1.1.
3. You change PC-DOS versions.

Failure to redo the configuring process could result in serious damage, not only to 1-2-3 files, but to entire disks or diskettes.

THE FIVE DISKETTES

The Lotus 1-2-3 programs are supplied on five diskettes. 1-2-3 performs many functions; the code to perform all these functions cannot fit on one diskette. The diskettes are as follows:

System Disk The system disk contains the 1-2-3 program, help, and configuration files. Since the system disk contains the program to develop spreadsheet, display graphs, and manage information, you will be using it most frequently.

System Disk (Backup Copy) Lotus Development Corporation provides a backup copy of the system disk. This backup copy is identical with the system disk. The reason Lotus provides you with two copies of the system disk is that 1-2-3 is *copy-protected.* Copy-protected means that you cannot use DISKCOPY to copy the system disk to your own diskette and run 1-2-3 from the copied diskette. *You must run 1-2-3 from the system disk or the backup copy. When you start 1-2-3, one of these diskettes must be in the A-drive.*

Utility Disk The utility disk contains programs which support 1-2-3. One support function is to configure 1-2-3; you will use the utility disk in this chapter to configure 1-2-3. Another function provided by programs on the utility disk is to convert files from other programs, such as VisiCalc or dBASEII, into worksheet files that can be used by 1-2-3. This function, known as Translate, lets you import data from these programs for 1-2-3 use. Translate is discussed in Chapter 18.

Tutorial Disk The tutorial disk is a set of 1-2-3 lessons which help you get acquainted with the power of 1-2-3. Running the tutorial is a good way to start 1-2-3. The tutorial disk is discussed in Chapter 6.

PrintGraph Disk Although you can display graphs while running the 1-2-3 program, you cannot print them. The PrintGraph disk contains the program to print 1-2-3 graphs. You will learn about these features in Chapter 21.

Lotus Development Corporation has automated the configuration process. The utility disk contains files, called *batch files* or *.BAT files*, which contain most of the commands for configuring 1-2-3. You simply run the .BAT file which pertains to your particular PC configuration and follow the directions as displayed.

CONFIGURING 1-2-3 FOR A TWO-DISKETTE PC

The installation procedure for a PC with two diskette drives consists of the following steps.

Step 1. Copy PC-DOS to the diskettes. Start up the PC with the PC-DOS diskette in the A-drive. Supply the date and time, and wait for the A-prompt.

Insert the utility disk into the B-drive and close the drive door. PC-DOS Version 1.1 produces erroneous results if you use DISKCOPY or DISKCOMP and your PC has more than 320K of RAM. The utility disk contains a program, FIXDOS, which fixes these problems. So if you are using PC-DOS Version 1.1 and have more than 320K of RAM, type the following command:

```
A>B:FIXDOS
```

This command runs the FIXDOS program on the utility disk. When the A-prompt displays again, the fixes have been applied to PC-DOS Version 1.1.

You are ready to copy PC-DOS to the diskettes. All the diskettes except the tutorial disk require a copy of PC-DOS. Insert the system disk into the B-drive, close the drive door, and type the following command:

```
A>B:INSTALL[ENTER]
```

The INSTALL procedure installs PC-DOS on the system disk. Repeat this procedure, installing PC-DOS on the system disk (backup copy), the PrintGraph disk, and the utility disk.

Step 2. Install the driver for your monitor configuration. The driver programs are on the utility disk. The following drivers can be installed:

- MONO for the IBM monochrome monitor
- HERCULES for the IBM monochrome monitor with the Hercules graphics card
- B&W for the IBM black-and-white graphics monitor
- COLOR for the IBM color monitor
- BOTH for two monitors, the IBM monochrome monitor and a monitor with the color/graphics adapter
- COMPAQ for the COMPAQ monitor

Insert the utility disk into the A-drive and close the drive door. Select the driver to be installed and specify B: to indicate that the driver files are to be copied to the diskette in the B-drive. Thus, to install the IBM color monitor driver, type the following command:

```
A>COLOR B:[ENTER]
```

You will install the driver on all five diskettes. Follow the directions as displayed.

Step 3. Format at least one diskette. You need at least one diskette in PC-DOS format to store your 1-2-3 models. Do the following:

- Place the PC-DOS diskette in the A-drive and close the drive door.
- Place an unformatted diskette, or a formatted diskette which contains no files you wish to keep, in the B-drive and close the drive door.
- Type the following command:

```
A>FORMAT B:[ENTER]
```

Press [ENTER] again to start formatting the diskette. You can format as many diskettes as you like—it's a good idea to have several formatted, blank diskettes handy.

CONFIGURING 1-2-3 FOR A PC WITH A HARD DISK

The installation procedure for a PC with a hard disk is even simpler. You copy files on all the five diskettes to the hard disk. You then access all the 1-2-3 program files from a directory on the hard disk. Remember, however, that because of 1-2-3s copy protection, the system disk or the backup copy of the system disk must be in the A-drive when you start 1-2-3.

The hard disk is typically installed on the C-drive. The following procedure assumes a new installation of 1-2-3 on a PC or PC/XT with the A-drive as a diskette drive and the C-drive as the hard disk drive. Do the following steps.

Step 1. Install PC-DOS Version 2 on the hard disk. This most likely has been done as part of the installation of the PC or PC/XT hardware itself. It is necessary for proper functioning of the hard disk.

Step 2. Start up the PC. Do not insert the PC-DOS diskette into the A-drive. The PC accesses PC-DOS directly from the hard disk. The following prompt displays:

```
C> _
```

This indicates that the files will be stored on the hard disk, installed in the C-drive.

Step 3. Create a directory. Although not necessary, it is advisable to create a separate directory which will contain the Lotus 1-2-3 programs. Use the **MKDIR** (make directory) command to create a directory; use **CHDIR** (change directory) to change the current directory. To create and change a directory called \LOTUS, type the following commands:

```
C>MKDIR \LOTUS[ENTER]        create a directory called LOTUS
C>CHDIR \LOTUS[ENTER]        make it the current directory
```

Step 4. Copy the 1-2-3 program files into the directory. Insert the system disk into the A-drive and close the drive door. Type the following command to copy *all* files to the \LOTUS directory on the hard disk:

```
C>COPY A:*.*[ENTER]
```

This command uses the wild card feature of PC-DOS to copy all files to the current directory. Follow the same procedure to copy the files on the PrintGraph disk, utility disk, and tutorial disk, to the \LOTUS directory.

Step 5. Install the driver for the appropriate monitor on the hard disk. Unlike the procedure for the two-diskette PC, in which you had to copy the driver files to each diskette, you need only copy the driver files once, into the \LOTUS directory. To install the color monitor driver, type the following command:

```
C>COLOR C:[ENTER]
```

This installs the driver for the color monitor into the \LOTUS directory. You are now ready to use 1-2-3 with the hard disk.

BEWARE ***Never Use 1-2-3 with Any Version of PC-DOS Other Than the one You Configured for 1-2-3 Use***

PC-DOS Version 1.1 is incompatible with PC-DOS Version 2. Incompatible means that it is possible to destroy disk files, created with PC-DOS Version 2, in PC-DOS Version 1.1. PC-DOS commands such as DIR and FORMAT operate slightly differently in the two versions. Although you might be lucky and escape trouble by mixing PC-DOS versions, you also run the risk of losing data. So play it safe and use the PC-DOS version you configured for 1-2-3.

OTHER PARTS OF THE LOTUS 1-2-3 PACKAGE

In addition to the diskette, Lotus 1-2-3 contains the following:

A function key template. Each function key carries a specific meaning in 1-2-3. Lotus supplies a brown plastic function key template which indicates the meaning of these keys. The template wraps around the function keys. While using 1-2-3, you should place the template around the keys to remind you of their meaning in 1-2-3.

An installation guide. The guide, called *Getting Started*, explains the installation process in detail. Refer to it, or to this chapter, if you must reconfigure 1-2-3.

A customer registration form. You should fill out and return the customer registration form to Lotus Development Corporation. In that way, as a registered user, you will get notices of new Lotus products and enhanced versions of 1-2-3 as they become available.

The reference manual. The reference manual is designed to provide a detailed answer to a specific Lotus 1-2-3 question. You will find that it is a comprehensive reference. After you have used this book to master 1-2-3 skills, you can use the reference manual to answer more specific questions. I have found the several indexes provided (alphabetical, functional, and by command tree) to be especially useful in locating an item of interest.

YOU'RE READY TO LEARN HOW TO USE 1-2-3!

Now you should feel comfortable with the IBM PC hardware configuration you are using. You should be able to use PC-DOS to operate the PC. You now have the 1-2-3 programs installed, either on a two-diskette PC or with the hard disk.

You're ready to learn how to use 1-2-3. Read on! Don't be afraid to experiment. Try the HOW TOs and the BEWAREs. Most of all, think about how what you are learning about 1-2-3 can help you be more productive.

PART II

The Lotus Access System and the Lotus Tutorial Disk

CHAPTER 5

The Lotus Access System

Lotus 1-2-3 contains many programs. There is the 1-2-3 program (the main program which allows you to create spreadsheets, display graphs, and manage information), the PrintGraph program (which prints 1-2-3 graphs), the file translation programs (which convert 1-2-3 worksheet files into files which can be read by other programs such as dBASEII), and so on. You could become quite confused if you were required to remember the names of each of these programs.

Fortunately, Lotus Development Corporation provides a way to run these programs without having to remember their names, through use of the Lotus Access System. The Lotus Access System is a program which resides on each of the disks, with the exception of the tutorial disk which is designed for instructional purposes rather than to develop models. After you have used PC-DOS to start up the PC, you can insert either the system disk, the system disk (backup copy), the PrintGraph disk, or the Utility disk, into the A-drive, close the drive door, and simply type:

```
A>LOTUS[ENTER]
```

Lotus Access System screen displays, as shown below:

```
Lotus Access System V.1A (c)1983 Lotus Development Corp.          MENU
1-2-3 File-Manager Disk-Manager PrintGraph Translate Exit
Enter 1-2-3--Lotus Spreadsheet/Graphics/Database Program


                          Sat 23-Jun-84
                            9:28:32am


 Use the arrow keys to highlight command choice and press [Enter]
Press [Esc] to cancel a choice; Press [F1] for information on command
choices
```

Figure 5.1

MENUS

The Lotus Access System displays a *menu* of choices. The *mode indicator*, at the upper right corner of the screen, shows that a MENU is being displayed. This menu is typical of Lotus 1-2-3 menus. The menu consists of two lines. The first line, 1-2-3 File-Manager Disk-Manager PrintGraph Translate Exit, is a list of your choices. The default choice, the leftmost choice of *1-2-3*, is highlighted.

The second line is a longer description of what happens if you accept the highlighted choice. You accept the proposed choice by pressing [ENTER].

What if you want another choice? You can use [LEFT], [RIGHT], [HOME], or [END] to travel to other choices. The keys are used as follows:

[LEFT]	Travel to choice at the left of the proposed choice. If at leftmost choice, travel to rightmost choice.
[RIGHT]	Travel to choice at the right of the proposed choice. If at rightmost choice, travel to leftmost choice.
[HOME]	Travel to leftmost choice.
[END]	Travel to rightmost choice.

From the *1-2-3* choice, [LEFT] takes you to *Exit* (the last choice), [RIGHT] takes you to *File-Manager*, [HOME] has no effect (you're already at the leftmost choice), and [END] takes you to *Exit* also.

Once you are positioned at the choice you want, pressing [ENTER] accesses it.

If you don't want to use the keys to point to your choice, you have another alternative: typing the first character of the choice. Within a Lotus 1-2-3 menu, each choice has a unique first character. By typing it (you do *not* have to press [ENTER]), you access the function.

GETTING HELP

You may want additional information about the choices available to you. This information is available without you having to refer to the manual. Simply press [F1/HELP]. The program will explain your options. The program is smart enough to know exactly what your choices are at any time and it displays the help information appropriate to the situation. This is very useful; it is available from any of the Lotus 1-2-3 programs.

WHAT YOU CAN ACCESS FROM THE LOTUS ACCESS SYSTEM

From the Lotus Access System, you can access any Lotus-provided function, except for the tutorial. Your choices are as follows:

1-2-3 1-2-3 is the main Lotus-provided program. You create all your spreadsheets in 1-2-3. The other functions support 1-2-3 operation. The 1-2-3 program file is on the system disk or the system disk (backup copy). You will be using 1-2-3 almost exclusively starting with Chapter 7.

File-Manager The file-manager lets you copy, erase, rename, backup, and sort the files in your directory. The file-manager lets you perform the functions of the PC-DOS commands COPY, ERASE, RENAME, DIR, and CHKDSK without either (a) learning the commands, or (b) leaving the Lotus Access System. Like the Lotus Access System itself, the file-manager displays a menu, and you select your choice from the options. You will use the file-manager in the exercise at the end of this lesson.

Disk-Manager The disk-manager lets you format, copy, compare, and check the status of diskettes. The disk-manager lets you perform the functions of the PC-DOS commands FORMAT, DISKCOPY, DISKCOMP, and CHKDSK using a menu, in the same user-friendly way as the file-manager. You will use the disk-manager in the exercise at the end of this lesson.

PrintGraph The PrintGraph functions are contained on the PrintGraph disk. Using the PrintGraph disk, you can print graphs created in 1-2-3. PrintGraph is discussed in Chapter 21.

Translate The translate functions let you convert 1-2-3 worksheet files to formats recognized by dBASEII, VisiCalc, and programs using the DIF file format (and to convert files created by these programs into the 1-2-3 worksheet file format). The translate programs are on the utility disk; they are discussed in Chapter 18.

Exit Exit leaves the Lotus Access System, returning to PC-DOS.

HOW TO: Enter the Lotus Access System Automatically

There's an easier way to enter the Lotus Access System. If PC-DOS finds a file called AUTOEXEC.BAT on the disk from which it is performing the PC startup, it runs the commands found in that file automatically. Each of the diskettes which contains LOTUS.COM also contains a file called AUTOEXEC.BAT, which contains the following commands:

```
DATE
TIME
LOTUS
```

You can use any of the four diskettes to start up the PC. Remember, this discussion does not apply to the tutorial disk. PC-DOS will run the commands in the AUTOEXEC.BAT file, which consist of the PC-DOS `DATE` and `TIME` commands, and start the Lotus Access System.

If you want to try this out, do the following:

1. Turn off the PC.
2. Insert any of the Lotus-supplied disks except the tutorial disk into the A-drive and close the drive door.
3. Turn on the PC.

You should be prompted for the date and the time, and then the Lotus Access System screen should display. You're ready to go!

HOW TO: Bypass the Lotus Access System

You can run many of the programs in the Lotus 1-2-3 packages directly from PC-DOS, rather than from the Lotus Access System. In PC-DOS, any file with an extension of .EXE, .COM, or .BAT can be run by typing its name and pressing **[ENTER]**. For example, the 1-2-3 program is contained in the file 123.EXE. If you insert the system disk in the A-drive, close the drive door, and type:

A>123[ENTER]

you will enter 1-2-3 directly, bypassing the Lotus Access System.

Why would you want to do this? For most people, menus are easier to use than commands. Some people prefer to use the PC-DOS commands rather than the file-manager or disk-manager menus. Not all PC-DOS commands are accessible from the Lotus Access System. These people could enter 1-2-3 by typing **123[ENTER]**; when they quit the 1-2-3 program, they would be returned to PC-DOS, rather than to the Lotus Access System.

There's another reason. Your 1-2-3 worksheet can be slightly larger if you enter 1-2-3 directly rather than from the Lotus Access System. The Lotus Access System, when operational, occupies 656 bytes of RAM. This RAM cannot be used by the 1-2-3 worksheet. Normally, this is not a problem. However, should your worksheet be close to the memory limit, try running 1-2-3 directly and see if it helps.

Exercise:

Using the File-Manager and the Disk-Manager

This exercise parallels the PC-DOS exercise at the end of Chapter 3. This time, however, you will use the Lotus Access System's file-manager and disk-manager. Be sure you have a blank diskette handy. After doing this exercise, I think most of you will agree that using the file-manager and disk-manager is easier than using the PC-DOS commands directly.

1. First, start up the system. Insert the utility disk, where the file-manager and disk-manager programs are located, into the A-drive and close the drive door. Turn on the PC. You should be prompted for the date and time, and then the Lotus Access System menu displays.

2. The proposed choice is 1-2-3. Enter the file-manager by pointing. press **[RIGHT]** to travel to the File-Manager choice and **[ENTER]** to confirm the choice. The file-manager displays a screen, prompting you to choose either the A-drive or the B-drive, as shown below:

If you are using PC-DOS Version 1.1, you can manage files on the diskette in the A-drive or the B-drive. If you are using PC-DOS Version 2, drive is the current directory at startup. Press **[ENTER]** to select the diskette on the A-drive (the utility disk).

```
Select source disk.                                           [DISK DRIVE]
[A] B
Use disk A as source.
```

Figure 5.2

3. The File Management System screen should display, as shown below:

```
LOTUS File Management System V.1A (C)1983 LOTUS Development Corp.   [MENU]
[COPY] Erase Rename Archive Disk-Drive Sort Quit
Copy selected files from the current disk to another.

  FILENAME   EXT    DATE      TIME    SIZE
  AUTOEXEC   BAT 01-JUL-83   1:23am     20
  B&W        BAT 01-JUL-83   1:23am   1036
  BOTH       BAT 01-JUL-83   1:23am   1036
  CHKDSK     COM 07-MAY-82  12:00pm   1720   Current Drive:     A
  COLOR      BAT 01-JUL-83   1:23am   1036   Number of Files:   38
  COMMAND    COM 07-MAY-82  12:00pm   4959   Total Bytes Used: 218112
  COMPAQ     BAT 01-JUL-83   1:23am   1036   Total Bytes Free: 104448
  CONTINUE   BAT 01-JUL-83   1:23am   3837
  CPQOTD     DRV 01-JUL-83   1:23am    745
  DBFWKS     EXE 01-JUL-83   1:23am  16000
  DIFWKS     EXE 01-JUL-83   1:23am  18304
  DISKCOMP   COM 07-MAY-82  12:00pm   1640
  DISKCOPY   COM 07-MAY-82  12:00pm   2008
  FILEMGR    COM 01-JUL-83   1:23am  17706
  FISDOS     COM 01-JUL-83   1:23am   1195
  FORMAT     COM 07-MAY-82  12:00pm   3816
  GD         DRV 01-JUL-83   1:23am   2139
  HERCULES   BAT 01-JUL-83   1:23am   1036
```

FIGURE 5.3

The filename, extension, date created, time created, and size (in bytes) of each file, displays. This display is similar to the display from the PC-DOS DIR command. Unlike the display from DIR, The File Management System automatically sorts the file names in alphabetical order; PC-DOS does not sort the file names. So if you are looking for an entry for a particular file, it's easy to scan down the FILENAME column until you see it.

As a bonus, the File Management System displays the current drive, the number of files, the total bytes used, and the total bytes free on the diskette.

The DIR command does not display this information automatically—you must use CHKDSK. So the File Management System is giving you the equivalent of two PC-DOS commands on one screen! Simply by specifying the diskette drive, without entering any commands, you see the status and the files on the diskette.

4. You can sort, or rearrange, the display of the files. For example, you could display the file names in descending order (from highest to lowest) by file size.

Instead of pointing, press the letter **S** for **S**ort. You needn't press [ENTER] —it's assumed. The Sort Menu should display, as shown below:

```
Select sort parameters.                                              SORT
Primary Key  Secondary Key Reset Go Quit
Set primary key

  FILENAME   EXT     DATE      TIME    SIZE
  AUTOEXEC   BAT  01-JUL-83   1:23am     20
  B&W        BAT  01-JUL-83   1:23am   1036
  BOTH       BAT  01-JUL-83   1:23am   1036
  CHKDSK     COM  07-MAY-82  12:00pm   1720   Current Drive:     A
  COLOR      BAT  01-JUL-83   1:23am   1036   Number of Files:   38
  COMMAND    COM  07-MAY-82  12:00pm   4959   Total Bytes Used:  218112
  COMPAQ     BAT  01-JUL-83   1:23am   1036   Total Bytes Used:  104448
  CONTINUE   BAT  01-JUL-83   1:23am   3837
  CPQOTD     DRV  01-JUL-83   1:23am    745
  DBFWKS     EXE  01-JUL-83   1:23am  16000
  DIFWKS     EXE  01-JUL-83   1:23am  18304
  DISKCOMP   COM  07-MAY-82  12:00pm   1640
  DISKCOPY   COM  07-MAY-82  12:00pm   2008
  FILEMGR    COM  01-JUL-83   1:23am  17706
  FISDOS     COM  01-JUL-83   1:23am   1195
  FORMAT     COM  07-MAY-82  12:00pm   3816
  GD         DRV  01-JUL-83   1:23am   2139
  HERCULES   BAT  01-JUL-83   1:23am   1036
```

FIGURE 5.4

Note that the mode indicator displays SORT. (Lotus knows what you are trying to do.) You can sort the entries by a particlar column—name, extension, date/time created, or size. Before sorting the entries, you must tell the File Management System on which column the entries are to be sorted. Press **P** to indicate that you wish to choose the *primary key* column, and **S** to indicate that the primary key is to be size. The entries can be sorted in ascending (*A*) or descending (*D*) order. Since you want to display the entries from highest-to-lowest size, select **D** for descending order. You could also specify a secondary key column used to break ties, although it is not necessary for the example.

Having specified the primary key, you can perform the sort by pressing **G** for **G**o. The sorted entries display, as shown below:

```
LOTUS File Management System V.1A (C)1983 LOTUS Development Corp.     MENU
COPY Erase Rename Archive Disk-Drive Sort Quit
Copy selected files from the current disk to another.

  FILENAME   EXT    DATE       TIME    SIZE
  VCWKS      EXE  01-JUL-83   1:23am  20224
  TRANSLAT   COM  01-JUL-83   1:23am  20187
  DIFWKS     EXE  01-JUL-83   1:23am  18304
  FILEMGR    COM  01-JUL-83   1:23am  17706
  WKSDBF     EXE  01-JUL-83   1:23am  16128
  DBFWKS     EXE  01-JUL-83   1:23am  16000
  WKSDIF     EXE  01-JUL-83   1:23am  14336
  LTSLOAD    COM  01-JUL-83   1:23am  10144
  IBMOB&W    DRV  01-JUL-83   1:23am   5294
  IBMOCOLO   DRV  01-JUL-83   1:23am   5294
  IBMOHERC   DRV  01-JUL-83   1:23am   5293
  COMMAND    COM  07-MAY-82  12:00pm   4959
  CONTINUE   BAT  01-JUL-83   1:23am   3837
  FORMAT     COM  07-MAY-82  12:00pm   3816
  IBM1G1     DRV  01-JUL-83   1:23am   2139
  IBM1G2     DRV  01-JUL-83   1:23am   2139
  GD         DRV  01-JUL-83   1:23am   2139
  IBM1HERC   DRV  01-JUL-83   1:23am   2038
```

Figure 5.5

Looks like VCWKS.EXE (the program to translate VisiCalc files to and from 1-2-3 worksheet files) has the largest size.

You will return to the file-manager soon. For now, quit the file-manager and return to the Lotus Access System by typing **Q** to quit the file-manager and **Y** to confirm.

5. To copy the utility disk to the diskette in the B-drive, press **D** to select **D** isk-Manager. The Disk-Manager menu screen displays, as shown below:
The proposed choice is Disk-Copy, which copies a diskette to another diskette. Insert a diskette, whose contents you don't care about, into the B-drive, and close the drive door. Press [ENTER] and **Y**.

Press any key to start the actual DISKCOPY. When the prompt Copy another (Y/N)? displays, DISKCOPY has completed. Answer **N** to return to the Lotus Access System. Note that you are not returned to the Disk-Copy menu, but to the menu above it.

6. To verify that DISKCOPY copied the diskette correctly, you must reenter the disk-manager. Press **D** to enter the Disk-Manager, 3**C** to start to

Compare the diskettes, and then any key. This sequence runs the PC-DOS DISKCOMP command, which does the verification. When the prompt Compare more diskettes (Y/N)? displays, answer **N**. You will be returned to the Lotus Access System.

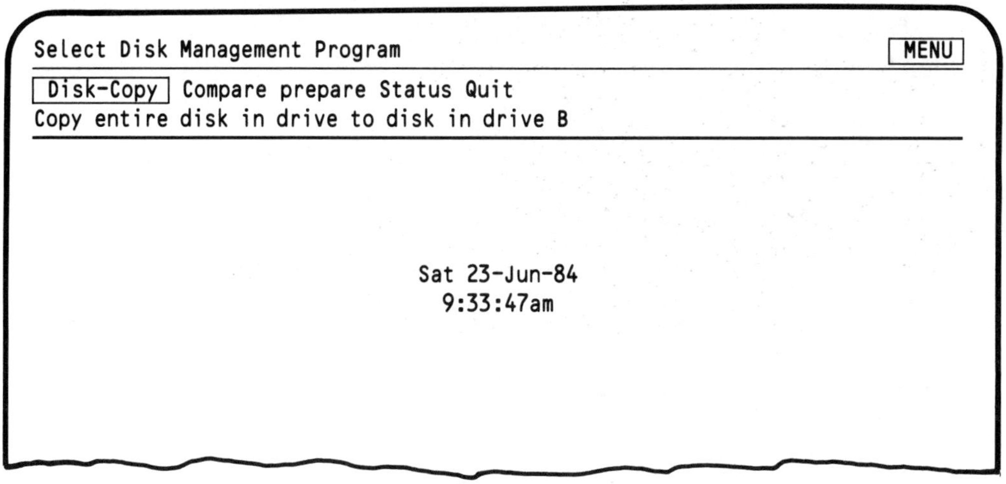

Figure 5.6

7. You can format a diskette using the **Prepare** option of the disk-manager. Prepare runs the PC-DOS FORMAT command. To format a diskette, press **D** to enter the disk-manager, **P** and **Y** to start the diskette preparation process. Press any key to start formatting the diskette. When the prompt Format another (Y/N)? displays, the diskette is formatted. Answer **N** to return to the Lotus Access System.

8. The **Status** option initiates the PC-DOS CHKDSK command to check the status of the diskette and verify its integrity. Press **D** to enter the Disk-Manager, **S** to initiate diskette status checking, and **B** to do the CHKDSK for the diskette in the B-drive. After the diskette status displays, press any key to return to the Lotus Access System.

9. You can use the File-Manager to copy some files from the utility disk to the newly formatted diskette. Press **F** to enter the File-Manager, **[ENTER]** to select the A-drive, and **[ENTER]** to begin the copying process. After you enter the File-Manager, the list of files in the directory displays.

You are going to copy the files AUTOEXEC.BAT, B&W.BAT, and BOTH.BAT, (the first three files), from the utility disk to the diskette in the B-drive. Since this diskette has just been formatted, it should contain no files.

A list of the files on the utility disk should display. The mode indicator has changed from MENU to COPY. You can now select the files you wish to copy.

The selection process is simple. First, position the cursor to the entry of the file you wish to copy by pressing **[DOWN]** (position to the next entry below), **[UP]** (position to the next entry above), **[HOME]** (position to the first entry, or **[END]** (position to the last entry). When you are positioned at the entry for a file you wish to copy, press [SPACE]. If you change your mind, and don't wish to copy this file, position yourself at that entry and press [SPACE] again. The number sign (#) displays to the left of the entry. Select as many files as you wish. To select the first three files, type the following:

[SPACE]	selects AUTOEXEC.BAT
[DOWN]	positions to B&W.BAT
[SPACE]	selects B&W.BAT
[DOWN]	positions to BOTH.BAT
[SPACE]	selects BOTH.BAT

Your screen should display as follows:

```
Copy the following files                                              COPY

Select files for processing.

  FILENAME   EXT    DATE       TIME    SIZE
# AUTOEXEC   BAT  01-JUL-83   1:23am     20
# B&W        BAT  01-JUL-83   1:23am   1036
# BOTH       BAT  01-JUL-83   1:23am   1036
  CHKDSK     COM  07-MAY-82  12:00pm   1720   Current Drive:     A
  COLOR      BAT  01-JUL-83   1:23am   1036   Number of Files:   38
  COMMAND    COM  07-MAY-82  12:00pm   4959   Total Bytes Used:  218112
  COMPAQ     BAT  01-JUL-83   1:23am   1036   Total Bytes Free:  104448
  CONTINUE   BAT  01-JUL-83   1:23am   3837
  CPQOTD     DRV  01-JUL-83   1:23am    745
  DBFWKS     EXE  01-JUL-83   1:23am  16000   Press [Space] to toggle mark.
  DIFWKS     EXE  01-JUL-83   1:23am  18304   Press [Enter] to process.
  DISKCOMP   COM  07-MAY-82  12:00pm   1640   Press [Esc] to return to menu.
  DISKCOPY   COM  07-MAY-82  12:00pm   2008
  FILEMGR    COM  01-JUL-83   1:23am  17706
  FIXDOS     COM  01-JUL-83   1:23am   1195
  FORMAT     COM  07-MAY-82  12:00pm   3816
  GD         DRV  01-JUL-83   1:23am   2139
  HERCULES   BAT  01-JUL-83   1:23am   1036
```

Figure 5.7

Press [ENTER] to start the copying process, and [ENTER] to confirm that the files are to be copied to the diskette in the B-drive. You will be asked to confirm the copy. Press Y to confirm. The copying process should then start, highlighting each file name as it is copied. At the end, you are returned to the File-Manager. Unlike the Disk-Manager, where you returned to the Lotus Access System when a function completes, you stay in the File-Manager after a function completes.

10. You can verify whether the files really did copy to the diskette on the B-drive. From the File-Manager menu, change the directory by selecting Disk-Drive. Press D to select Disk-Drive, and then B to select the B-drive. The screen displays as follows:

```
LOTUS File Management System V.1a (C)1983 LOTUS Development Corp.      MENU
Copy  Erase Rename Archive Disk-Drive Sort Quit
Copy selected files from the current disk to another.

  FILENAME  EXT    DATE      TIME     SIZE
  AUTOEXEC  BAT  01-JUL-83   1:23am     20
  B&W       BAT  01-JUL-83   1:23am   1036
  BOTH      BAT  01-JUL-83   1:23am   1036
                                              Current Drive:    B
                                              Number of Files:  3
                                              Total Bytes Used: 5120
                                              Total Bytes Free: 317440
```

Figure 5.8

11. You can erase files, as well. To erase AUTOEXEC.BAT from the diskette in the B-drive. From the File-Manager menu, select Erase. Press E to erase a file, [SPACE] to select AUTOEXEC.BAT, [ENTER] to start the erase process, and Y to confirm. After the file has been erased, the following screen displays:

```
LOTUS File Management System V.1A (C)1983 LOTUS Development Corp.      MENU
Copy  Erase Rename Archive Disk-Drive Sort Quit
Copy selected files from the current disk to another.

  FILENAME  EXT    DATE      TIME     SIZE
  B&W       BAT  01-JUL-83   1:23am   1036
  BOTH      BAT  01-JUL-83   1:23am   1036
                                              Current Drive:    B
                                              Number of Files:  2
                                              Total Bytes Used: 4096
                                              Total Bytes Free: 318464
```

Figure 5.9

12. You can also rename files. To rename B&W.BAT to BLAKWHIT.BAT type the following:

```
R[SPACE][ENTER]YBLAKWHIT.BAT[ENTER]
```

After B&W.BAT has been renamed, the directory should display as shown below:

```
LOTUS File Management System V.1A (C)1983 LOTUS Development Corp.        MENU
Copy Erase Rename Archive Disk-Drive Sort Quit
Copy selected files from the current disk to another.

  FILENAME   EXT    DATE       TIME    SIZE
  BLAKWHIT   BAT  01-JUL-83   1:23am   1036
  BOTH       BAT  01-JUL-83   1:23am   1036
                                              Current Drive:     B
                                              Number of Files:   2
                                              Total Bytes Used:  4096
                                              Total Bytes Free:  318464
```

Figure 5.10

13. Archive creates a copy of the file on the same directory. To archive BLAKWHIT.BAT to B&W.BAT, creating two copies of the file in the directory, type the following:

```
A[SPACE][ENTER]YB&W[ENTER]
```

After the archive has been performed, the directory should display as shown below:

```
LOTUS File Management System V.1A (C)1983 LOTUS Development Corp.        MENU
Copy Erase Rename Archive Disk-Drive Sort Quit
Copy selected files from the current disk to another.

  FILENAME   EXT    DATE       TIME    SIZE
  B&W        BAT  01-JUL-83   1:23am   1036
  BLAKWHIT   BAT  01-JUL-83   1:23am   1036
  BOTH       BAT  01-JUL-83   1:23am   1036
                                              Current Drive:     B
                                              Number of Files:   3
                                              Total Bytes Used:  6144
                                              Total Bytes Free:  316416
```

Figure 5.11

Note that even though you didn't specify the .BAT extension for B&W, it was carried over.

14. You've already seen how to sort the entries in a directory in Step 4. You've seen everything the File-Manager and the Disk-Manager can do. When you're done, you must quit the File-Manager. To return to the Lotus Access System, type **Q** to quit and **Y** to confirm. To exit to PC-DOS, type **E** to exit and **Y** to confirm.

You really know your way around the PC now! You can either use PC-DOS or the Lotus Access System to manage your files and diskettes. Congratulations!

Armed with these survival skills, you're ready to become proficient in 1-2-3. To give you a preview of 1-2-3's capabilities, I'll first introduce you to Lotus' interactive tutorial. Then, you'll explore these capabilities systematically, and in depth.

CHAPTER 6

The Lotus 1-2-3 Tutorial Disk

Lotus Development Corporation has provided a superb demonstration of many of 1-2-3's commands. It's called the tutorial disk. It's fun to use: you feel as if there's a friendly person talking to you, instead of the computer!

The tutorial disk contains 6 entertaining lessons, which are:

LESSON A: Getting Started
LESSON B: The Loan-Analysis Worksheet I
LESSON C: The Loan-Analysis Worksheet II
LESSON D: The Loan-Analysis Worksheet III
LESSON E: Using a 1-2-3 Database
LESSON F: 1-2-3 Graphing

Lesson A introduces you to the 1-2-3 worksheet and gives you the opportunity to move around it and enter information into it. Lessons B, C, and D develop a loan payment worksheet from scratch. Lesson E introduces the concept of information management in 1-2-3, using a database of music compositions as an example. And Lesson F demonstrates the potential of displaying graphs in 1-2-3.

The Lotus tutorial introduces a lot of concepts. It's a good starting point. Don't worry if you don't understand everything the first time. You will thoroughly explore all of these concepts and many others. After you have completed this book, try the Lotus tutorial again. It's my hope that you'll understand *everything*.

The tutorial was designed to simulate an actual 1-2-3 session. It is interactive: you participate in the learning. The tutorial is programmed to accept *only* those keys which it directs you to press, except for the following which have special meaning:

[ESC] means "I'd like to stop here—stop the lesson".
[PGUP] means "Go to the next screen—I understand this".
[PGDN] means "Go back one screen—I want to review it".

You can also press [SPACE]. The tutorial accepts pressing [SPACE] as a speed typing key. Instead of hunting and pecking to find the keys, you can press the space bar and the tutorial will prompt for the next key. When a screen contains information about an entire concept, the tutorial pauses for your review. Press [ENTER] to continue to the next screen.

So let's go! Do the following:

1. Start up your PC using the correct version of PC-DOS. I hope you can do this by now. If you have problems, refer to Chapter 4.
2. Insert the tutorial disk into the A-drive and close the drive door.

3. Type the following command to start the tutorial: A>TUTOR[ENTER]
4. Do Lesson A completely. By doing Lesson A, you get a flavor for 1-2-3's operation. Type the keys as the tutorial directs you.
5. Skim through the other lessons. Don't expect to understand everything. You might consider using [SPACE] as a speed typing key.

After you have completed the exercise, proceed to Chapter 7, where you'll be formally introduced to 1-2-3.

PART III

Basic Worksheet Skills

CHAPTER 7

Introducing the 1-2-3 Worksheet

This chapter is designed to familiarize you with the 1-2-3 worksheet, traveling from one part of the worksheet to another, and entering labels (text like words in this book) and values (numbers used in calculations) into the worksheet.

STARTING THE 1-2-3 PROGRAM

Assuming that you have configured 1-2-3 properly, you can start the 1-2-3 program in one of three ways.

From the Lotus Access System. Insert any of the Lotus-supplied disks, except the tutorial disk. Type the following:

```
A>LOTUS[ENTER]
```

The Lotus Access System screen displays, proposing that you enter 1-2-3. Press [ENTER] to confirm. If one of the copies of the system disk is not in the A-drive, you will be prompted to insert it. When you have done so, press any key to start 1-2-3. The Lotus copyright message screen displays; press any key to clear the display and see the first 1-2-3 screen.

From the PC-DOS A> Prompt. Insert one of the copies of the system disk into the A-drive and type the following:

```
A>123[ENTER]
```

This command runs the program 123.EXE (the 1-2-3 program). The Lotus copyright message screen displays; press any key to clear the display and see the first 1-2-3 screen.

Automatically after PC Startup. You can start up the PC with one of the copies of the system disk, using it like the PC-DOS diskette. These disks contain the information to start up your PC and enter the Lotus Access System. You are prompted for the date and time; after you have entered these items, you automatically enter the Lotus Access System. Press [ENTER] to start running the 1-2-3 program.

The initial 1-2-3 screen is illustrated in Figure 7.1.

HOW 1-2-3 DISPLAYS THE WORKSHEET

The IBM PC monitors can display 25 rows of text. The 1-2-3 worksheet displays in 20 of these rows. It is displayed on screen rows 5 to 24. The control

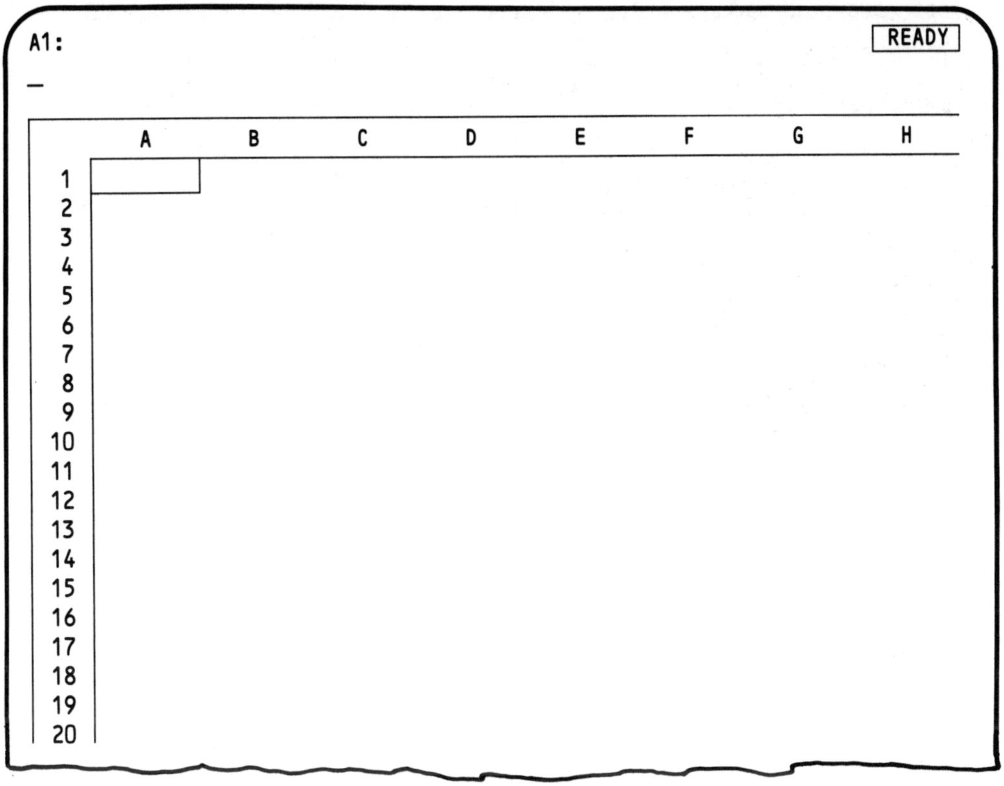

Figure 7.1

panel occupies screen rows 1 to 3 and the border row occupies row 4. The bottom row (row 25) is used by 1-2-3 for displaying special indicators and messages. The first part of this chapter describes how 1-2-3 uses these screen areas. Then you will learn how to enter information into the worksheet.

How the Worksheet is Arranged

The 1-2-3 worksheet consists of a grid of *cells*. The cells are identified by one or two column letters (from A to IV) and a row number (from 1 to 2048). There are 256 columns labeled alphabetically; the column labels are displayed in the border row. The first 26 columns are labeled A, B, C, . . . ,Z. Then, 1-2-3 labels column 27 with the *two* letters AA. Columns 27-52 therefore are labelled AB, AC, AD, . . . ,AZ. This labelling continues with BA, BB, BC, . . . ,BZ, CA to CZ, and so on, until Column 256 (Column IV). The first cell is labeled A1; the last cell is labeled IV2048.

How many cells is this? With 2,048 rows and 256 columns, there are a maximum number of 524,288 cells.

The screen cannot display all 524,288 cells, however. You see the first 20 rows (labeled down from 1 to 20) and the first 8 columns (labeled across from A to H): 160 cells in all. If you divide the maximum number of cells (524,288), by the number of cells which display on one screen (160), you will discover that you would need more than 3,000 screens to display a worksheet with the maximum number of cells.

The Active Worksheet

Even though the theoretical maximum number of cells is 524,288, you cannot create a worksheet this size on your PC. The reason is that your worksheet must fit in RAM. The maximum size of the worksheet depends on how much RAM is in your PC. The PC has a maximum capacity of 640K RAM; 1-2-3 can use up to 544K of this for expanding the active worksheet.

What has to fit is not the entire worksheet, but the part of the worksheet where you have made entries to affect cells. Lotus calls this part of the worksheet the *active worksheet*. The active worksheet is the rectangle whose top left corner is Cell A1 and whose bottom right corner is the last cell in which you have made an entry. Figure 7.2 is a diagram of the active worksheet.

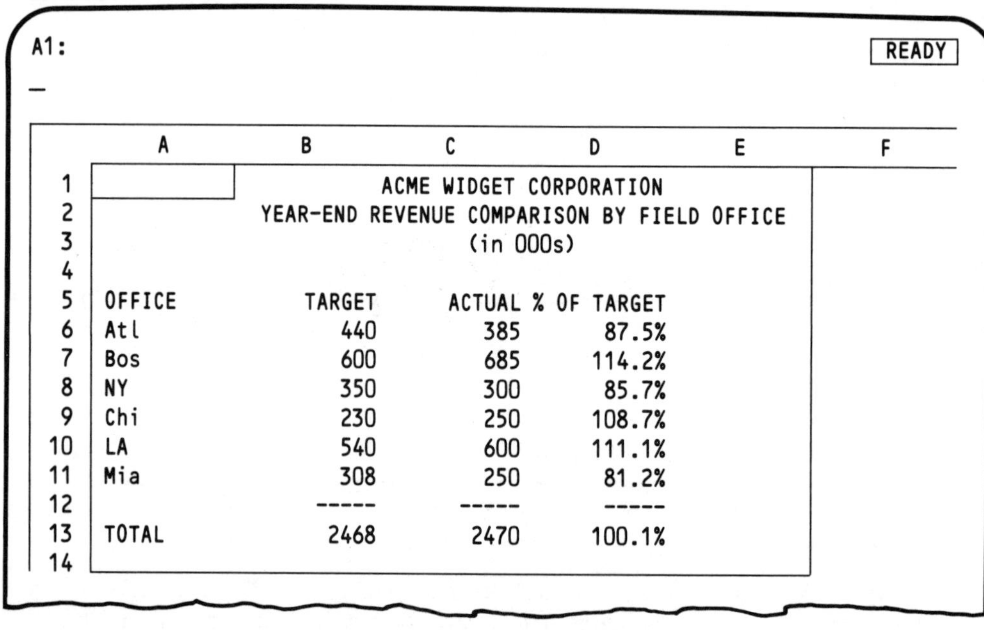

Figure 7.2 The Active Worksheet

You should always design your models to make this rectangle as small as possible—a process called *shrinking the active worksheet*. Why? Because the smaller the active worksheet, the less RAM is required. In later chapters, you will see several techniques for shrinking the active worksheet.

The Cell Pointer and the Active Cell

The highlighted rectangle indicates where the next data to be entered will be stored in the worksheet, and it is called the *cell pointer*. When 1-2-3 starts, the worksheet is empty and the cell pointer is positioned at Cell A1. As you travel around the worksheet to other cells, the cell pointer indicates the cell where data is to be entered. This cell is called the *active cell*. Thus, when you enter 1-2-3, the active cell is Cell A1.

THE CONTROL PANEL

The top three rows are used by 1-2-3 to help you control the worksheet. That's why Lotus Development Corporation calls these three rows the *control panel*. The control panel contains the following information:

The first row contains information about the active cell, such as its address, its contents if any, and format and protection indicators if any. Additionally, at the upper-right corner of the first row, there is the *mode indicator*, which tells you what 1-2-3 expects from you next. You have seen the mode indicator in Chapter 5 when we explored the Lotus Access System.

The second row is used for two purposes. If you are entering data into the active cell, or changing data that is already in it, the second row displays what you are entering or changing as you type it. If 1-2-3 is presenting you with a menu or other list of choices, the second row displays the options available to you. Again, this is similar to the Lotus Access System menus.

The third row is used only when 1-2-3 is presenting you with a menu or other list of choices. It displays a long description of the highlighted menu choice, as in the Lotus Access System.

THE BOTTOM ROW

The bottom row of the display is also used by 1-2-3 to give you additional information. The left part of the row is for error messages. Most of the time, 1-2-3 can do what you ask it. There are times, however, when you ask 1-2-3 to do something it cannot do. For example, if you ask 1-2-3 to print your worksheet and your printer is not turned on, 1-2-3 displays a `Printer error` message. If you turn on the printer and reissue the request, 1-2-3 will print your worksheet.

The right part of the row is for additional indicators. Some PC keys have two meanings. These meanings are switched, or *toggled* on and off. These special toggle keys are [NUM LOCK] (controlling the meaning of the keys on the numeric keypad), [CAPS LOCK] (controlling the meaning of shifted and nonshifted typewriter keys), and [SCROLL LOCK] (controlling cell pointer movement). If these keys are toggled on, 1-2-3 displays an indicator; if these keys are toggled off, 1-2-3 does not display the indicator for that key. The indicator for [NUM LOCK] is `NUM`; the indicator for [CAPS LOCK] is `CAPS`; and the indicator for [SCROLL LOCK] is `SCROLL`. You will encounter other indicators later on.

GETTING HELP

From anywhere in 1-2-3, you can get additional help if you're stuck. As you saw in the Lotus Access System, you simply press [F1/HELP]. (After you press [F1/HELP], the mode indicator changes to HELP.) Getting help is like having the 1-2-3 manual on-line. In fact, each help screen is cross-referenced to a page in the reference manual, should you need additional information.

From every help screen, you can get additional information. Each help screen leads you to additional screens related to that topic. From any screen, you can go to the help index to learn about any 1-2-3 topic. Figure 7.3 is the help index.

```
A1:                                                          HELP
_
------------------------------------------------------------------
Help Index                    Select one of these topics for additional Help
 How to use The Help Facility       How to Start Over
"Beep!"--Errors and Messages        How to End a 1-2-3 Session

Special Keys                        Moving the Cell Pointer
The Control Panel                   Cell Entries
Modes and Indicators                Erasing Cell Entries

Formulas                            Operators
"@" Functions

Cell Formats--Number vs. Label      Column Widths

1-2-3 Commands                      Keyboard Macros
Command Menus                       Function Keys

Ranges                              Menus for File, Range, and Graph Names
Pointing to Ranges                  Filenames
Range-Editing Keys
```

Figure 7.3 The Help Index

As an added convenience, 1-2-3 remembers the last 15 help screens you have seen. Press [BACKSPACE] to review a previous help screen.

When you have completed reading the help information, press [ESC]. 1-2-3 returns you to where you were before you asked for help.

MOVING AROUND THE WORKSHEET

Moving to Adjacent Cells

You use [DOWN], [UP], [RIGHT], and [LEFT] to move from one adjacent cell to another. [DOWN] moves down one cell, [UP] moves up one cell, [RIGHT] moves right one cell, and [LEFT] moves left one cell. When you try to go beyond the worksheet boundaries, 1-2-3 beeps. If you press the keys shown below, 1-2-3 performs a little square dance.

[DOWN]	Go to next cell down (Cell A2)
[RIGHT]	Go to next cell on right (Cell B2)
[UP]	Go to next cell up (Cell B1)
[LEFT]	Go to next cell on left (Cell A1)
[LEFT]	1-2-3 beeps, since you can't go left

Taking Giant Steps

Suppose you want to take larger steps. Pressing [DOWN] 2,047 times to go from Row 1 to Row 2048 is a bit tedious and time-consuming. 1-2-3 has several methods for taking larger steps through the worksheet. Instead of using [UP] or [DOWN] to travel one row at a time, you can use [PGUP] and [PGDN] to travel 20 rows at a time. Instead of using [RIGHT] or [LEFT] to travel across the worksheet, you can use [TAB] (or [CTRL]-[RIGHT]) to travel 8 columns to the right, or [SHIFT]-[TAB] (or [CTRL]-[LEFT]) to travel 8 columns to the left. If you press the keys shown below, 1-2-3 does a larger square dance.

[PGDN]	Go down 20 rows (A1 to A21)
[CTRL]-[RIGHT]	Go right 8 columns (A21 to I21)
[PGUP]	Go up 20 rows I21 to I1)
[CTRL]-[LEFT]	Go left 8 columns (I1 to A1)

Using [END]

[END] is used to travel to a boundary of entries. [END] can be very useful when you have entered a large amount of information in adjacent cells and you want to position yourself at some boundary (left, right, top, or bottom) of this information. Suppose you have developed a worksheet with several parts, as shown in Figure 7.4.

Instead of pressing [DOWN] many times you can press [END], followed by [DOWN] to travel to the last row of the first group. [END] acts as a toggle. After you press it, you'll see the **END** indicator in the indicators area. If you press [END] again, the **END** indicator turns off. Figure 7.5 illustrates the effect of pressing [END] followed by [DOWN]. Pressing [END] followed by [DOWN] again, causes you to jump to the *first* row of the *next* group. Figure 7.6 shows what happens when you press [END] and [DOWN] again. [END] can also be used in conjunction with [LEFT] and [RIGHT] to do column jumps.

HOW TO: Use [END] to Find the Active Worksheet Boundary

If you press [END], followed by [HOME], you travel to the active worksheet boundary. You can see how much of your worksheet must fit in RAM by doing

A1: 'REVENUES READY

_

	A	B	C	D	E	F
1	REVENUES	TARGET	ACTUAL	% OF TARGET		
2	Atl	440	385	87.5%		
3	Bos	600	685	114.2%		
4	NY	350	300	85.7%		
5	Chi	230	250	108.7%		
6	LA	540	600	111.1%		
7	Mia	308	250	81.2%		
8						
9						
10	COSTS	TARGET	ACTUAL,	% OF TARGET		
11	Atl	385	500	129.9%		
12	Box	500	450	90.0%		
13	NY	300	325	108.3%		
14	Chi	200	200	100.0%		
15	LA	450	500	111.1%		
16	Mia	250	200	80.0%		
17						
18						
19						

Figure 7.4 Worksheet With Two Groups of Rows

this. You may be surprised that the boundary cell is empty. This is because the active worksheet must include *any* column and *any* row in which you entered data. Since you cannot see the entire worksheet on the screen at once, you may have to travel up or left to see what entries have been made. There are other ways you can inadvertently expand the active worksheet; you'll get to them in later chapters.

HOW TO: Find the Maximum Number of Cells in Which You Can Enter Data

This technique will show you how to create the largest possible worksheet (i.e., the largest active worksheet), and will tell you how many cells can possibly have data. Along the way, you will discover creative uses for the [END] key.

Use the /Data Fill command. /Data Fill enters a series of numbers, in increments, into consecutive cells. You are going to attempt to fill the entire worksheet with the values 1, 2, 3, 4, and so on. The filling may take a while. The more RAM you have, the longer it will take. While /Data Fill is working, you'll see a blinking WAIT mode indicator. Don't worry—that means /Data Fill is doing its job. Type the following:

```
A7: 'Mia                                                     READY
_

        A              B           C          D          E          F
 1   REVENUES       TARGET      ACTUAL % OF TARGET
 2   Atl               440         385      87.5%
 3   Bos               600         685     114.2%
 4   NY                350         300      85.7%
 5   Chi               230         250     108.7%
 6   LA                540         600     111.1%
 7   Mia               308         250      81.2%
 8
 9
10   COSTS          TARGET      ACTUAL, % OF TARGET
11   Atl               385         500     129.9%
12   Box               500         450      90.0%
13   NY                300         325     108.3%
14   Chi               200         200     100.0%
15   LA                450         500     111.1%
16   Mia               250         200      80.0%
17
18
19
```

Figure 7.5 Pressing [End] Followed by [DOWN]

`/DF`	Start the /Data Fill command
`A1..IV2048[ENTER]`	The fill range (the area to fill with numbers) is the entire worksheet (the rectangle with corners A1 (the first cell) and IV2048 (the last cell))
`1[ENTER]1[ENTER]999999[ENTER]`	Start the filling with the number 1, increment by 1, and end with 999999.

Eventually (probably several minutes later, so get a cup of coffee if you like), 1-2-3 displays the `Memory full` error message on the bottom row. When that happens press `[ESC]` to clear the message.

You have now filled the worksheet with consecutive numbers, starting from 1. How many cells is that? You can use `[END]` to find out, as follows:

`[END][RIGHT]`	Go to rightmost column of entries
`[END][DOWN]`	Go to last entry in this column

A10: 'COSTS READY

	A	B	C	D	E	F
1	REVENUES	TARGET	ACTUAL	% OF TARGET		
2	Atl	440	385	87.5%		
3	Bos	600	685	114.2%		
4	NY	350	300	85.7%		
5	Chi	230	250	108.7%		
6	LA	540	600	111.1%		
7	Mia	308	250	81.2%		
8						
9						
10	COSTS	TARGET	ACTUAL	% OF TARGET		
11	Atl	385	500	129.9%		
12	Bos	500	450	90.0%		
13	NY	300	325	108.3%		
14	Chi	200	200	100.0%		
15	LA	450	500	111.1%		
16	Mia	250	200	80.0%		
17						
18						

Figure 7.6 Pressing [END] Followed by [DOWN] Again

The number that displays is the maximum number of cells you can enter. The number is, in practice, significantly less than this. Memory is used by many other 1-2-3 features, such as storing labels, values, and formulas. Any memory used subtracts from the amount that can be used by the worksheet.

You probably are not at the end of the active worksheet. The active worksheet is a rectangle whose top corner is Cell A1 and whose bottom corner cell coordinates are the highest column letter and highest row number you've entered. To see the active worksheet boundaries, type the following:

[HOME]	Go to Cell A1
[END][HOME]	Go to the end of the active worksheet

Unless you have filled in a complete rectangle, this cell is probably empty. That's because the active worksheet includes the entire rectangle, not just the cells in which you have entered data. Every time you enter information in a new column or row, you have expanded the active worksheet rectangle.

Moving with Special Keys

If you happen to know what cell you want to go to, you can go there directly using a function key. Simply press [F5/GOTO]. For example, to go to the last cell of the worksheet (Cell IV2048), type the following:

```
[F5/GOTO]IV2048[ENTER]
```

In addition to [F5/GOTO], there are many occasions when you want to see what's at the beginning of the worksheet. 1-2-3 provides an easy way of going home to Cell A1. You simply press [HOME] and voila, you're at Cell A1.

A final special key is [SCROLL LOCK]. When you press [SCROLL LOCK], the cell pointer freezes on the active cell and the arrow keys pull the worksheet display. When the cell pointer is at the edge of the worksheet display, the cell pointer is pulled in the direction of the movement. [SCROLL LOCK] is used when you want to focus on a particular cell which may contain important information such as total revenue, and display the cells around it. When the scroll lock feature is on, you will see the SCROLL indicator display in the bottom row.

ENTERING LABELS

Having toured the worksheet, you are ready to enter information into it. Labels are used as text, such as column or row headings. You will enter the label SALES in cell A1. When you enter 1-2-3, the mode indicator indicates READY. READY means that 1-2-3 is ready for you to enter information into the active cell.

To start, type the first character (the S). The worksheet displays as shown in Figure 7.7. The mode indicator changes from READY to LABEL? How does 1-2-3 know that you want to enter a label? It takes a guess from the first character you type. Most commonly, you start a label with a letter; if the first character is a letter, 1-2-3 assumes you are entering a label. To finish entering the SALES label, type the following:

```
ALES[ENTER]
```

The worksheet displays as shown in Figure 7.8. The label is stored in the cell and the mode indicator returns to READY.

Using the Label Prefix

Look at the first row of the control panel. Do you see the apostrophe (') before the entry SALES? You did not enter this apostrophe; 1-2-3 automatically added it.

The apostrophe is called a *label prefix*. The label prefix affects how the label displays relative to the column-width. When you start 1-2-3, the column-width is 9 (in Chapter 12, you'll learn how to change the column-width). 1-2-3 has four label-prefixes, which are:

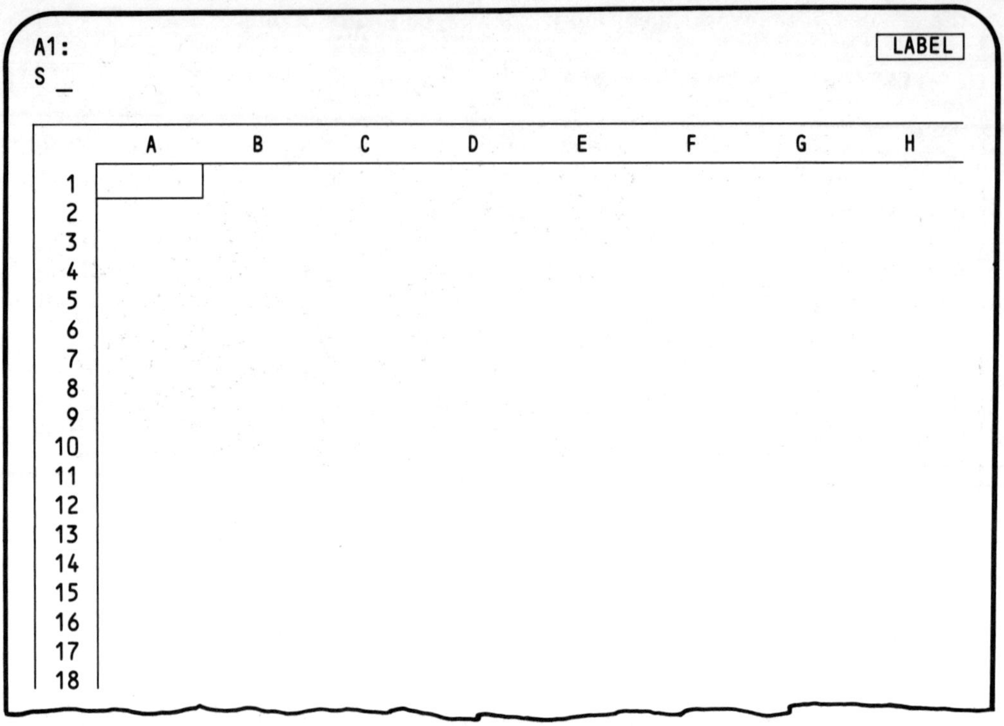

Figure 7.7 Starting a Label Entry

' left-adjust the label relative to the column width
" right-adjust the label relative to the column width
^ center the label relative to the column width
\ repeat the label for the column width

1-2-3's automatic, or *default* assumption is to left-adjust all labels. In Chapter 11, you will learn how to change this default.

BEWARE ***The Label Prefix Is Stored with the Label***

1-2-3 stores the label prefix as the first character of the label. If you enter a label prefix as the first character of a label, 1-2-3 stores it as a label prefix rather than as the first character. If the first character is not a label prefix, 1-2-3 automatically starts the label prefix with the default. Typing **SALES** will produce the same display, a left-adjusted label, as typing **'SALES**.

HOW TO: Start a Label with a Label Prefix

So what happens if you want to enclose the label, such as "SALES" in quotes? If you type **"SALES"**, in cell A1, you get the display of Figure 7.9.

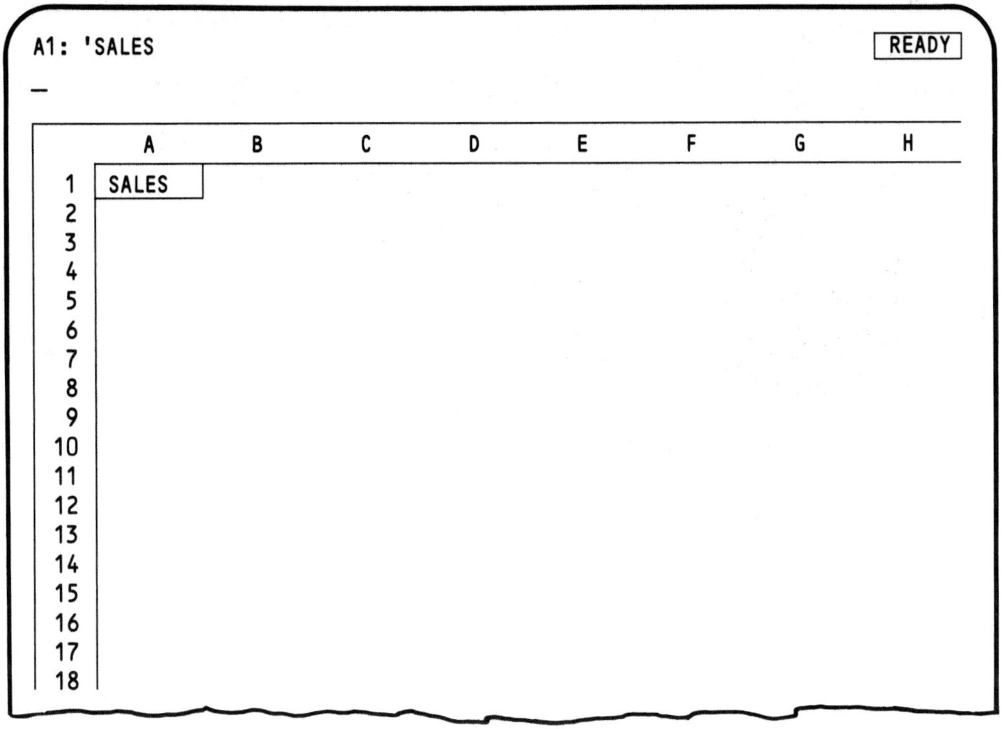

Figure 7.8 Completing a Label Entry

1-2-3 interpreted the first double-quote to be the right-adjust label prefix, rather than part of the label. So 1-2-3 right-adjusted the label **SALES"**, omitting the first double-quote. This is rather unexpected, to say the least.

How, then, do you do it? Simple! Start the label with the left-adjust label prefix (the apostrophe). Type the following:

```
'"SALES"[ENTER]
```

1-2-3 interprets the apostrophe to be the left-adjust label prefix. Follow the label prefix with the label as it is to display.

BEWARE *Displaying and Storing Long Labels*

If a label is longer than the column width, and the next cell on the right is empty, the label will display in the area used by that cell. You can enter up to 240 characters in a label; it displays in all the non-empty cells to its right that it can.

Figure 7.10 illustrates how the long label ACME QUARTERLY SALES FOR 1984 displays, entered in Cell A1.

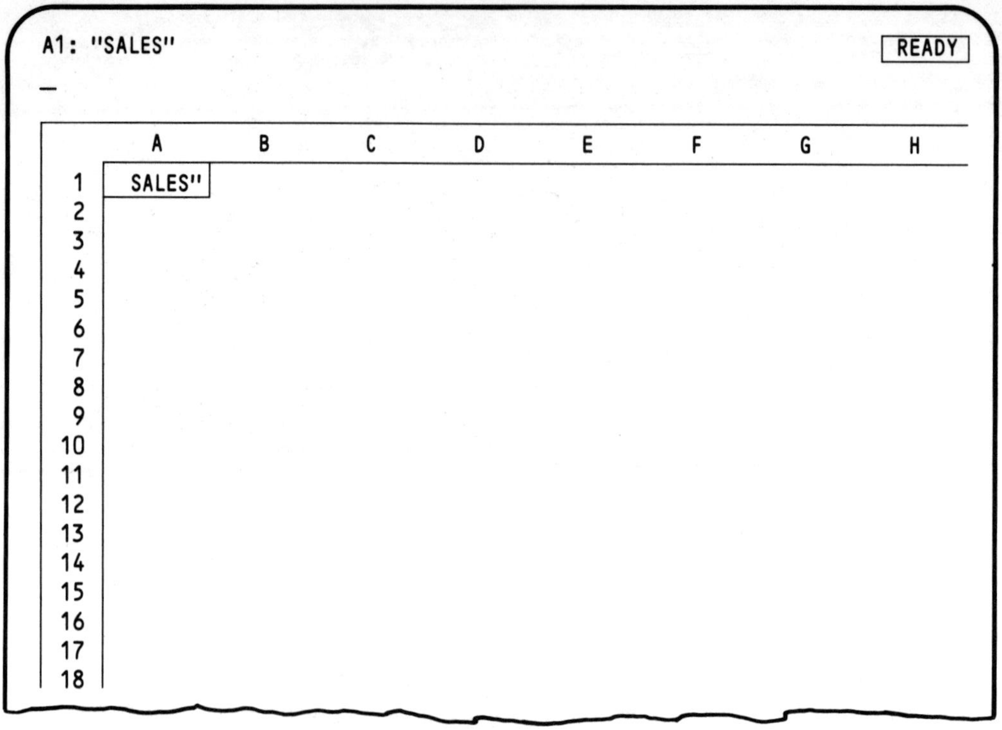

Figure 7.9 A Strange Label

In Cell B1, if you enter the value 123, the label displays as shown in Figure 7.11. You might think that part of the long label was destroyed by entering the value in Cell B1. This isn't true. There's a subtle difference between how a long label *displays* and what 1-2-3 *stores*. If you go to Cell A1 and look at the control panel, you will find that the *entire* label is still stored. Here is an instance where the information displayed looks different from the information stored.

Combining Entering with Moving

Pressing [ENTER] enters information into the cell but does not move the cell pointer. However, pressing a pointer-movement key when information is being entered has the effect of pressing [ENTER], to enter the information into the cell, and then pressing the key, to move the cell pointer. If you enter, in Cell A1, SALES[DOWN], the following occurs:

1. 1-2-3 displays SALES with the left-adjust label prefix, in Cell A1.

2. The cell pointer travels down, to Cell A2.

This combination of entering with moving works not only for [DOWN] but also

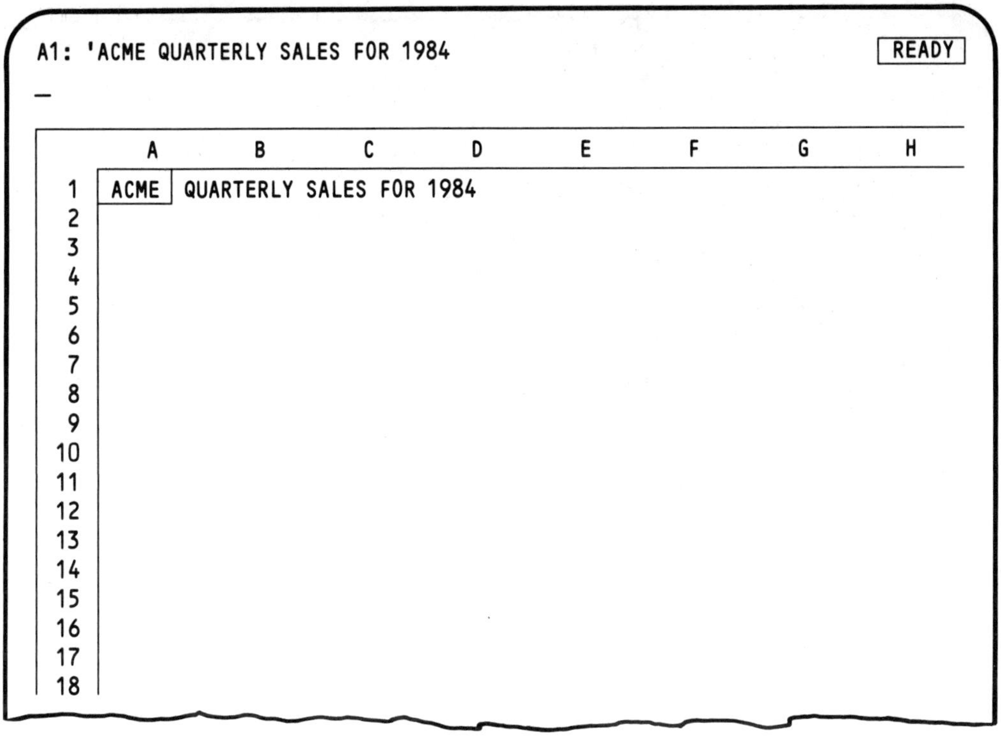

Figure 7.10 A Label Displaying Across Several Cells

for [LEFT], [RIGHT], [PGUP], [PGDN], and [HOME].

BEWARE ***You May End Up Where You Don't Want To Be***

If you are far away from [HOME], enter information into a cell, and press [HOME] by mistake, you enter the information into the far away cell, and you go home, to Cell A1. If you want to go back to that cell, you'll have to find your way there, since 1-2-3 doesn't remember where you were before you pressed [HOME].

MAKING CHANGES WITH [F2/EDIT]

What if you want to change an entry? You have two alternatives:

1. You can enter the new data in the cell, destroying the old data forever.
2. You can press [F2/EDIT]. You know you're editing a cell when the mode indicator displays EDIT.

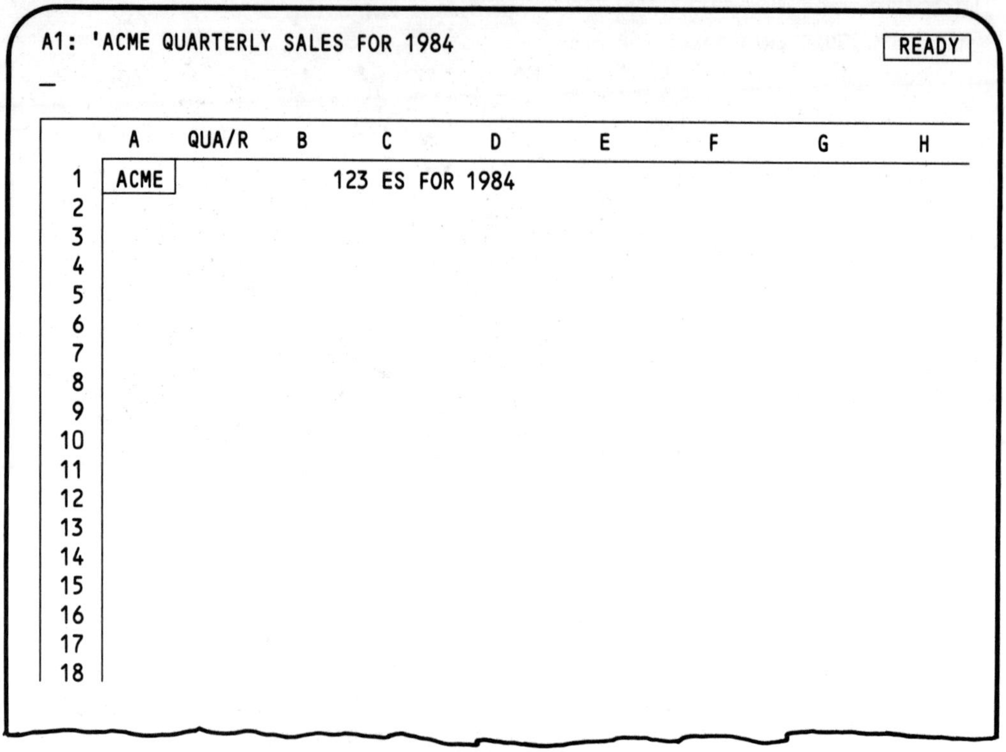

Figure 7.11 A Value Seemingly Destroying Part of the Label

Pressing [F2/EDIT] causes the entry to be copied into row 2 of the control panel. You can then change the entry, using the following keys:

[BACKSPACE]	delete the character to the left of the cursor
[DEL]	delete the character at the cursor
[LEFT]	move cursor one character to the left
[RIGHT]	move cursor one character to the right
[TAB]	move cursor 5 characters to the right
[SHIFT]-[TAB]	move cursor 5 characters to the left
[HOME]	move cursor to beginning of entry
[END]	move cursor to end of entry

If you make the changes and press [ENTER], the changed entry replaces the original entry. You can also press [UP], [DOWN], [PGUP], and [PGDN], to combine entering with moving. When you try to enter invalid information into a cell, 1-2-3 automatically places you in EDIT mode.

Entering Values

Values are numbers, used in calculations. If the first character is any of the following: 0 1 2 3 4 5 6 7 8 9 + - . (@ # $ 1-2-3 assumes you are entering a value. If the first character is anything else, 1-2-3 assumes you are entering a label. When 1-2-3 is assuming you are entering a value, the mode indicator displays VALUE.

You enter a number without any dollar signs or commas. (You will see how to make the numbers look pretty—or *format* them—in Chapter 11.) The only exception to entering numbers unformatted is the use of the percent sign (%). If you type 100%, 1-2-3 interprets that the same as the number 1. You enter a decimal point to separate the integer from the decimal part. You can also enter a number in exponential format. Some examples of entering numbers are:

123
0.50
50%
-5.77
2.54E+3 (2.54 * 1000 or 2,540)

1-2-3 remembers numbers to approximately 15 decimal places.

BEWARE *Entering Numbers with the Numeric Keypad*

The numeric keypad on the IBM PC has two meanings. If [NUM LOCK] is on, the keys have numeric values; if [NUM LOCK] is off, they are used to travel around the worksheet. If you want to enter numbers with the numeric keypad, and [NUM LOCK] is off, you wind up traveling! (You also may wind up entering a number when you want to travel.) Whenever you use the numeric keypad, check for the **NUM** indicator displaying in the bottom row.

You'll hardly ever go wrong if you use the numbers on the top row of the typewriter keyboard, which always mean numbers unless you press [SHIFT].

HOW TO: Use 1-2-3 as a Calculator

It's very simple to use 1-2-3 as a calculator. 1-2-3 will let you enter any calculation involving numbers in a cell and will display the answer. 1-2-3 uses the following mathematical symbols:

+	(addition)
-	(subtraction)
*	(multiplication)
/	(division)
^	(exponentiation—raise to a power)

The following are some simple calculations you can have 1-2-3 perform:

400*3	(displays 1200)
-6/3	(displays -2)
2^3	(2 to the third power, or 8)
(5+4)*3	(9*3, or 27)

BEWARE *You May Not Always Want to Calculate a Value*

I've run into situations where this automatic calculator feature has gotten me into trouble. Consider the case of entering a telephone number (say 617-

555-1212) as a label. You might want to do this if you are sending your worksheet to someone at another office and you want to display your phone number if a problem arises.) If you enter **617-555-1212** in Cell A1, 1-2-3 displays the number **-1150**.

Why? 1-2-3 calculated the formula 617−555−1212 and entered the answer (−1150) in Cell A1. How do you get around this? Read the HOW TO below to find out.

HOW TO: Start a Label with a Number

Suppose you want to start a label with a number? You might want to title your worksheet 1984 SALES. If you try to enter **1984 SALES** in Cell A1, 1-2-3 beeps and puts you in **EDIT** mode, with the cursor after the 4 in 1984.

Since the first character of the entry is **1** 1-2-3 thought you were trying to enter a value! 1-2-3 has to calculate a number from what you enter. Since it could not calculate a number from the label 1984 SALES 1-2-3 placed you in **EDIT** mode. The cursor is positioned at the point where 1-2-3 gave up.

Then how do you start a label with a number? Simple! Start the label with a *label prefix*. From where 1-2-3 placed you, if you type the following:

3[HOME]	get to beginning of entry
'	start entry with the left-adjust label prefix
[ENTER]	enter it into the cell

you will enter the 1984 SALES label into the cell. If the first character of a label is a label prefix, 1-2-3 ignores it and interprets the second character as the beginning of the label. Earlier in this chapter, we discovered that this was a potential problem when starting a label with a label prefix. Here, it saves us.

The telephone number problem is solved in the same way. You must start the telephone number entry with a label prefix, and then enter the number.

Leaving the 1-2-3 Program

To leave 1-2-3, the mode indicator should display **READY**. Enter the following keys:

/QY

The slash character (/) invokes the main 1-2-3 menu, which you will learn about in the next chapter. The **Q**uit option starts the process of leaving 1-2-3; the **Y** confirms that you really want to leave.

BEWARE ***When You Leave 1-2-3, the Data You Have Entered Is Lost***

That's right, it's gone forever. In addition to learning about menus, you'll learn how to save the worksheet data in the next chapter.

Where you go after you leave 1-2-3 depends on how you got into the program. There are two possibilities:

1. If you entered 1-2-3 through the Lotus Access System or by turning on the PC through using the system disk to startup the PC, you are returned to the Lotus Access System.
2. If you entered 1-2-3 through PC-DOS, you are returned to PC-DOS.

Congratulations! You already know quite a bit, although you must admit you have created nothing worth saving. You're ready for Chapter 8, where you will create a worksheet and save it in a more permanent form, as a disk file.

CHAPTER 8

Saving and Retrieving Your Work

In this chapter, you will learn how to use 1-2-3 menus and to save and retrieve disk files using the 1-2-3 /File commands.

THE MAIN 1-2-3 MENU

From 1-2-3, if the mode indicator displays READY, you can invoke the main 1-2-3 menu by pressing the slash character (/). Although you have used the 1-2-3 menu in several of the exercises, you have not been formally introduced to it. The main 1-2-3 menu has the following options:

```
Worksheet Range Copy Move File Print Graph Data Quit
```

As in the Lotus Access System, when you are in a menu, the mode indicator displays MENU. The menu choices display in the second row of the control panel; row 3 of the control panel is a longer explanation of the highlighted choice.

All the Lotus 1-2-3 programs are consistent in display and in how you choose from the options. As in the Lotus Access System, you can either:

1. Point to the option. Use [HOME], [END], [LEFT], or [RIGHT] to point to the option. Press [ENTER] to select the option. Or,
2. Type the first character of the option. For each menu, all the choices have a different first character. Simply type that letter (you needn't press [ENTER]) to select the option.

LEVELS OF MENUS

Most menus have several levels. When you select an option, there's a good chance you'll see another menu with additional options. For example, the /File menu, which lets you control disk files and which you will use in this chapter, contains several options depending on what you wish to do with the files.

You may have made a mistake and want to go to a previous level, as for example to return to the 1-2-3 main menu from the /File menu. To do so, simply press [ESC]. [ESC] returns you to the previous menu.

You may have to select from as many as 5 menus to have 1-2-3 perform a particular function. (Don't worry. This is only for the most complicated functions.) Perhaps you decided you didn't really want to do this and you want to return to entering information in the worksheet. You could press [ESC] 5 times. Or, you could take a short-cut: pressing [CTRL]-[BREAK] once. [CTRL]-[BREAK] means aborts the function you were in.

THE /FILE MENU

From the main 1-2-3 menu, you can choose from 9 options. This chapter deals with saving your work on disk files. To save your work, you use the /File menu. From the main 1-2-3 menu, press F (or use the pointer movement keys to highlight the File option and press [ENTER]). The /File menu has the following options:

```
Retrieve Save Combine Xtract Erase List Import Directory
```

/File Save, /File Retrieve, /File Erase, /File List, and /File Directory are discussed in this chapter. The other /File commands are discussed in Chapter 18.

When you enter information into the worksheet, it is stored in RAM. RAM, you will recall, is temporary memory. It is erased when you quit 1-2-3. Using the /File commands, you can store your worksheet onto a more permanent medium—the disk.

Worksheets are stored as PC-DOS disk files. As such, they must adhere to the rules for naming PC-DOS files—rules discussed in Chapter 3. Each file must be named with a directory (or disk) name, a filename, and an extension. You need only enter the filename. 1-2-3 fills in the directory name and the extension for you.

Saving Your Worksheet to the Disk

/File Save saves the worksheet in memory to a disk file. Create a filename containing from 1 to 8 characters; 1-2-3 adds the directory name, and the .WKS extension.

BEWARE ***Save Your Worksheet Frequently***

You should use /File Save any time you have entered information you wish to keep from one 1-2-3 session to another. You should also use /File Save several times within a session if you are making many changes. My rule of thumb is *if it's hard to reconstruct the changes, save the file.* You never know when some unforseen event, like a power failure, will destroy the information in RAM and cause you to lose your worksheet.

If you have previously issued a /File Save in this session, 1-2-3 remembers the last filename you used and proposes that as the new filename. This is usually what you want because you probably are going to use /File Save for the same file several times during a session. If the specified filename does not exist, using /File Save will automatically create it on the disk.

BEWARE ***If a File with the Same Name Already Exists, the Old Contents Are Lost***

If the filename already exists on the disk, 1-2-3 asks whether you really want to replace the file with the contents of your worksheet. If you replace the file, the old contents are lost and cannot be retrieved. If you decide not to replace the file, specifying Cancel returns you to READY mode, cancelling the command. In most cases, you really do want to replace the file, because the old information is out of date. However, if you want to keep the old information, type another filename. 1-2-3 erases its proposed filename, letting you type the name you choose. Press [ENTER]. If your filename doesn't exist, 1-2-3 will save the worksheet with the name you chose rather than the name it proposed. You'll then have two versions of the worksheet.

BEWARE ***Save Your Worksheet Before Using /Worksheet Erase or /Quit***

/Worksheet Erase erases the worksheet. Before you do it, save your worksheet if you wish to keep its contents. Of course, if you don't need to save your worksheet, then don't do a /File Save. If you /Quit 1-2-3, you also lose the worksheet unless you issue a /File Save beforehand.

/File Save saves all the information related to the worksheet. It even saves the position of the cell pointer!

Retrieving Your Worksheet from the Disk

You probably will have many worksheets stored on a disk. The command to retrieve a saved worksheet file is /File Retrieve. When you issue /File Retrieve (if any worksheets exist in the directory), 1-2-3 displays them as a one-row menu. You can use [HOME], [END], [RIGHT], or [LEFT] to point to the file you wish to retrieve, or you can simply type the filename.

BEWARE ***/File Retrieve Erases the Previous Memory Contents***

Before you use /File Retrieve, be sure that you use /File Save if you wish to save the worksheet in memory to disk. /File Retrieve destroys the worksheet in memory before retrieving the worksheet from the disk file.

Listing the Worksheet Files

/File List Worksheet lists worksheet files on the directory. You can also list graph pictures (which have the .PIC extension) and print files (which have the .PRN extension). You cannot list any other files on the directory with /File List. If you want to list *all* files in your directory, you must use either the File-Manager or PC-DOS. In addition to displaying the file names, /File List displays the amount of space (in bytes) remaining on the disk. If this amount is small, you might consider using the command discussed below.

Erasing Worksheet Files

You can use /File Erase to erase (delete or remove) unwanted files from the disk, thus creating more room for other files.

BEWARE *Files Erased with /File Erase Cannot Be Recovered*

Since 1-2-3 cannot reconstruct files which have been erased, be sure that when you erase a file, you really don't need the information in it.

You can erase .PIC and .PRN files, as well as .WKS files, with /File Erase. You can also use a wild card file designation to erase multiple files. The wild card designators are:

? (matches a single character: H?T matches HOT, HAT, and HIT)

* (matches all characters to end of filename: C* matches any filename starting with the letter C)

BEWARE *You May Erase More Files Than You Want*

For example, the command /FEW * (/File Erase Worksheet) erases *all* worksheet files. Wild cards are convenient, but be careful!

Changing the Default Directory or Disk

/File Directory displays the name of the directory in which your data files are being saved. In PC-DOS Version 1.1, the drive designator is the letter of the diskette drive where 1-2-3 accesses and stores data files (usually the B-drive). If you are using PC-DOS Version 2, you can specify a directory. /File Directory displays the current directory path where 1-2-3 stores and retrieves data files.

You can change either the drive designator, or the directory, either for the duration of this 1-2-3 session, or permanently. If you are using a hard disk, you probably have multiple directories resident on it. You may store one type of worksheet (your budget data) in one directory, and another type of worksheet (your invoices) in another directory. Use /Worksheet Global Default Directory to point to another directory for this session. Use /Worksheet Global Default Update to change the directory permanently.

Exercises

The following exercises should familiarize you with using the disk to save your work. If you are storing your worksheets on diskette, be sure to have at least one blank, formatted diskette handy. Refer to Chapter 3 for how to use the PC-DOS FORMAT command to format the disk. You can also use the Lotus Access System's File-Manager to prepare a disk—refer to Chapter 5. If you are storing worksheets on a hard disk, the disk has already been formatted.

1. Enter 1-2-3 so that the initial 1-2-3 screen displays. If you are storing data files on diskette, insert the blank, formatted diskette in the B-drive and close the drive door.

2. Start by entering a row of data, in preparation for saving it. Type the following:

SALES[RIGHT]	Enter SALES label in A1 and go to B1
100[RIGHT]	Enter value 100 in B1 and go to C1
200[RIGHT]	Enter value 200 in C1 and go to D1
300[ENTER]	Enter value 300 in D1

3. To save the file, giving it the name SALES, type the following:

/FSSALES[ENTER]	Use /File Save to file SALES.WKS

4. To see if the worksheet file exists in the directory, use **/File List Worksheet**. Type the following:

/FLW	List the worksheet files in the directory

The entry for the file SALES displays, as well as a display of the number of bytes available for storage of additional files. Press any key to clear the display and return to the worksheet display.

5. To erase the worksheet in RAM, use **/Worksheet Erase**. Type the following:

/WEY	Use /Worksheet Erase and confirm

The worksheet should be empty.

6. To retrieve the file just saved, use **/File Retrieve**. Type the following:

/FRSALES[ENTER]	Retrieve SALES.WKS from the disk

The SALES row, as originally entered, should display in the worksheet. It was retrieved from the disk file. Note that the cell pointer is positioned at Cell D1—its position when the worksheet was saved to SALES.WKS.

7. If you change a value and save the file again, 1-2-3 saves the change. Type the following:

[LEFT]150[ENTER]	Change Cell C1 to 150
/FS[ENTER]	Save the file (1-2-3 remembers your previous **/File Save** was to the SALES file)
R	Confirm that you want to replace the file with new information

You have now changed the SALES.WKS file on disk, changing Cell C1 from 200 to 150.

8. To erase the file from within 1-2-3, use **/File Erase Worksheet**. Type the following:

/FEWSALES[ENTER]	Erase the worksheet file SALES.WKS
Y	Confirm that you reall want to erase it
/FLW	/File List SALES.WKS is erased

SALES.WKS is gone; 1-2-3 cannot reconstruct it. Press any key to clear the display and return to the worksheet display.

9. Finally, use /Worksheet Global Default Directory to display the current directory in which data files will be stored. Type the following:

/WGDD	Show the default directory
[ENTER]Q	Back to the worksheet display

If you are using PC-DOS Version 1.1 a two-diskette PC, the default directory is probably B: which indicates the diskette in the B-drive. If you are using PC-DOS Version 2, the default directory is the full path name of the directory in which your data files are kept.

If you change the default directory, any data files saved in this session will be saved on it. If you do not save the change, the default directory remains in effect for this session only. You must use /Worksheet Global Default Update to make this new directory for data files permanent. 1-2-3 saves the new default directory in the file 123.CNF, the 1-2-3 configuration file, on the system disk. If you update the configuration file, the directory stored in it becomes the default directory for the next 1-2-3 session.

Now that you know how to save your work on disk, you are ready to learn how to enter formulas and create useful worksheets. In Chapter 9, you will enter a simple worksheet for Acme Widget and save it to disk.

CHAPTER 9

Entering Formulas

This chapter introduces several methods of entering formulas into the 1-2-3 worksheet. You will create a worksheet comparing Acme Widget's budgeted and actual sales, and save it for later modification.

WHAT IS A FORMULA?

A *formula* is simply a generalization of the HOW TO in which we used 1-2-3 as a simple calculator. Instead of entering a calculation referencing numbers, you enter a formula referencing cells which contain a number. If Cell A1 contained the value 2, and Cell A2 contained the value 3, if Cell A3 contained the formula +A1+A2, the formula would evaluate to 5.

Why go to the trouble of creating formulas? Because if a cell referenced in a formula is changed, 1-2-3 automatically recalculates the formula. In other words, if you changed the value in Cell A1 to 5, Cell A3 would automatically change to 5+3, or 8. Formulas are the reason spreadsheet software is so popular. Simply by changing one number, such as the rate of inflation, you can see the effect on thousands of formulas which depend on it, such as costs for each of your raw materials.

ENTERING A FORMULA BY TYPING

One way to enter a formula is to type it in the cell. Consider the following worksheet:

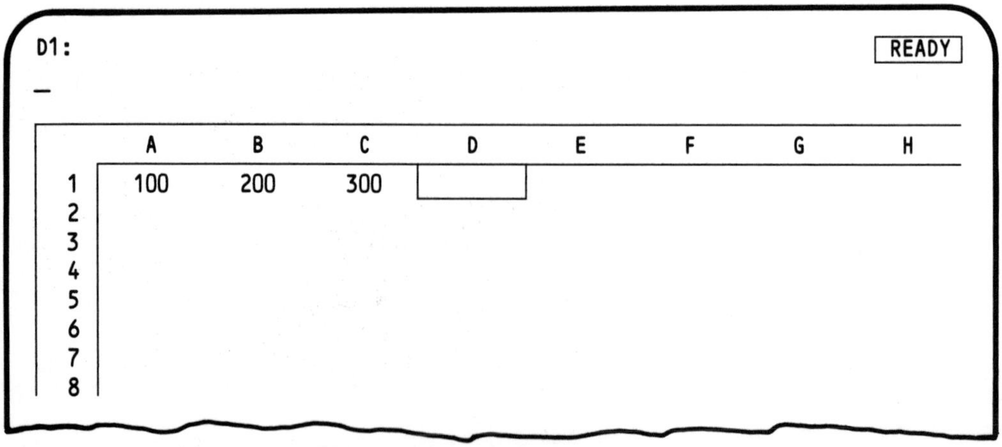

Figure 9.1

Cell A1 contains the value 100; Cell B1 the value 200; and Cell C1 the value 300. You could enter, in Cell D1, a formula which instructs 1-2-3 to add the contents of Cells A1, B1, and C1. The following formula instructs 1-2-3 to do just that:

```
+A1+B1+C1[ENTER]
```

You must start the formula entry with an arithmetic operator, such as +, to prevent 1-2-3 from thinking that we want to enter the *label* A1+B1+C1. The worksheet displays as shown below:

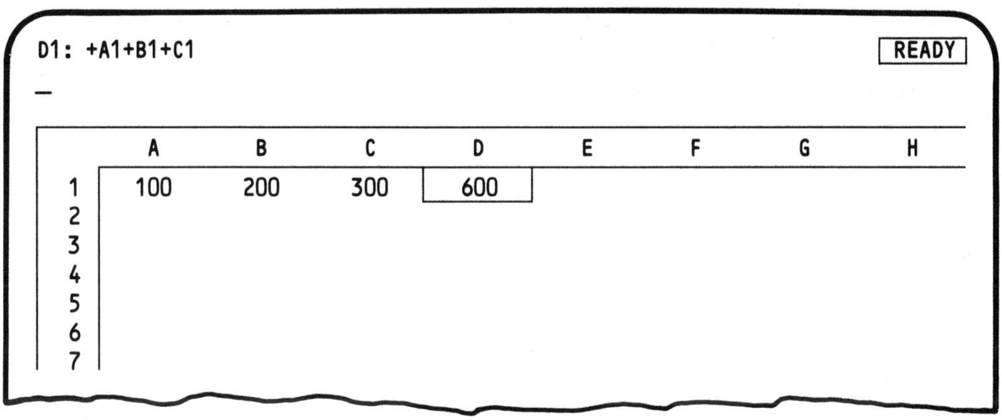

Figure 9.2

This formula *automatically* changes when the values in A1, B1, or C1 change. This feature is called *automatic recalculation*. In Chapter 15, you will learn how to turn off automatic recalculation, as well as the other recalculation methods used by 1-2-3.

Entering a Formula by Pointing to Cells

Instead of entering a formula directly in the cell, you can point to the cells referenced in the formula. You use the pointer-movement keys to point to these cells. In Cell D1, you can enter the formula as follows:

`+[LEFT][LEFT][LEFT]`	Point to Cell A1
`+`	The cell pointer is back at Cell D1
`[LEFT][LEFT]`	Point to Cell B1
`+[LEFT][ENTER]`	Point to Cell C1; enter the formula

using `[LEFT]` to point to the cells in the formula.

Whenever 1-2-3 expects a cell reference, you can either type it in or point to it. If you point to a cell reference, the mode indicator changes to **POINT**.

You can mix typing and pointing, if you wish. You can start by typing cell references and end by pointing to them; or vice versa. The exercises at the end of this chapter will give you practice in mixing these ways of entering formulas.

BEWARE ***If You Enter an Invalid Formula, 1-2-3 Places You in EDIT Mode***

If you make a mistake in entering a formula, and try to enter it, 1-2-3 places you in EDIT mode. You *must* complete the formula by typing—you cannot go back to POINT mode. So be careful when entering formulas!

WHAT IS A FUNCTION?

1-2-3 provides many pre-written formulas, or *functions*. Functions are extremely valuable because they can save you from entering time-consuming and complex formulas.

All 1-2-3 functions begin with the at-sign (@). To use a function, you supply values, called *arguments*. The meaning of an argument varies from one function to another. In one case, an argument can be an individual cell; in another, a column number; in another, group of cells. Not only can the meaning of an argument vary, but so can the number of arguments. Some functions take one argument, some take two. Some even take as many as you want to supply! The arguments are enclosed in parentheses, so that a function is coded as follows:

```
@functionname(argument1,argument2,argument3,...)
```

All of the 1-2-3 functions and their arguments, except for the database statistical functions, are discussed in Chapter 17. The database statistical functions are discussed in Chapter 23, which discusses 1-2-3 databases as well.

USING THE @SUM FUNCTION

Functions are powerful short-cuts, aiding in the efficiency of your models. To give you a preview of the power of functions, 1-2-3 provides a function to add the contents of adjacent cells—the @SUM function. @SUM's arguments are one or more *cell-ranges*. Cell ranges are discussed in detail in Chapter 10. A cell-range is a rectangular array of cells. You specify a cell range by identifying the corners of the rectangular array. In Cell D1, you could have coded the formula to add the contents of Cells A1, B1, and C1, as follows:

```
@SUM(A1..C1)[ENTER]
```

The two periods are used to identify a cell-range, with A1 and C1 as its corners.

Using the @SUM function for a cell range of three cells doesn't save much coding. However, consider the coding involved in summing the contents of the first 20 rows for Column A. Would you rather code

```
@SUM(A1..A20)[ENTER]
```

or

```
+A1+A2+A3+A4+A5+A6+A7+A8+A9+A10+A11+A12+A13+A14+A15+A16+A17+A18+A19+A20
```

HOW TO: Find the Value of a Cell Without Traveling to It

Did you know that you don't have to travel to a cell to find out its value? You can enter a formula referencing that cell. If you press [F2/EDIT], followed by [F9/CALC], 1-2-3 converts the cell formula into its value. The following example shows how you can enter a value in Cell A21, then go [HOME] to Cell A1 (Cell A21 does not display). While you are at Cell A1, you can find Cell A21's value, which displays in the control panel. When you're done, simply press [ESC] to prevent the formula + A21 to be stored in Cell A1, and you're done. Enter the following:

[F5/GOTO]A21[ENTER]	Go to Cell A21
5000[HOME]	Enter 5000 and go to Cell A1
+A21	Start as if you are entering formula
[F2/EDIT][F9/CALC]	The value in Cell A21 displays in the control panel
[ESC]	Just fooling! You didn't want to put that value in Cell A1

Exercises

You probably need some practice before you become proficient in 1-2-3's methods of entering formulas. Start with a fresh worksheet. Use /Worksheet Erase Yes if you have any leftover data from the previous exercise; or simply restart 1-2-3. If you are using a diskette to store files, insert it into the B-drive and close the drive door.

You will practice the methods of entering a formula to sum the values in three cells in a row. Enter 100 in Cell B1, 200 in Cell C1, and 300 in Cell D1. Position the cell pointer at Cell E1, where you will enter the formula to sum these values. Your worksheet should display as shown in Figure 9.3.

1. First, enter a formula into Cell E1 by typing it. The formula will calculate the sum of the values in Cells B1, C1, and D1, and store the result in Cell E1. Type the following:

[F5/GOTO]E1[ENTER]	Go to the cell to enter the formula
+B1+C1+D1[ENTER]	Type the formula E1=B1+C1+D1

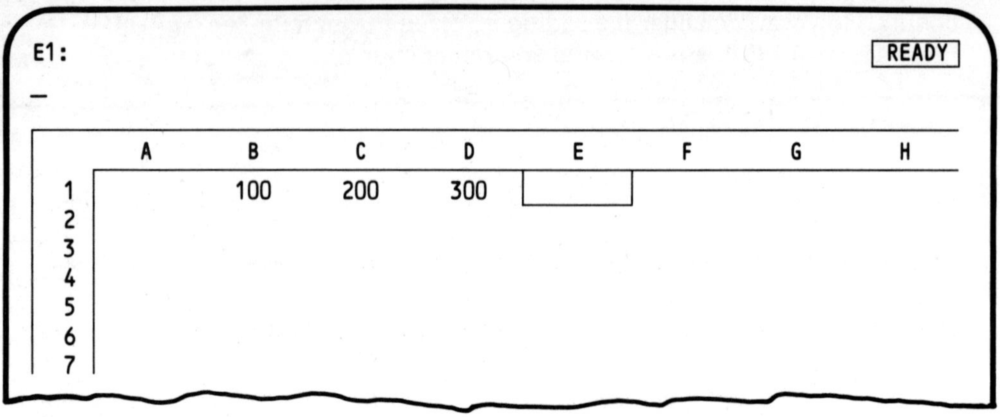

Figure 9.3

See what happens if the contents of Cell D1 are changed by typing the following:

`[LEFT]400[ENTER]` Change Cell D1 to 400

1-2-3 automatically recalculates the formula in Cell E1 (to 700) to reflect the changed value in Cell D1. That's the beauty of formulas. When you change a cell referenced in the formula, the formula is automatically recalculated.

Your worksheet should display as follows:

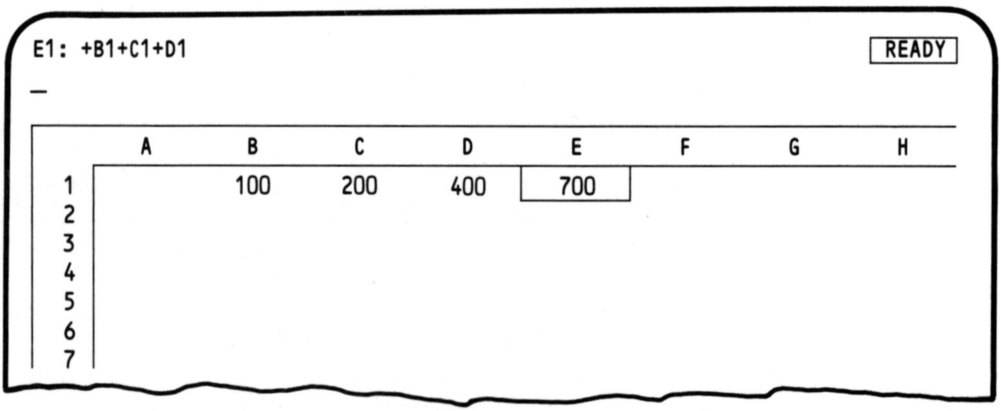

Figure 9.4

2. Appearances can be deceiving. Even though the formula in Cell E1 displays as a value, it's quite different from a simple number in the cell. If a number were stored in Cell E1, the formula would be destroyed; if you made a change to Cell D1, the change would not be reflected in Cell E1. Type the following and see what I mean:

[RIGHT]650[ENTER]	Change Cell E1 to the value 650
[LEFT]600[RIGHT]	Now change Cell D1

Cell E1's value did not change. In general, once you enter a formula, you would like to prevent it from being destroyed. In Chapter 12, we will explore some techniques which help to preserve formulas.

3. In addition to letting us type in the formula, 1-2-3 lets us enter the formula by pointing to cells. Type the following:

+[LEFT][LEFT][LEFT]	Point to Cell B1
+	The cell pointer is back at Cell E1
[LEFT][LEFT]	Point to Cell C1
+[LEFT][ENTER]	Point to Cell D1; enter the formula

Were you able to point to the cells which are referenced in the formula?

4. 1-2-3 lets you be even more creative in entering formulas. You can either start typing the formula and finish by pointing to cells; or you can start pointing to cells and finish with typing the formula. To start typing and finish by pointing, enter the following:

+B1+C1+	Start by typing part of the formula
[LEFT][ENTER]	Finish by pointing to Cell D1

To go the other way, starting by pointing and finishing by typing, enter the following:

+[LEFT][LEFT][LEFT]	Start by pointing to Cell B1
+C1+D1[ENTER]	Finish by typing the rest of the formula

5. You can also sum the values in Cells B1, C1, and D1 using the @SUM function. Enter the following:

[F5/GOTO]E1[ENTER]	Go to the cell to enter the function
@SUM(B1..D1)[ENTER]	Sum the values in Cells B1, C1, and D1

6. It's time for you to enter a simple model shown in Figure 9.5. The worksheet consists of 4 columns. Column A contains Acme's branch office names; Column B the target revenues (in thousands); Column C the actual revenues, and Column D the percent of the target that each office achieved. Enter the data shown below Figure 9.5. Each line shows the cell reference, followed by a colon, followed by what you type. The worksheet contains two formulas: a division calculation for cells in Column D, which calculates actual revenue as a percent of target revenue; and two @SUM function calculations in Row 13, which sum target and actual revenues for all offices.

```
A1:                                                              READY
_

        A        B        C        D        E        F        G        H
  1                            ACME WIDGET CORPORATION
  2                   YEAR-END REVENUE COMPARISON BY FIELD OFFICE
  3                                     (in 000s)
  4
  5  OFFICE      TARGET   ACTUAL % OF TARGET
  6  Atl            440      385      0.875
  7  Bos            600      685   1.141666
  8  NY             350      300   0.857142
  9  Chi            230      250   1.086956
 10  LA             540      600   1.111111
 11  Mia            308      250   0.811688
 12
 13  TOTAL         2468     2470   1.000810
 14
 15
 16
 17
 18
```

Figure 9.5

```
C1: ACME WIDGET CORPORATION
B2: YEAR-END REVENUE COMPARISON BY FIELD OFFICE
B3: '(in 000s)
A5: OFFICE
B5: TARGET
C5: ACTUAL
D5: % OF TARGET
A6: Atl
B6: 440
C6: 385
D6: +C6/B6
A7: Bos
B7: 600
C7: 685
D7: +C7/B7
A8: NY
B8: 350
```

```
C8: 300
D8: +C8/B8
A9: Chi
B9: 230
C9: 250
D9: +C9/B9
A10: LA
B10: 540
C10: 600
D10: +C10/B10
A11: Mia
B11: 308
C11: 250
D11: +C11/B11
A13: TOTAL
B13: @SUM(B6..B11)
C13: @SUM(C6..C11)
D13: +C13/B13
```

Since you will use this worksheet later, save it to the disk file ACME.WKS. Enter the following, after you have completed the worksheet:

```
/FSACME[ENTER]
```

Congratulations! You've created your first worksheet. You're well on your way to being able to create your own 1-2-3 worksheets. You now know the fundamentals. The rest of the chapters in this part of the book are intended to hone these skills so you can become even more creative with 1-2-3. So proceed to Chapter 10, where you'll learn all about cell ranges, one of the keys to effective use of 1-2-3.

CHAPTER 10

Using Cell Ranges

The ability to define and manipulate cell ranges is one of the most powerful parts of the 1-2-3 worksheet. After you understand how to use cell ranges, you will have much more control over creating and modifying worksheets. You will learn several techniques for defining and manipulating cell ranges. We will use these techniques many times in other chapters. At the end of this chapter, you will use cell ranges creatively to print the entire Acme worksheet using a few simple commands.

WHAT IS A CELL RANGE?

A cell range is a rectangular block of cells. You identify a range by naming the cells in the two diagonally opposite corners, of the rectangle, such as B5..B9 or A1.C5. You can define the following types of cell ranges: *A single-cell range.* A single-cell range is a cell range consisting of one cell. For example, the cell range A1..A1 contains only Cell A1. Figure 10.1 illustrates this.

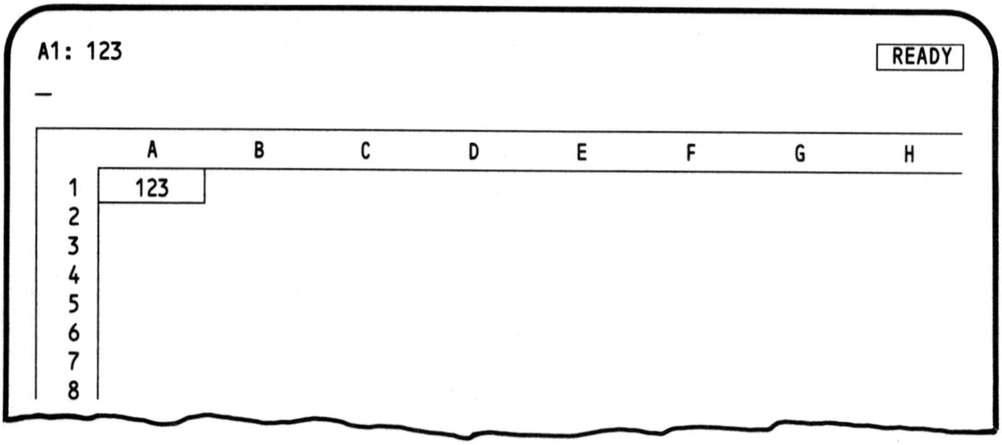

Figure 10.1 A Single-Cell Range

A cell range consisting of one column or one row. For example, the cells Column B, Rows 3 to 12, are contained in the cell range B3..B12. Or, the cells in Row 1, from Columns A to F, are contained in the cell range A1..F1. Figure 10.2 illustrates one-row cell range.

```
F1: 123                                                          POINT
Enter Print Range: A1..F1

         A        B        C        D        E        F        G        H
  1     123      123      123      123      123      123
  2
  3
  4
  5
  6
```

Figure 10.2 A Cell Range Consisting of One Row

A cell range consisting of more than one column and more than one row. For example, all the cells in Columns A through D and Rows 1 to 8 are contained in the cell range A1..D8. Figure 10.3 illustrates a cell range with multiple rows and columns.

```
F8: 123                                                          POINT
Enter Print range: A1..F8

         A        B        C        D        E        F        G        H
  1     123      123      123      123      123      123
  2     123      123      123      123      123      123
  3     123      123      123      123      123      123
  4     123      123      123      123      123      123
  5     123      123      123      123      123      123
  6     123      123      123      123      123      123
  7     123      123      123      123      123      123
  8     123      123      123      123      123      123
  9
 10
```

Figure 10.3 A Cell Range Consisting of Several Columns and Rows

HOW ARE CELL RANGES USED?

Cell ranges are used in a wide variety of situations. 1-2-3 uses them in many formulas. For example, the interest rate and the term arguments of the @PMT function (which calculates the payment for a loan) are single-cell ranges.

The @SUM function can sum the values in any number of cell ranges, although the most common situation is summing values in a one-column or one-row cell range.

Cell ranges are also used in *commands*. For example, when you print a worksheet using the /Print command, 1-2-3 requires that you specify a *print range* consisting of the block of cells you wish to print. Cell ranges used in commands are called *command ranges*. Many of the powerful 1-2-3 features depend on command ranges—you will encounter them many times.

DEFINING A CELL RANGE BY TYPING CELL ADDRESSES

The simplest way of defining a cell range is by typing in the addresses of the cells at the opposite corners of the rectangle. In typing cell addresses, note the following:

1. You must use at least one period to separate the two cell addresses. @SUM(B1.D1) is equivalent to @SUM(B1..D1). 1-2-3 displays the cell range using exactly two periods, regardless of the number of periods you use.
2. Upper case and lower case letters are interchangeable in referencing the cells.
3. You can reference any of the opposite corners of the rectangle.

All of the following reference the same cell range: A1..D3

D3..A1
A3..D1
D1..A3
a1..d3
a1.D3
A1.......d3

And, for a single-cell range, you can omit the second cell altogether. Thus, A1 is equivalent to A1..A1.

In the exercises of Chapter 9, you defined cell range for @SUM by typing it as the argument of the function. Whenever 1-2-3 requires a cell range, you can type it in.

DEFINING A CELL RANGE BY POINTING

Rather than typing the cell addresses, you can use the pointer-movement keys. As you define the range, 1-2-3 highlights it, filling in the cell addresses.

Defining cell ranges seems tricky at first, but it's really easy once you get the hang of it. You'll get the most benefit out of this description by entering 1-2-3 and pressing the keys that I indicate. You can also read the description and do the exercises for review. You'll need some practice before pointing at cell ranges becomes second-nature.

Enter the values 100, 200, and 300 in Cells B1, C1, and D1. Suppose you are at Cell E1 and want to use **@SUM** to sum the values in B1, C1, and D1. Start by typing the following:

```
@SUM(
```

The worksheet displays as shown below:

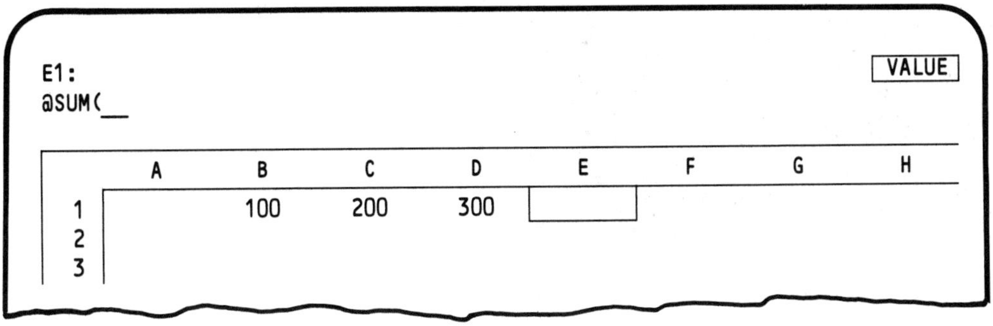

Figure 10.4

At this point, **@SUM** expects a cell range. You have a choice. You can enter it directly, as you did before. Or, you can use **[LEFT]** to *point* to the start of the range.

Press **[LEFT]**. (Note that the mode indicator switches to **POINT** mode.) The worksheet displays as shown below:

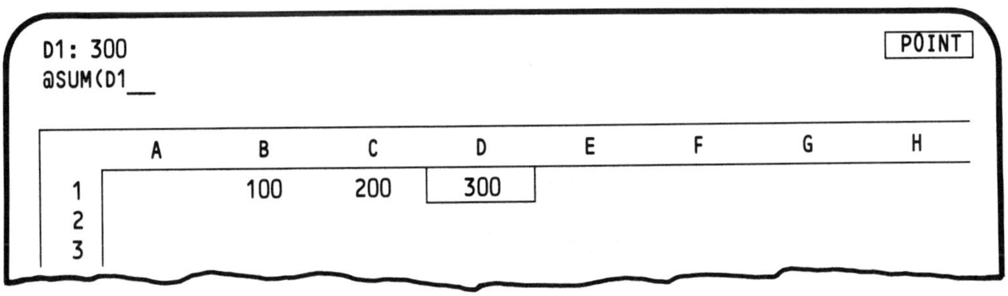

Figure 10.5

You have reached a corner of the cell range. To anchor the cell range, use the period. The period indicates the beginning of the cell range.

Enter **[PERIOD]**. The worksheet displays as shown below:

Note that 1-2-3 automatically fills in two periods and proposes the single-cell range D1..D1. The two dots mean that the cell address on the left (the first D1) is anchored.

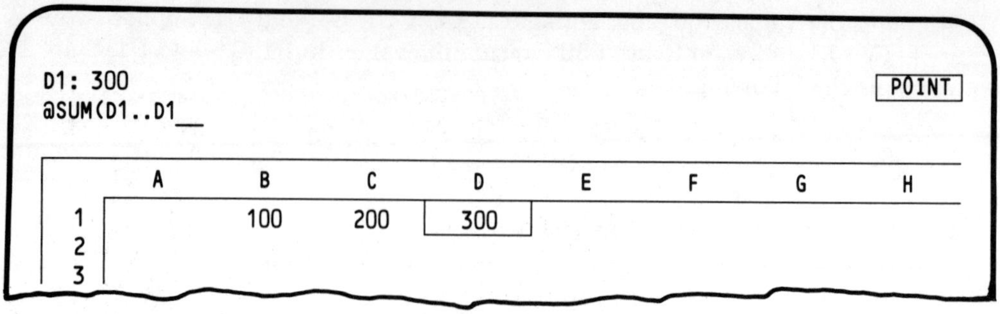

Figure 10.6

Press **[LEFT]** twice. Note that 1-2-3 highlights an expanded cell range. While the cell address D1 on the left is anchored, the cell address on the right changes as you travel. The cell range D1..B1 is highlighted; this is the range which you want **@SUM** to use. Enter a right parenthesis **)** to complete the range specification and **[ENTER]** to complete the formula. The worksheet displays as shown below:

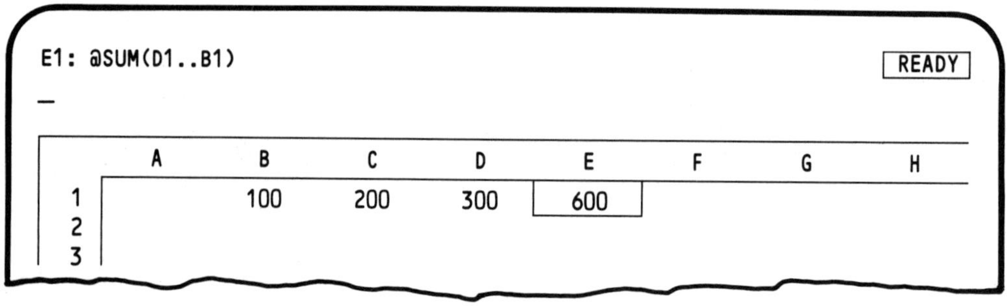

Figure 10.7

You're back at Cell E1, having entered the formula successfully!

The period has another use. If the cell pointer is anchored already, you can use the period to define a new anchor cell and free cell. This is called *riding the range.*

Using [ESC]

[ESC] has a special use in pointing to cell ranges. If the cell pointer is not already anchored, pressing **[ESC]** causes the cell pointer to return to the cell in which you are entering the formula and erases the cell address from the end of the formula. If the cell pointer is already anchored, pressing **[ESC]** shrinks the range back to the anchor cell, and removes the anchor. **[ESC]** is performing its usual role—backing up one step.

Using [BACKSPACE]

[BACKSPACE] also has a special use. When pointing at a cell range, [BACKSPACE] tells 1-2-3 to forget the cell range. If you want 1-2-3 to forget the cell range you had pointed to, press [BACKSPACE] to return to the cell in which you are entering the formula. From there, you can use the pointer-movement keys to define a new range. Of course, if you don't want to point, you can type in the cell addresses.

USING RANGE NAMES

cell ranges, you can define a named
ne rather than by cell addresses.
select the Range option. The Range
which work on cell ranges. One of
nich creates a name for a cell range.
SALESNUMBERS, identifying the

NTER]

ayed as @SUM(D1..B1), now dis-
pl ge name makes the formula more
ur a that you're adding up the sales
nu ing of adding up the numbers if
the

instead of its cell addresses. If a
ran range 1-2-3 displays it in formulas. You can define more than one name for a cell range; however, one name can point to only one cell range.

HOW TO: Use Range Names to Go To Another Part of the Worksheet

You can use a range name, in conjunction with [F5/GOTO], to go to another part of the worksheet. If you use a range name with [F5/GOTO], you will go to the top-left corner of the range. This is very useful if different parts of the worksheet store different types of information. For example, suppose you use one part of the worksheet to enter revenue items, and another part to enter expense items. Use /Range Name Create, naming the cell which starts the revenue section REVENUE and the cell which starts the expense section EXPENSES. When you want to go to the revenue section, enter the following:

```
[F5/GOTO]REVENUE[ENTER]
```

And when you want to go to the expense section, enter the following:

```
[F5/GOTO]EXPENSES[ENTER]
```

If you forget the range names, you can use [F3/NAME] to display a list of range names and select from them. You can enter the following:

[F5/GOTO]	Go to another part of the worksheet
[F3/NAME]	Show me all the range names

Whenever you're in POINT mode, you can press [F3/NAME] to display a menu of range names.

BEWARE *Don't Use Range Names That Are Cell Addresses*

1-2-3 can get confused if you enter a range name that is a cell address. If you specify a range name called B2 (which really points to Cell F1), and you attempt to go to B2 (intending to go to the cell range starting at F1), you may wind up at Cell B2 instead!

You should define meaningful range names. For example, a cell range containing 1984 expense data should be named EXP84.

/Range Name Delete

You can use /Range Name Delete to delete a range name. If you enter the following:

```
/RNDSALESNUMBERS[ENTER]
```

the SALESNUMBERS range name is deleted. Any formulas which referenced SALESNUMBERS would reference the cell addresses again. Thus, the display of the formula would revert to @SUM(D1..B1).

BEWARE *Once You Delete a Range Name, You Cannot Restore It*

If you accidentally delete a range name, (it's easy enough to do; 1-2-3 does not warn you with a confirmation message) you must remember the cell range it pointed to and use /Range Name Create to re-create the range name.

BEWARE *Using /Range Name Reset*

/Range Name Reset is potentially even more dangerous—it resets *all* range names. If you are building a complex model, it is entirely likely that you may create many range names. (I have seen 1-2-3 worksheets with over 100 range names.) /Range Name Reset will erase all of them at once. Again, as with /Range Name Delete, 1-2-3 does not warn you. So make sure you really want to reset your range names before you do it.

/Range Name Labels

/Range Name Labels lets you define many single-cell range names at once. You enter a column of labels and tell 1-2-3 to create single-cell range names to the left, right, above, or below the labels. /Range Name Labels is used primarily to make formulas display more clearly. It is also a powerful tool in writing sophisticated macros and in streamlining 1-2-3's data management.

HOW TO: Make 1-2-3 Remember Ranges

Save your worksheet with /File Save. When 1-2-3 saves your worksheet, it saves all the cell ranges and range names as well as the worksheet data itself. This means that when you retrieve your file in another session, the cell ranges and range names you have created are retrieved along with it.

/RANGE AND /WORKSHEET COMMANDS

Now that you understand what a range is, it's easy to understand the difference between /Range and /Worksheet commands. The /Range commands apply to cell ranges. /Worksheet commands, however, apply to the entire worksheet.

Several of the /Worksheet commands and /Range commands seem to perform the same function. A good example is /Range Erase, which erases the contents of cells in a cell range. The comparable /Worksheet command is /Worksheet Erase, which erases the entire worksheet.

But do they perform the same functions? No. /Worksheet Erase has more drastic effects. Using /Worksheet Erase is like starting 1-2-3 from scratch, erasing all your work. Among other things, /Worksheet Erase erases your range names! /Range Erase does not affect range names. You will see other examples of how /Range and /Worksheet commands, while appearing to be similar, have quite different effects, in the next chapter.

BEWARE ***/Range Erase Is Not the Same As Entering Blanks in a Cell***

Entering blanks in a cell is different from an empty cell. A cell with blanks stored is actually a *label* consisting of the label-prefix and blanks. A truly empty cell contains no label-prefix.

This difference is important. When you learn about the /Data commands, you will see cases where not knowing the difference between a a cell containing blanks and a truly empty cell can cause problems.

Exercises

If you read this chapter without following along by pressing the keys in 1-2-3, enter 1-2-3. Have your diskette with the ACME.WKS worksheet file handy, because you will print it at the end of this chapter.

1. Let's define a single-cell range. The cell range consists of the Cell A1, where you were when you saved the ACME.WKS file. Type the following:

```
/RNCONECELL[ENTER][ENTER]
```

2. You can define another cell range called ONEROW consisting of the first four cells in Row 1 (A1..D1). This is the type of cell range you will most frequently create, for functions such as **@SUM**. Create range by pointing, by typing the following:

```
/RNCONEROW[ENTER]
[RIGHT][RIGHT][RIGHT][ENTER]
```

3. Finally, define a block of cells called FIVEBYFOUR consisting of all the cells in the first five rows and the first four columns (A1..D5). Type the following:

```
/RNCFIVEBYFOUR[ENTER]A1..D5[ENTER]
```

4. **@SUM** will take any number and type of cell range as arguments. You can use **@SUM** to sum various columns of the FIVEBYFOUR cell range.

First, put some numbers in the cell range. The easiest way to do this is to use the /Data Fill command. (Remember how you used /Data Fill in Chapter 7 to fill the entire active worksheet with numbers?) Instead of typing the cell addresses, you can specify the FIVEBYFOUR cell range, as follows:

```
/DFFIVEBYFOUR[ENTER]1[ENTER]1[ENTER][ENTER]
```

Each cell should be numbered consecutively, columnwise, from 1 to 20.

Go to Cell A6. To use **@SUM** to sum the numbers in Column A by pointing, type the following:

```
@SUM([UP].[HOME])[ENTER]
```

To define the cell range, use [UP] to point to the last cell in the column, [PERIOD] to anchor the cell pointer, and [HOME] to expand the cell pointer to Cell A1.

The **@SUM** formula should evaluate to 15.

Just for fun, let's sum the values in the three ranges you created—ONECELL (A1..A1), ONEROW (A1..D1), and FIVEBYFOUR (A1..D5). Type the following:

```
@SUM(ONECELL,ONEROW,FIVEBYFOUR)[ENTER]
```

The **@SUM** formula should evaluate to 245 (the sum of the values in each of these cell ranges).

5. This shows how [ESC] and [BACKSPACE] work. Suppose you want to add the values in Column A, as follows:

```
@SUM([UP].[HOME]
```

and then decide that you really wanted to add the value in Row 5. How can you cause 1-2-3 to forget the range that is currently highlighted? Simple! Press **[ESC]**. The formula which formerly displayed as **@SUM(A5..A1** now displays as **@SUM(A5** with the anchor removed. To continue, press **[PERIOD]** (to create the anchor cell at A5, and then **[END][RIGHT]** (to get to the end of the values in Row 5). Complete the formula by typing **)[ENTER]**. The formula **@SUM(A5..D5)** evaluates to 50.

While **[ESC]** causes 1-2-3 to forget the range, **[BACKSPACE]** goes one more step—it gets you back to the cell where you started entering the formula! Type the following starting at Cell A6:

```
@SUM([UP].[HOME][BACKSPACE]
```

You're back at Cell A6, with **@SUM(A6** displaying! The anchor has been removed; you can use the arrow keys to travel to another part of the worksheet. If you wanted to type the cell addresses, you could press **[ESC]** and type them in. For the purpose of the exercise, press **[CTRL]-[BREAK]** to start over.

6. Deleting and resetting range names affect the formula display. Let's recreate the **@SUM** function with three cell ranges as arguments, delete a range name, reset all range names, and see how these actions affect formula display. Type the following:

@SUM(ONECELL,ONEROW,FIVEBYFOUR)[ENTER]	
/RNDONECELL[ENTER]	(ONECELL is replaced by A1 in formula)
/RNR	(All the range names are gone!)

When a range name is deleted, 1-2-3 goes back to referencing the cell range by the cell addresses.

7. You can travel to the beginning of a range. Create a range name called RANGENAME, which starts at Cell A4, and use **[F5/GOTO]** to travel to it. Type the following:

/RNCRANGENAME[ENTER]	Create range name called RANGENAME
A4..F5[ENTER]	Upper-left corner at Cell A4
[F5/GOTO]RANGENAME[ENTER]	You've traveled to Cell A4!

You can run into trouble if the range name is a cell address, such as A6. Type the following to see:

/RNCA6[ENTER]A4..F5[ENTER]	Range name A6 names the same range
[F5/GOTO][F3/NAME]	Go to a named range
[ENTER]	Pointing to range name A6, confirm

Where did you wind up? At Cell A6, although you should have stayed put! This mixup can occur in other situations, such as arguments to functions. Moral: don't name ranges that can be confused with cell addresses.

8. Finally, to see the effect of erasing values, but not the function, use /Range Erase. Type the following:

```
/REA1..D5[ENTER]
```

Unfortunately, since the FIVEBYFOUR range name was wiped out with the /Range Name Reset, you had to identify the range with cell addresses. The @SUM function in Cell A6 now calculates to 0.

9. Ranges can be used with many commands, such as printing the worksheet. From the main 1-2-3 menu, the /Print command starts the process of printing a worksheet. The simplest way to print a worksheet is to define a *print range* and then print it. Make sure the disk containing the ACME.WKS file is accessible by 1-2-3, and type the following:

/FRACME[ENTER]	Retrieve the ACME.WKS file
/RNCWORKSHEET[ENTER]	Create WORKSHEET range name
[ESC]	[ESC] unanchors cell pointer
[HOME].[END][HOME][ENTER]	WORKSHEET references active worksheet
/PPR	Access the /Print commands
WORKSHEET[ENTER]	WORKSHEET is to be printed
G	Start printing
Q	Quit printing; return to the worksheet
/FS[ENTER]R	Save the file with range name

The secret of printing the entire worksheet so easily is the definition of the WORKSHEET range name as the entire worksheet. Using the sequence [HOME].[END][HOME], we defined a range which included the entire active worksheet (which in most cases is what we would like to print). When you save the file, 1-2-3 remembers the WORKSHEET range name you have created. If you retrieve the worksheet file again, you need not redefine the range name. Simply type /PPG (/Print Printer Go).

Using range names effectively is the secret of 1-2-3. Use them whenever you can. Make the names meaningful. A range name which sums individual costs should be called COSTS; a range name for a cell containing an interest rate should be called INTERESTRATE. In this way, you will be able to understand the formulas. This makes the worksheet easier to change. Almost all the features you will use from now on can benefit from use of range names.

In the next chapter, you will learn how to make the numbers display with commas, dollar signs, percent signs, and so on using *numeric formats* and discover some interesting interactions between /Range and /Worksheet commands.

CHAPTER 11

Numeric Formats

This chapter introduces you to the numeric display formats supported by 1-2-3. After reading this chapter and practicing a bit, you should be able to control the manner in which numbers display. You will learn about the /Worksheet Global Format, /Range Format, /Worksheet Global Label-prefix, and /Range Label-prefix commands. All of the formats except for Date formats will be covered in this chapter. Date formats are a special case and will be covered in the discussion of date functions, in Chapter 17.

This chapter contains a large number of BEWAREs. That's because it's easy to confuse how the number displays with how it is stored. For some formats, the displayed number corresponds with the stored number; for others, the displayed number appears to be rounded, even though the number is stored to its true accuracy. 1-2-3 can store a number with up to 15 digits of accuracy. So it's easy to be misled into thinking that 1-2-3 made a calculation error, when in fact a number is simply displayed in rounded form. Some formats, as you will see, get away from displaying numbers entirely.

HOW ARE NUMERIC FORMATS USED?

You use numeric formats to change the way the numbers *display* or *print*. Formatting does not affect calculations. You may want to print your worksheet with numbers preceded by dollar signs, or with percent signs after the numbers. This prettying up function is accomplished by formatting the numbers.

Using /Range Format

You use /Range Format to format cells which contain values or formulas which evaluate to a value. Formatting has no effect on labels.

If a cell was formatted with /Range Format, a *format indicator* (a letter followed, in some formats, by a number), enclosed in parentheses, displays in the control panel when the cell pointer is positioned at that cell. For example, if a number is formatted as percent with 2 decimal places, the format indicator displays (P2) for that cell.

What if you never used /Range Format to format a cell? 1-2-3 uses the *worksheet global format* as the cell's format. You will see in this chapter how the worksheet global format interacts with cells which have been formatted with /Range Format.

General

1-2-3 uses General format as the worksheet global format, unless you change it. This means that any number not formatted with /Range Format is displayed with General format.

With General format, numbers are displayed to their full accuracy. As many digits as required, up to 15, to display the number precisely will be used. When 1-2-3 starts, each column has a width of 9 characters. (You will learn how to change the column width in the next chapter.) If the number you enter cannot fit in the column width, the number displays in scientific notation (a number between 1 and 10, followed by E+, followed by a power of 10). Some examples of General format:

123	displays as	123
00.123	displays as	0.123
1234567890	displays as	1.2E+0E+
123.450	displays as	123.45

You can use /Range Format General to format a cell range to General format. In that case, the format indicator for these cells is (G). Since numbers in general format are not rounded, no number displays after the G. You would format a cell range to General format if the worksheet global format is different from the general format and you want those numbers to display to their full accuracy.

Fixed

Fixed format is useful for displaying a number rounded to a fixed number of decimal places. The format letter for Fixed is F; the letter is followed by the number of decimal places (0-15) to round. Thus, (F0) format displays a number rounded to its integer value; (F2) format displays a number rounded to 2 decimal places. Figure 11.1 illustrates (F0) and (F2) format.

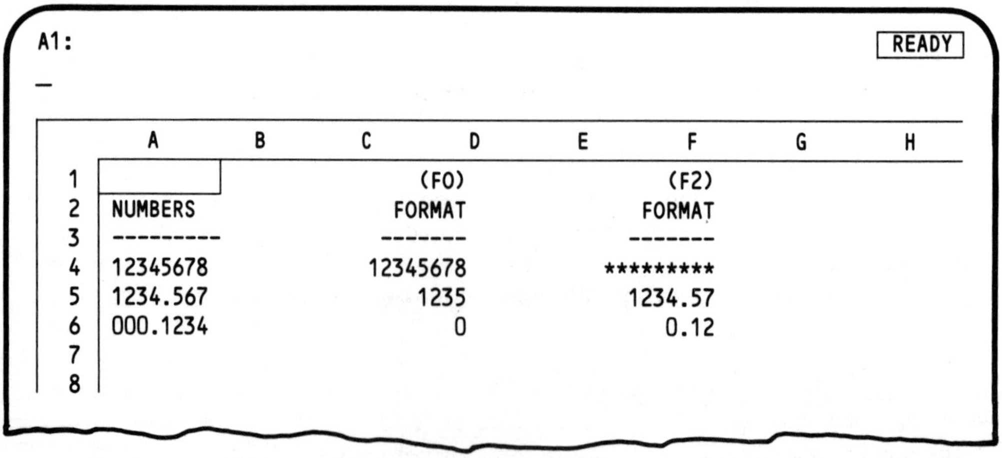

Figure 11.1 Fixed Format

The number is stored to its full 15-digit accuracy. However, you may want to display the number rounded to whole numbers or to two decimal places (say, to round to the nearest dollar or cent.)

If the number cannot fit in the column width, 1-2-3 displays a row of asterisks in the cell.

BEWARE ***The Numbers May Display with Rounding Errors***

If your worksheets contain formulas, and you use Fixed format, the formula cells may display as if a rounding error was introduced. Figure 11.2 illustrates this situation.

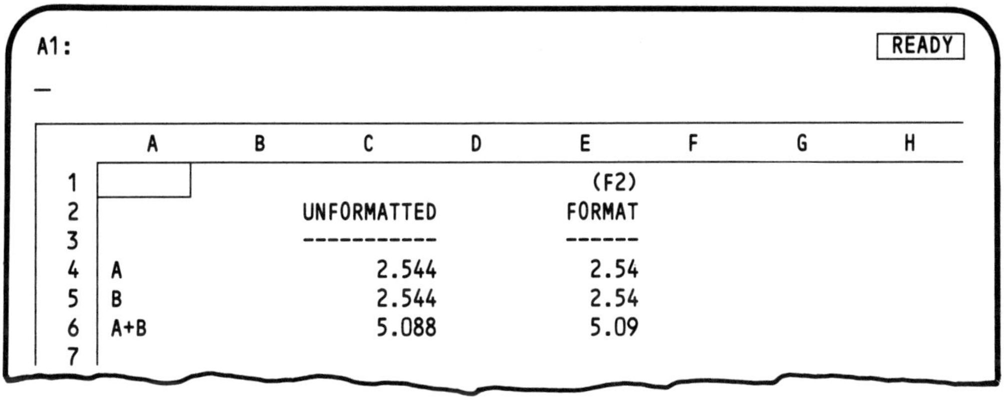

Figure 11.2 Rounding Error With (F2) Format

Cell C6 displays the result of adding 2.544 and 2.544 to its full value of 5.088. Cell E6 shows the same result rounding the numbers to two decimal places, using (F2) format. The answer (5.09) seems to indicate that the formula miscalculated. The formula, in fact, calculated correctly. Its *display*, however, is rounded to 2 decimal places. In Chapter 17, you will learn how to use the @ROUND function, which rounds calculated results, to avoid this problem.

Currency

Currency format has the following characteristics.

1. Like Fixed format, Currency format displays a number rounded to the specified number of decimal places.
2. Commas separate each group of three digits to the right of the decimal point, for readability.
3. Negative numbers display enclosed in parentheses.
4. A dollar sign is placed before the number.

5. If the number cannot display in the column width, 1-2-3 displays a row of asterisks in the cell.

The format letter for Currency is C; the letter is followed by the number of decimal places to round. You'll probably use Currency format frequently. It's the easiest way of representing whole dollars (C0) or dollars and cents (C2). Figure 11.3 illustrates (C0) and (C2) formats.

```
A1:                                                          READY
_

      A           B         C         D         E         F         G         H
 1                                  (C0)                (C2)
 2  UNFORMATTED                    FORMAT              FORMAT
 3  -----------                    ------              ------
 4            0                        $0               $0.00
 5  123.4567                         $123             $123.46
 6  -123.456                       ($123)           ($123.46)
 7
```

Figure 11.3 Currency Format

Since Currency format, like Fixed format, does rounding, a calculation may appear to have introduced a rounding error in Currency format.

Comma

Comma format displays as Currency format, except for the absence of the dollar sign before the number. You will also use Comma format quite often, to display non-dollar numbers with commas separating them.

The format indicator for Comma is (,); the comma is followed by the number of decimal places to be rounded. Figure 11.4 illustrates the (,0) and (,2) formats.

Like Fixed and Currency formats, a calculation may appear to have produced a rounding error in Comma format.

Percent

Percent format lets you enter a number as a percentage. (You enter the value 50%; the number is stored as .5.) 1-2-3 always lets you enter a number as a percentage. For example, if you type 100% into a cell which has General format, the number will display as 1.

You use Percent format only if you want the number to *display* with the percent sign. In other words, to display 100% in a cell, you must format the

```
A1:                                                          READY
_

       A          B          C          D          E          F          G          H
  1                                    (,0)                  (,2)
  2  UNFORMATTED                      FORMAT                FORMAT
  3  -----------                      ------                ------
  4            0                           0                  0.00
  5  123.4567                            123                123.46
  6  -123.456                          (123)              (123.46)
  7
```

Figure 11.4 Comma Format

cell in Percent format. So the Percent format is really equivalent to entering an unformatted number, and displaying it multiplied by 100 and with the percent sign added. The displayed number is equivalent to the stored number.

The format character for Percent is P; the character is followed by the number of decimal places to be rounded. Figure 11.5 illustrates (P0) and (P2) formats.

```
A1:                                                          READY
_

       A          B          C          D          E          F          G          H
  1                                    (P0)                  (P2)
  2  UNFORMATTED                      FORMAT                FORMAT
  3  -----------                      ------                ------
  4            0                          0%                 0.00%
  5           -1                       -100%              -100.00%
  6            1                        100%               100.00%
  7  123.4567                        123456%             12345.67%
  8  -123.456                        -12346%             *********
  9
```

Figure 11.5 Percent Format

You can, of course, introduce the same display rounding errors with Percent format as for Fixed, Currency, and Comma formats.

Text

Text format displays cell formulas rather than their values. If the cell has a value rather than a formula, the value displays in General format. Text format is useful for seeing which cells contain formulas and which cells contain just numbers. The format indicator for Text format is (T). (Since Text format displays formulas, there is no rounding involved.) Figure 11.6 illustrates Text format.

```
A1:                                                          READY
_

        A            B          C          D     E     F     G     H
 1                                        (T)
 2   UNFORMATTED                        FORMAT
 3   -----------                        ------
 4         4                                4
 5         6                                6
 6         7                                7
 7         8                                8
 8
 9        15                   +C7+C6
10        25                   @SUM(C4.
11
```

Figure 11.6 Text Format

In Figure 11.6, Cell A9 actually contains the formula **+A7+A6**. Cell A9, which is unformatted, displays the result of the formula, 7+8, or 15. Column C cells have Text format. The numbers 4, 6, 7, and 8 are unaffected by Text format. However, instead of the *result* of the formula (15) being displayed in Cell C9, the *formula itself* (+C7+C6) is displayed.

In practice, if the formula is even a bit complex, the entire formula won't display in the cell. For example, Cell A10 contains the function **@SUM(A4..A7)** to add 4 cells. The corresponding formula **@SUM(C4..C7)**cannot display in Cell C10. (Cell C10 actually contains a relatively simple formula and 1-2-3 still cannot display it.) You can find out the complete cell formula either by widening Column C's column width (discussed in Chapter 12) or by printing the worksheet cell formulas (discussed in Chapter 16).

An additional drawback to Text Format is that values displayed in Text format revert to General format, losing Currency, Comma, or Percent attributes.

Scientific

Scientific format causes 1-2-3 to display the number in scientific (exponential) notation—a number between 1 and 10 multiplied by an exponent (E) of 10. The format letter for Scientific format is S; the letter is followed by the number of decimal places to round. Some examples of Scientific format are as follows:

123 in (S2) format displays as 1.23E+2
123 in (S0) format displays as 1E+2
0.123 in (S2) format displays as 1.23E-1

+/−

The +/− format is a primitive method of drawing a horizontal bar graph with plus and minus signs, with a period representing 0. The number of plus or minus signs is the integer part of the number. If the number cannot fit into the column, asterisks display. The +/− format character is (+). Figure 11.7 illustrates the +/− format.

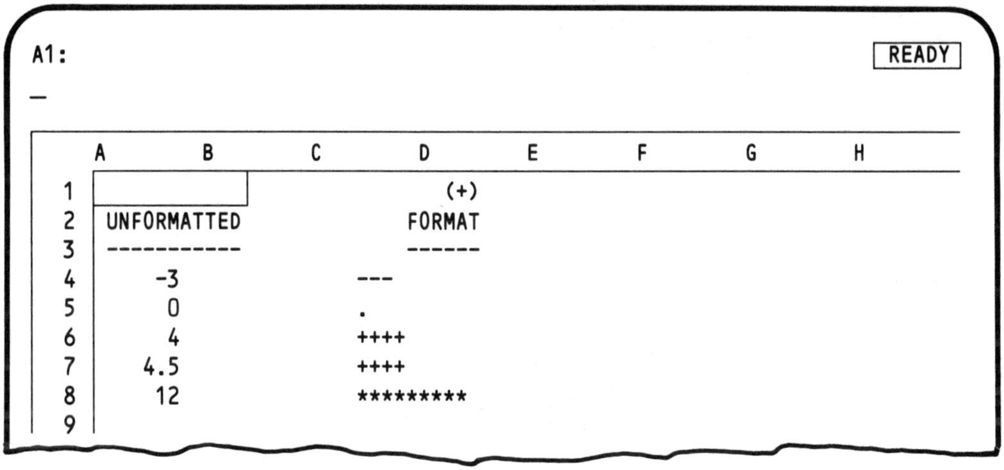

Figure 11.7 +/− Format

Note the 0 formats to .; the -3 to ---; the 4 to ++++; the 4.5 to ++++ (ignoring the fractional part of the number); and the 12 to all asterisks (the number is too large to fit in the column). Additionally, +/− formatted numbers left align (whereas all other numeric formats right align), making for a strange display indeed! In practice, (+) format has limited and specialized use. For most applications, it's easier to create a bar graph (as you will do in Chapter 20).

INTERACTION OF /RANGE FORMAT AND /WORKSHEET GLOBAL FORMAT

/Worksheet Global Format controls how the numbers display for cells which have not been explicitly formatted with /Range Format. If you do not change the global format, all cells are formatted with the General format.

If you want most of your numbers to display with dollar signs, rounded to the nearest integer, use /Worksheet Global Format to specify Currency, with no decimal places. As you enter numbers, they are automatically displayed with dollar signs, rounded to the nearest integer. You need not use /Range Format to get the numbers to display as you want.

If you change the worksheet global format, all numbers not specifically formatted with /Range Format display using the new global format. So, if you suddenly decided to display your worksheet in Currency format and two decimal places (rounded to the nearest cent), use /Worksheet Global Format to specify Currency, with two decimal places, and all cells not specifically formatted with /Range Format will display in the new format.

If you decide to reset cells you have formatted with /Range Format to the global format, you can use /Range Format Reset.

BEWARE *Formatted Cells Are Part of the Active Worksheet*

Even if a cell is empty, if you have used /Range Format to format a cell range, 1-2-3 counts it as part of the active worksheet. This means you have less memory to use for entering data. To shrink the active worksheet, one of the steps should be to use /Range Format Reset for all cells which appear to be empty but which, in fact, are formatted. This procedure is discussed in the next chapter.

INTERACTION OF /RANGE LABEL-PREFIX AND /WORKSHEET GLOBAL LABEL-PREFIX

1-2-3 formats labels differently from numbers. As with formats, 1-2-3 has a /Range Label-prefix command which lets you format a cell range containing labels to be aligned either left, right, or center, relative to the column width.

Unlike formats, however, 1-2-3 has no label prefix indicator. There is no /Range Label-prefix Reset command corresponding to the /Range Format Reset command. /Worksheet Global Label-prefix has no effect on labels you have already entered. The global label prefix only affects labels entered afterwards. Thus, after using /Worksheet Global Format, you are likely to see many numbers change their formats, while after using /Worksheet Global Label-prefix, no labels will change their display.

SOME MORE BEWARES

BEWARE *Numeric Formats Cannot Be Combined*

Perhaps you would like to have your numbers display with dollar signs (like (C2) format), but with negative numbers displaying with a - sign (rather than the parentheses allowed by (C2). You're out of luck! 1-2-3 numeric formats are an all or none proposition. You cannot combine parts of the Currency format and General format (as would be appropriate here), or combine Percent and Comma format to display a number with % and commas.

BEWARE ***/Range Erase Does Not Erase the Cell Format***

/Range Erase erases only the cell contents. The cells, if formatted by /Range Format, remain formatted (although empty). To remove the cell format, use /Range Format Reset.

BEWARE ***You Cannot Center or Left Justify Numbers***

This is a particularly nasty problem. Numbers can only be right-justified. If you want to align numbers with left-justified labels (typically used as column headings), you will have a problem. The best circumvention to this problem is to right-justify the labels (using /Range Label-prefix Right), aligning them with the numbers.

Exercises

1. Enter 1-2-3. Using /Range Format, reproduce the illustrations in this chapter.
2. After you feel comfortable with 1-2-3's numeric formatting capabilities, erase the worksheet (use /Worksheet Erase Yes). This exercise will show the interaction of the worksheet and range format commands. You should be at Cell A1. Type the following:

```
123[ENTER]
```

The number **123** should display in Cell A1. To use /Worksheet Global Format, Type the following:

```
/WGFC2[ENTER]
```

Cell A1's contents now display as **$123.00**. Since Cell A1 is unformatted, it takes the worksheet global format.

To format Cell A1 to (C2) format, type the following:

```
/RFC2[ENTER][ENTER]
```

Note the (C2) format indicator (for Currency, with two decimal places). Cell A1 is now formatted.

Go to Cell B1 and type **123[ENTER]**. Cell B1's contents also display as **$123.00**, as it takes the worksheet global format.

Now, let's change the worksheet global format back to General. Type the following:

```
/WGFG
```

Cell A1 still displays as **$123.00**, while Cell B1 displays as **123**. Since Cell B1 was not formatted, it took the new worksheet global format. Cell A1, which was formatted, retained its range format.

3. When a cell is erased, its format remains. Type the following:

```
/REA1..B1[ENTER]
```

Go to Cell A1. Do you see that the (C2) format is still there? That's because /Range Erase erases only the cell contents, not its format. This is a good lead-in to the next exercise.

4. You can produce a Memory full message with a blank worksheet! How? By using /Range Format. Type the following:

```
/RFC2[ENTER]A1..IV2048[ENTER]
```

You tried to format the entire worksheet with (C2) format. 1-2-3 expands the active worksheet to accommodate the formatted cells. However, there isn't enough RAM to do it, and 1-2-3 produced the message. This command shows that formatted cells take up memory, even though they're empty. Press [ESC] to clear the error message and return to the worksheet.

5. How does erasing the worksheet affect cell formats? Type the following to find out:

/WEY	Erase the worksheet
123[ENTER]	Enter the number 123

The number displayed as 123! What happened? /Worksheet Erase, in addition to erasing the worksheet, resets all cell formats, and resets the worksheet global format to General. 1-2-3 has reset the cell formats to their state at the start of the program.

6. Worksheet and range label prefixes interact as well. Type the following in Cell A1:

```
SALES[ENTER]
```

You've entered a left-aligned label, with a left-adjust label prefix as the global label prefix. To change the global label prefix to center labels, type the following:

/WGLC	/Worksheet Global Label-prefix Center

Only labels entered subsequently are affected. The SALES label is still left-adjusted.

Go to Cell B1, and type the following:

```
SALES[ENTER]
```

The SALES label is centered with respect to the column width. Note the ^ prefix to indicate a centered label. Changing the global label prefix does not affect any labels you have previously entered.

Now you can use /Range Label-prefix to change the label prefix of a cell range. To left-justify the SALES label in Cell B1, type the following:

```
/RLL[ENTER]
```

The SALES label in Cell B1 is now left-justified.

The difference between global and range formats and label prefixes is that whereas changing the global format changes all values in cells in which /Range Format has not been used, changing the global label prefix has absolutely no effect on any labels in the worksheet. The global label prefix only affects labels you will subsequently enter—not any that are already entered.

7. It's time to make the ACME worksheet numbers look more presentable by formatting the target and actual revenues to (C0) format, and the percent of target numbers to (P1) format. Make sure the ACME.WKS file is accessible to 1-2-3 and type the following:

`/FRACME[ENTER]`	Retrieve ACME.WKS from the disk
`/RFP1[ENTER]D6..D13[ENTER]`	Make the % OF TARGET column (P1) format
`/RFC0[ENTER]B6..C13[ENTER]`	Make TARGET and ACTUAL revenue columns (C0) format
`/FS[ENTER]R`	Save ACME.WKS to the disk

You have taken the first step towards controlling the display of the worksheet. You now can control how numbers display. In the next chapter, you will learn several other techniques for controlling the worksheet display.

CHAPTER 12

Controlling the Worksheet Display

In this chapter, you will learn additional ways to gain tighter control over how the worksheet displays. This chapter discusses the following:

Controlling the column width. When you start 1-2-3, the column widths for all columns are set to 9. This means that a number containing a maximum of 8 digits (one character position is used to separate the columns, preventing the numbers from running into each other) or a label containing 8 characters (if the cell to the right is not empty) can display. Use /Worksheet Column-width Set to expand the column width for a column to display a larger number or a bigger label. If you want to expand the column width for all columns, use /Worksheet Global Column-width Set.

Splitting the screen into a horizontal or vertical window. To enable you to visually compare monthly revenue with yearly revenue, as you are looking at your individual monthly revenue numbers in one window, you would like the yearly revenue numbers to display in another window. 1-2-3 lets you split your worksheet into two windows, either horizontally or vertically. Use /Worksheet Window to accomplish this.

Freezing the worksheet titles. If you have a large worksheet, you may want certain rows and/or columns to be frozen as you are moving about the worksheet. This makes the meaning of the numbers clearer. Use /Worksheet Titles to freeze row names and/or column headings.

Protecting cells from inadvertent modification. To preserve the integrity of the worksheet, cells containing formulas and labels should not be modified. At the same time, you should be able to change the values in cells which require data entry.

1-2-3 provides several commands which help to protect formulas while allowing numbers to be modified. These commands are /Worksheet Global Protection, /Range Unprotect, /Range Protect, and /Range Input.

CONTROLLING THE COLUMN WIDTH

Setting the Column Width for One Column

Use /Worksheet Column-width Set to expand or contract the width of cells in a particular column. Suppose. when you first start 1-2-3, you enter the number 1234567.89 in Cell A1, and then use /Range Format to format the cell to (C2) format. The number displays as shown below:

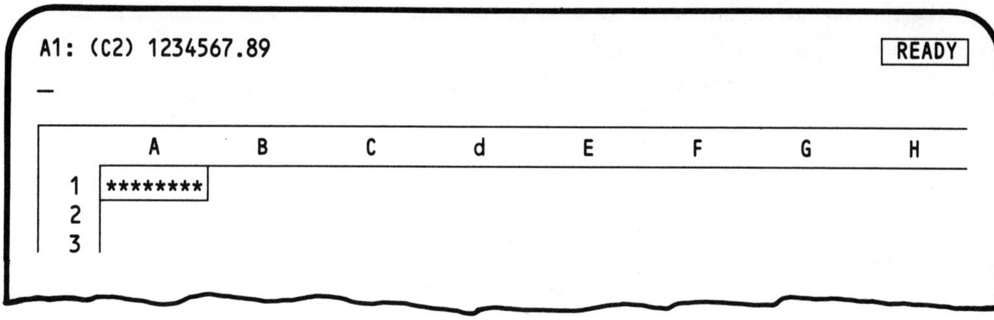

Figure 12.1

1-2-3 displays asterisks because the number is too large (remember, you must include the dollar sign, two commas, and a decimal point in the 9 characters allowed for the column width) to fit in the column width. You can change the column width to accommodate this 13-character number, by typing the following command:

```
/WCS14[ENTER]
```

Now the entire number displays—with the dollar sign, the commas, and the decimal point.

You can also use [LEFT] and [RIGHT] with /Worksheet Column-width Set to preview the display. Using these keys, you see how the worksheet display changes before you press [ENTER] to confirm.

You also can use /Worksheet Column-width Set to display additional characters of a long label where the cell to the right is not empty. Remember how, in Chapter 3, the entry 123 in Cell B1 appeared to destroye the label ACME QUARTERLY SALES FOR 1984? The problem was not that 1-2-3 forgot part of the label entry. Rather, it was in how 1-2-3 displayed it. (Look at Figure 7.11 to refresh your memory.)

There are two techniques for making 1-2-3 display the entire label again. One technique is to use /Worksheet Column-width Set to expand Column A's width. If you type the following, with the cell pointer at any cell in Column A:

```
/WCS29[ENTER]
```

the worksheet would display as shown in Figure 12.2. Column A's column width is now large enough to display the entire label.

The second technique, which does not involve expanding Column A's column width, is to erase the contents of Cell B1 using /Range Erase. After Cell B1's contents are erased, the label in Cell A1 can overflow into Cell B1, since Cell B1 is now empty.

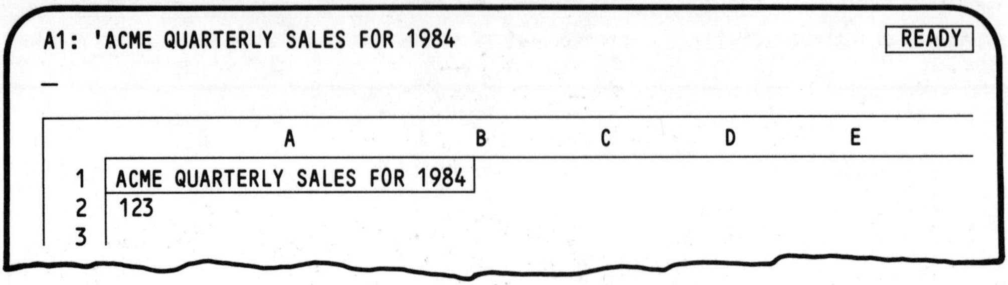

Figure 12.2

BEWARE ***/Worksheet Column-width Set Applies to the Entire Column***

In these examples, setting Cell A1's column width would have been sufficient to correct the problem in displaying the cell contents. 1-2-3, however, will not let you set the column width of one individual cell. You must set the column width for an entire column of cells. After the /Worksheet Column-width Set command, all of the cells in Column A now have a column width of 29. This can be a problem if you want to reproduce a form, such as an IRS Form 1040, where the column widths vary from one row to the next.

BEWARE ***You Cannot Hide Cells***

If your worksheet contains sensitive data such as employee salaries, you might want to hide this information. In other situations, the cell formulas may be confidential. 1-2-3 does not allow you to hide cells or formulas. All columns must have a column width of at least 1 character. Additionally, if you travel to a cell, its contents display in the control panel.

Setting the Column Width for All Columns

Instead of changing the column width of just one column, you can change it for many columns using /Worksheet Global Column-width. /Worksheet Global Column-width sets the column width for all columns whose width has not been specifically changed with /Worksheet Column-width Set. (The interaction of these commands is similar to the /Worksheet Global Format and /Range Format commands. The global command affects all cells except those which you have specifically set.)

Use /Worksheet Global Column-width when you start creating a worksheet in which all (or nearly all) of the columns require a different width from 1-2-3's default of 9 characters. For example, suppose your worksheet, consisting of 12 monthly revenue columns which total to a yearly revenue amount, requires a column width of 15 characters for all columns except Column N (where you're going to calculate the yearly revenue). Column N requires a column width of 17 characters to display the total accurately. Use the following commands when you start creating the worksheet.

/WGS15[ENTER]	Set the global column width to 15
[F5/GOTO]N1[ENTER]	Go to a cell in Column N
/WCS17[ENTER]	Set its column width to 17

You can also shrink the global column width if you are working with smaller numbers. One benefit of doing this is that more worksheet columns display.

Resetting the Column Width

Like /Range Format, you can reset a particular column back to the global column width. Use /Worksheet Column-width Reset.

CREATING WINDOWS

In addition to controlling column widths and titles, you can split the worksheet into two *windows*. You can split the worksheet into two horizontal windows with /Worksheet Window Horizontal. Or, you can split the worksheet into two vertical windows with /Worksheet Window Vertical. This is an either/or proposition; you cannot split the worksheet into two horizontal and two vertical windows at once. After you have created the two windows, you can use the [F6/WINDOW] key to switch between the windows.

Why use windows? To view parts of the worksheet which normally could not display together. For example, in creating that 13-column worksheet (12 columns containing revenue for each month, and the thirteenth containing the yearly revenue) you might want the yearly revenue column to display all the time, while you are looking at each month's revenue. Without windows, this is not possible (unless your numbers are very small and you shrink the column width). By splitting the screen into two vertical windows, however, you can display the monthly revenue columns in the window on the left, and the yearly revenue column in the window on the right. Figure 12.3 illustrates this.
Similarly, if you were adding your revenue numbers *down* instead of across, you could split the screen into two horizontal windows, displaying the yearly revenue *row* on the bottom window while you look at the monthly revenue numbers in the upper window. Figure 12.4 illustrates this.

Horizontal Windows

To split the screen into two horizontal windows, position the cell pointer at the row where you wish the screen to be split, and use /Worksheet Window

```
A1:                                                                READY
_

          A          B        C        D        E             N       O
 1                  ACME WIDGET REVENUES (1984)         1
 2                                                      2
 3                 Jan-84   Feb-84   Mar-84   Apr-84    3     TOTAL
 4   Atlanta          200      220      240      260    4      1820
 5   Los Angeles      150      160      170      180    5      1260
 6   Boston           340      355      370      385    6      2695
 7   New York         324      359      394      429    7      3003
 8   Chicago          546      551      556      561    8      3927
 9   Miami            189      209      229      249    9      1743
10                -------  -------  -------  -------   10   -------
11   TOTAL           1749     1854     1959     2064   11     14448
12                                                     12
13                                                     13
14                                                     14
15                                                     15
16                                                     16
17                                                     17
18                                                     18
```

Figure 12.3 A Vertical Window

Horizontal. Where the window is created depends on the position of the cell pointer. The top window contains all rows *above* the cell pointer. A horizontal window must contain at least one row; if you attempt to create a horizontal window when the cell pointer is at the top or bottom screen row, 1-2-3 beeps. The cell pointer will display at the bottom row of the upper window, in the same column it was before the screen was split.

Vertical Windows

To split the screen into two vertical windows, position the cell pointer at the column where you wish the screen to be split, and use /**W**orksheet **W**indow **V**ertical. Where the window is created also depends on the position of the cell pointer. The window on the left contains all columns *to the left of* the cell pointer. A vertical window must contain at least one column; if you attempt to create a vertical window when the cell pointer is at the leftmost or rightmost screen column, 1-2-3 beeps. The cell pointer will display at the rightmost column of the window on the left, in the same row it was before the screen was split.

A1: READY

	A	B	C	D	E	F	G
1			ACME WIDGET REVENUES (1984)				
2							
3		Jan-84	Feb-84	Mar-84	Apr-84	May-84	June-84
4	Atlanta	200	220	240	260	280	300
5	Los Angeles	150	160	170	180	190	200
6	Boston	340	355	370	385	400	499
7	New York	324	359	394	429	464	499
8	Chicago	546	551	556	561	566	571
9	Miami	189	209	229	249	269	289

	A	B	C	D	E	F	G
30	TOTAL	1749	1854	1959	2064	2169	2274
31							
32							
33							
34							
35							
36							
37							

Figure 12.4 A Horizontal Window

Synchronizing Windows

In addition to creating windows, you can *synchronize* or *unsynchronize* them. If a window is synchronized, when you move the cell pointer in one window, the other window travels in step. For a horizontal window, if the windows are synchronized, pressing [LEFT] or [RIGHT] in one window causes the second window to scroll left or right as well. For a vertical window, if the windows are synchronized, pressing [UP] or [DOWN] in one window causes the second window to scroll up or down as well. You might use synchronized windows if your worksheet contains columns of information (such as comparisons of last year's with this year's revenue) which you would like to compare visually and therefore which should move in tandem.

When you initially create a window, 1-2-3 assumes it is synchronized. You need issue no additional command after you have created the window if you wish to synchronize it.

You may, however, want the windows to be unsynchronized. In our revenue worksheet, you probably want the yearly revenue numbers to be frozen while you check out the monthly numbers. In this case, you would use

/Worksheet Window Unsynchronized. If windows are unsynchronized, moving the cell pointer in one window has no effect on the display in the other window.

What if your windows were unsynchronized but you later decide to synchronize them? In that case, you use /Worksheet Window Synchronized. After issuing the command, the windows are synchronized again.

Clearing the Window Display

Can you return to displaying one worksheet, eliminating the windows? Sure! Use /Worksheet Window Clear to view the worksheet without windows.

FREEZING THE TITLES

You may want the column headings or the labels in Column A of the rows to remain displayed on the screen as you move around the worksheet. It makes the meaning of a cell which contains September Revenues clearer if the September column and the Revenue row contains a title or heading label.

Normally, when you move the cell pointer around the worksheet, the columns and rows containing the labels also move offscreen with the cell pointer. For example, the worksheet illustrated below shows Acme Widget revenues for the first 6 months.

A1: READY

	A	B	C	D	E	F	G
1			ACME WIDGET REVENUES (1984)				
2							
3		Jan-84	Feb-84	Mar-84	Apr-84	May-84	June-84
4	Atlanta	200	220	240	260	280	300
5	Los Angeles	150	160	170	180	190	200
6	Boston	340	355	370	385	400	415
7	New York	324	359	394	429	464	499
8	Chicago	546	551	556	561	566	571
9	Miami	189	209	229	249	269	289

Figure 12.5

When you move to see the numbers in Column H (the July, 1984 Revenues) label in Column A disappears, as illustrated in Figure 12.6. If your worksheet contains many numbers, you may not know that the number represents Atlanta's Revenue.

B1: READY

	B	C	D	E	F	G	H	I
1				ACME WIDGET REVENUES (1984)				
2								
3	Jan-84	Feb-84	Mar-84	Apr-84	May-84	June-84	Jul-84	Aug-84
4	200	220	240	260	280	300	320	340
5	150	160	170	180	190	200	210	220
6	340	355	370	385	400	415	430	445
7	324	359	394	429	464	499	534	569
8	546	551	556	561	566	571	576	581
9	189	209	229	249	269	289	309	329
10								
11								
12								
13								
14								
15								
16								
17								
18								

Figure 12.6

/Worksheet Titles provides a solution to this. You can position the cell pointer *to the right of* any columns you wish to freeze while the cell pointer moves and use the /Worksheet Titles Horizontal command. Or, you can position the cell pointer *under* any rows you wish to freeze while the cell pointer moves and use the /Worksheet Titles Vertical command. You can even freeze *both* the horizontal and vertical titles.

Thus, to freeze the Revenue label in Column A, position the cell pointer at any cell in Column B, and use /Worksheet Titles Vertical. Figure 12.7 illustrates the worksheet when you are at Column H and the Revenue title is frozen.

When titles are frozen, you cannot use the pointer-movement keys to move into the frozen rows and/or columns. There are, however, two exceptions, which are:

When Using [F5/GOTO]. You can use [F5/GOTO] to go to a cell in a frozen area. The worksheet displays *two* columns or rows containing the frozen titles. They really represent the same cells. If you change the titles, you'll see two columns or rows with the same information change at once. This can be confusing, so avoid it.

When Using POINT Mode to Indicate a Range. You include frozen cells in ranges when using POINT mode. POINT mode is used (among other

```
E1: 'ACME WIDGET REVENUES 1984                                    READY
_

        A           C         D         E         F          G          H
 1                                 ACME WIDGET REVENUES (1984)
 2
 3                 Feb-84    Mar-84    Apr-84    May-84     Jun-84     Jul-84
 4  Atlanta           220       240       260       280        300        320
 5  Los Angeles       160       170       180       190        200        210
 6  Boston            355       370       385       400        415        430
 7  New York          359       394       429       464        499        534
 8  Chicago           551       556       561       566        571        576
 9  Miami             209       229       249       269        289        309
11
12
13
14
15
16
17
18
```

Figure 12.7

places) in commands such as /Range Erase. It's especially handy in building cell formulas. By including frozen cells in /Range Erase, you could erase them.

HOW TO: Set Titles in Two Windows

If you use /Worksheet Window to split the worksheet into two windows, you can set /Worksheet Titles in each window. You could make cells frozen in one window, and not frozen in the other window! To do this, simply use the /Worksheet Titles command in one window, press [F6/WINDOW] (to switch windows), and then use /Worksheet Titles in the other window.

CONTROLLING CELL PROTECTION

When building a worksheet, you want to prevent destroying formulas while making it possible to change the numbers in cells referenced by these formulas. You want to change the monthly revenue numbers while not destroying the @SUM formula for calculating the yearly revenue. How can 1-2-3 help?

1-2-3 lets you *protect* cells (such as cells containing formulas) from inadvertent modification. At the same time, 1-2-3 lets you *unprotect* cells (such as cells referenced in the formulas) so that you can modify them. You have several options.

One option is to protect all cells. If you want to protect *all* cells in the worksheet, you can do so with one command: /Worksheet Global Protection Enable. After you issue this command *you cannot enter any data anywhere in the worksheet!* If you try, 1-2-3 displays the error message Protected cell.

Of course, if you do this, you cannot modify your worksheet data. And that's probably the reason you built the worksheet in the first place! 1-2-3 provides a way for you to designate which cells can be changed. Use /Range Unprotect to unprotect these cells before you use /Worksheet Global Protection Enable, because /Worksheet Global Protection Enable protects all cells *except those which were made unprotected with /Range Unprotect.* For added emphasis, unprotected cells display in brighter green than protected cells if you use a monochrome monitor. With a color monitor, unprotected cells display in green, providing a nice contrast with the protected cells which display in white.

To summarize, in order to install protection properly, do the following:

1. Use /Range Unprotect to unprotect cells which you want to change. You can see which cells are unprotected because they display contrasted from the protected cells. In addition a U displays in the first row of the control panel.
2. Use /Worksheet Global Protection Enable to make all cells protected, except those in ranges for which you used /Range Unprotect.

If you change your mind, you can reverse both range unprotection and worksheet global protection. /Range Protect, when used on unprotected cells, removes their unprotected status. /Worksheet Global Protection Disable turns off worksheet global protection.

When you start 1-2-3, worksheet global protection is disabled and all cells are protected. Unlike unprotected cells, there is no letter to indicate that a cell is protected. If no U protection indicator displays in the control panel, the cell is protected. Thus, using /Worksheet Global Protection Enable when you start 1-2-3 will prevent you from entering any data into the worksheet.

WHAT /FILE SAVE REMEMBERS

/File Save saves much more than the data in the worksheet. It saves all the settings you have created, including:

1. the global column width
2. the column widths of each column
3. the window settings
4. the title settings
5. the global protection status
6. the protection status of all cells.

You could then create worksheet with individually tailored column widths, two vertical windows (each with separately frozen titles), and with formulas protected and cells which you want to change unprotected. After you use /File Save, when you use /File Retrieve to access the worksheet, it would display precisely as you saved it.

BEWARE *You Can Use /Worksheet Erase When Global Protection Is Enabled*

Here's an easy way to get rid of all this stuff! If you enter the following command:

/WEY Worksheet Erase Yes

you've erased not only all the data, but all the format and display commands which make the worksheet look pretty. You can erase the worksheet even when global protection is enabled! So be careful.

BEWARE *Unprotected Cells Are Part of the Active Worksheet*

Like cells on which /Range Format is in effect, cells on which /Range Unprotect is in effect are part of the active worksheet. This means your active worksheet may be larger than necessary, which brings me to the first method of shrinking the active worksheet.

HOW TO: Shrink the Active Worksheet (Method One)

To shrink the active worksheet, you must be sure that any cells which are blank also are not range formatted or unprotected. If you want to be absolutely sure that a blank cell range is not part of the active worksheet, do the following steps:

- /Range Erase the cell range, to blank them out. Use [END][HOME] to find the end of the active worksheet.
- /Range Format Reset the cell range to the worksheet global format.
- /Range Protect the cell range, removing any unprotection from the cell range.
- Save the file.

CONTROLLING CELL POINTER MOVEMENT

1-2-3 provides one additional feature to ensure that the worksheet remains as you wanted it. /Range Input lets you control where the cell pointer can travel. With /Range Input, you can ensure that the cell pointer moves only to cells in which data is to be entered. /Range Input works like a data entry form in which you tell the clerk where to enter data. To implement this, do the following:

- /Range Unprotect those cells for which you will allow changes.
- Use /Worksheet Titles to freeze title rows and/or columns in the form, preventing them from disappearing as data is being entered.
- Use /Range Input to specify the form.

The cell pointer will move only to unprotected cells of the /Range Input range. The pointer-movement keys [HOME], [END], [UP], [DOWN], [LEFT], and [RIGHT] can be used to move about the unprotected cells of the range. The only function keys which can be used are [F1/HELP], [F2/EDIT], and [F9/CALC].

It's easy to cancel /Range Input. If you enter data and press [ENTER], the data is entered into the cell and the cell pointer stays where it is. However, if you enter no data and press [ENTER], you cancel /Range Input. You can also press [ESC] or [CTRL]-[BREAK] to cancel /Range Input.

BEWARE ***/File Save Does Not Save /Range Input Status***

Since you cannot access the main 1-2-3 menu while in /Range Input, you cannot save the file while /Range Input is active. Therefore, you cannot use /File Retrieve to start entry using a /Range Input-type form without writing a macro.

In my experience, the fact that you can so easily cancel /Range Input and that you cannot enter form mode directly, seriously limit its use. /Range Input is more commonly used to control cursor movement in worksheets under macro control, rather than being used directly.

Exercises

Experiment with the ACME.WKS worksheet. Try the following:

1. Increase Column A's column width, so that the full name of the field office (rather than its abbreviation) can display as a label, without overflowing into adjacent columns. Use /Worksheet Column-width Set. Increase the column width of all the other columns to 14, to allow for larger numbers, using /Worksheet Global Column-width Set.
2. Use /Worksheet Titles Both to prevent the field office names (in Column A) and the heading rows, from being lost in the display as you move about the worksheet. Experiment with the other /Worksheet Titles options.
3. Split the screen horizontally and vertically using /Worksheet Window.
4. Create a form for data entry. Allow changes only to the values, and prevent changes to the formulas. Use /Range Unprotect first (to define the cell ranges which can be changed). Then use /Worksheet Global Protection Enable (to turn on cell protection.) Finally, use /Range Input to prevent the cell pointer from moving to protected cells.

Your 1-2-3 confidence level should be very high by now. You're ready to tackle some of the trickier parts of 1-2-3: copying and moving labels, values, and formulas. In the next chapter, you'll learn all about these topics, and how to be creative in using relative and absolute addressing.

CHAPTER 13

Using /Copy and /Move

This chapter deals with how to use /Copy and /Move to make copies (/Copy) or to move (/Move) the contents of a cell range.

WHEN TO USE /COPY

You will find many occasions when you will want to make a duplicate copy of the *labels* in a cell range to another cell range. For example, you have defined your column headings (JANUARY, FEBRUARY, MARCH, and so on) in a row (to label the Revenue numbers in your worksheet), and you would like to copy them to another row (to label the Expense numbers in your worksheet). In addition, you will also want to use /Copy to copy labels in order to use advanced 1-2-3 features, such as database management.

In addition to copying labels, you will frequently want to copy *values*—the numbers in your worksheet. For example, you could calculate revenue for a group of part numbers in one part of the worksheet, and expenses for the same group in another part. You would use /Copy to copy the product numbers from the revenue to the expense part. When you use /Copy to copy numbers 1-2-3 makes every effort to copy the *appearance* of the number, as well as its *contents.* Numeric formats and protection status, which control the appearance of a number, as well as the number itself, are copied. Thus, the copied numbers display in the same form as the original numbers.

BEWARE ***Cell Column Widths Are Not Copied***

The one characteristic of cells which is *not* copied is the column width. 1-2-3 does not give individual cells their own column width. Rather, the cell automatically takes the column width of its column. So, if you copy a cell from Column A (which has a column width of 9) to Column B (which has a column width of 15) the copied cell has a column width of 15. This may affect the display of a number. For example, if a cell in (C2) format is copied from a cell wide enough for dollar signs and commas to display in a cell which is not wide enough, the copied cell will contain asterisks (*****). To get the copied cell to display the value, you would have to expand the column width for the *entire* column, which may cause other cells not to display as you would like.

Finally, you use /Copy to copy *formulas.* You will be copying formulas often. For example, you might use the @SUM function to sum the monthly revenue cell contents to produce the yearly revenue. You want to use the same @SUM function down the column to sum 100 individual expense items. Instead of entering the @SUM function 100 times, you can use /Copy to copy the formula down the column.

Copying formulas is one of the trickiest and, at the same time, most powerful functions of the 1-2-3 worksheet. As with labels and values, 1-2-3 makes every effort to copy the meaning of the formulas as well as their contents. You tell 1-2-3 once (when you define the formula) how the cell range referenced in the formula is referenced, and 1-2-3 preserves this meaning when it copies the formula. In this chapter, you will discover several ways of referencing cells so that the formula you enter is meaningful when you copy it.

HOW TO: Copy Cell Ranges

You start the /Copy command by selecting the Copy option from the main 1-2-3 menu. You can copy any type of cell range. You can create single copies or multiple copies of the contents of the cell range.

Copying is really very simple: you tell 1-2-3 what cell range you want to copy (the FROM range), and where you want to start copying (the start of the TO range). You can make one copy of the FROM range, or you can make several copies. In this section, you will learn how to use /Copy to copy one cell, a cell range consisting of a row or a column, and a cell range consisting of a rectangular block of multiple rows and columns.

BEWARE ***/Copy Destroys the Contents of Cells in the TO Range***

The copying process overwrites the former contents of cells in the TO range. You cannot uncopy (restore the worksheet to its contents before you started /Copy). If you are going to use /Copy, and you are unsure whether you will overwrite parts of the worksheet that you wish to keep, save the worksheet with /File Save first. If you make any errors using /Copy, you can restore the worksheet to its former state by retrieving the worksheet with /File Retrieve.

Copying One Cell

You can copy the contents of one cell to another cell, to a cell range consisting of a row or column, or to a block of cells consisting of several rows and columns.

Suppose you have entered the label **SALES** in Cell A1, and you want to copy this label to Cell B1. Start the copying process when the mode indicator displays READY.

If the cell pointer is at Cell A1, and you start copying by typing **/C**, the screen displays as shown in Figure 13.1. Note that 1-2-3 places you in POINT mode. You can expand the cell range to copy. Since you only wish to copy one cell, press [ENTER] to indicate that the FROM range is A1..A1. The screen displays as shown in Figure 13.2. Now indicate the start of the TO range. Since you wish to copy the SALES label to Cell B1, press [RIGHT]. Alternatively, you could type in the cell addresses of the TO range. You *cannot*, however, use [F5/GOTO], since [F5/GOTO] is not operational in POINT mode. The screen displays as in Figure 13.3.

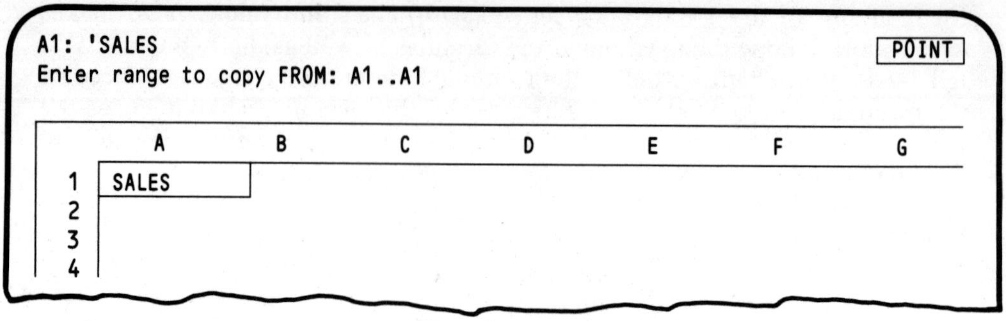

Figure 13.1 Starting /Copy

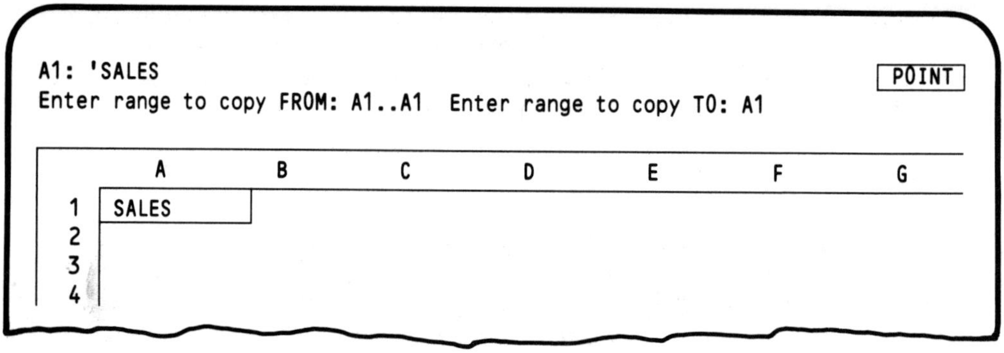

Figure 13.2 A One-Cell FROM Range

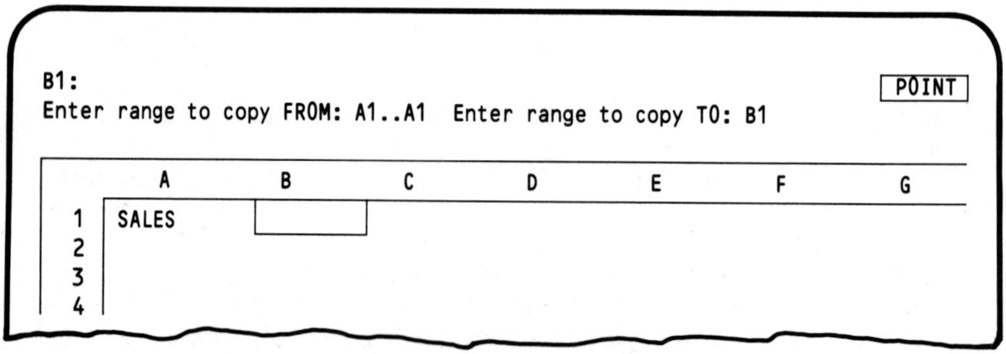

Figure 13.3 Pointing to TO Range

The start of the TO range is Cell B1 (which is what you want), so press [ENTER] to complete the /Copy operation. The screen displays as follows:

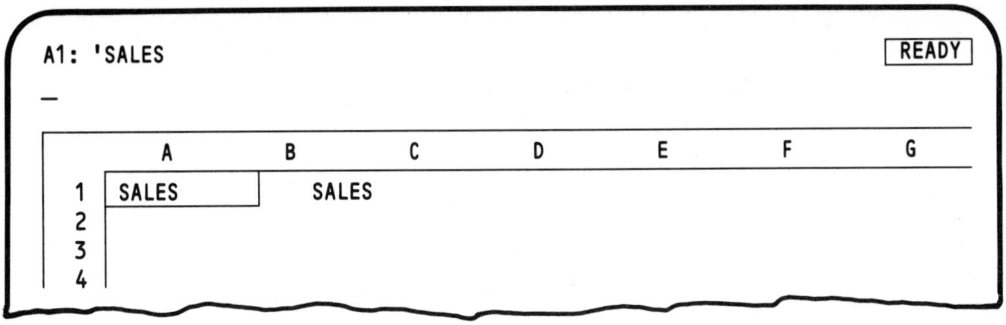

Figure 13.4 Completing Copying One Cell to Another

You can use /Copy to make more than one copy of the contents of Cell A1. How? By expanding the TO range! If, instead of pressing [ENTER], you had pressed [.] and expanded the TO range to B1..D1, you would make three copies of the SALES label, rather than one. By expanding the TO range, the screen displays as follows:

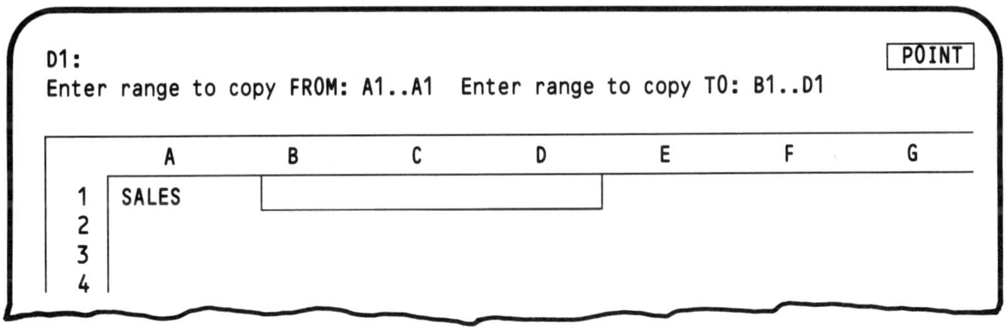

Figure 13.5 Expanding the TO Range

By pressing [ENTER], you would complete the copying, and the screen displays as shown in Figure 13.6.

Finally, you can expand the TO range to point to a rectangular block. For example, if you wanted to copy the SALES label to the range A2..C4, specify the TO range as shown in Figure 13.7 and press [ENTER]. This results in the display as shown in Figure 13.8.

HOW TO: Create a Row of Asterisks (Or Single Or Double Underscores)

You may need to create a row of asterisks, or single or double underscores, to separate one part of the worksheet from another. It's simple to do with /Copy combined with the repeat label-prefix (\). Here's how:

1. In the leftmost cell of the row enter a repeating label. To start creating a row of asterisks in Row 1, enter *[ENTER] in Cell A1.

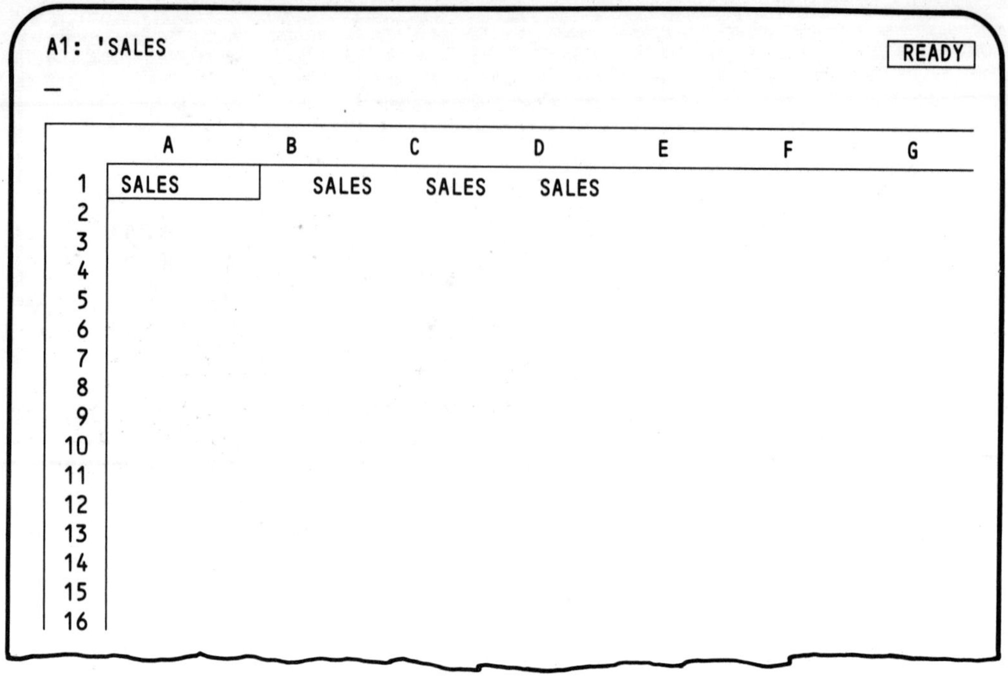

Figure 13.6 Completing Copying One Cell to a Row.

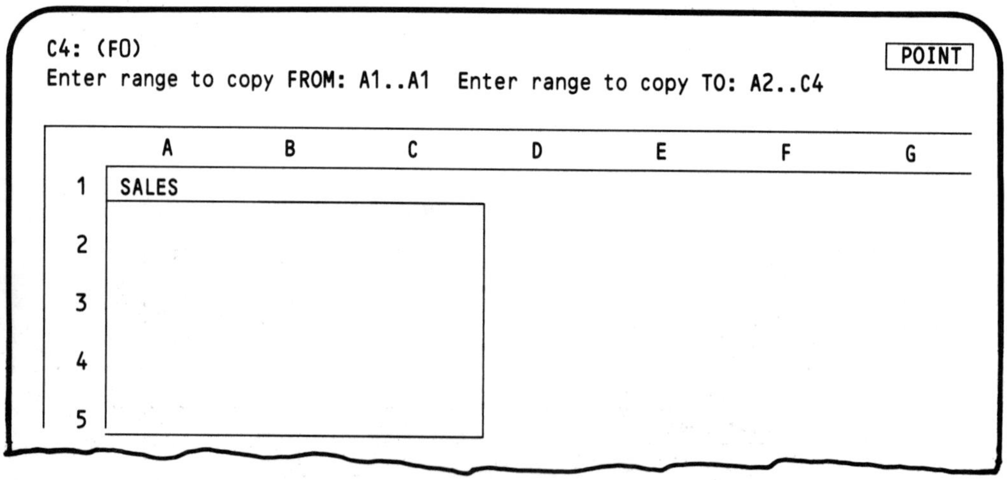

Figure 13.7 Copying a Cell to a Block of Cells

2. Copy this cell across Row 1, by typing the following:

`/C[ENTER]`	Start /Copy, FROM range is A1..A1
`B1..E1[ENTER]`	TO range is B1..E1

The row of asterisks is copied across Row 1.

```
A1: 'SALES                                                       READY
_

        A           B           C           D           E           F           G
  1  SALES
  2  SALES               SALES       SALES
  3  SALES               SALES       SALES
  4  SALES               SALES       SALES
  5
```

Figure 13.8 Completing /Copy

If you want to create a row with some other character, use that character as the character to repeat. For example, to enter a row of double underscores, enter \= instead of * in Cell A1, and copy the cell across the row.

Copying a Row or a Column of Cells

In addition to copying one cell, you can copy the contents of an entire row or column of cells. For example, you might want to copy the row of asterisks created with the HOW TO, to another row.

How to do it? Simple! Expand the FROM range.

If you position the cell pointer at the start of the row of asterisks, and type the following:

```
/C[RIGHT][RIGHT][RIGHT][RIGHT]
```

The FROM range is highlighted, as follows:

```
E1: \*                                                           POINT
Enter range to copy FROM: A1..E1

        A           B           C           D           E           F           G
  1  *************************************************
  2
  3
  4
```

Figure 13.9 Highlighting the FROM Range

To copy this row of asterisks to row 3, press [ENTER] to complete definition of the FROM range, and use the pointer movement keys to position the cell pointer at A3. The screen displays as follows:

```
A3:                                                              POINT
Enter range to copy FROM: A1..E1  Enter range to copy TO: A3

        A         B         C         D         E         F         G
   1  **************************************************
   2
   3  [         ]
   4
   5
```

Figure 13.10 Highlighting the Start of the TO Range

To copy a row of cells to another row, you need specify only the *start* of the TO range. So you need only press [ENTER] after you have arrived at Cell A3, and the /Copy will complete, as follows:

```
A1: \*                                                           READY
_

        A         B         C         D         E         F         G
   1  **************************************************
   2
   3  **************************************************
   4
   5
   6
   7
   8
   9
  10
  11
  12
  13
  14
  15
  16
  17
```

Figure 13.11 Completing /Copy

You could also create *multiple* copies of the row in adjacent rows of the FROM range. Simply give the TO range depth. For example, to create three copies of the row of asterisks, on rows 3, 4, and 5, define the TO range as A3..A5 (rather than simply A3) and press [ENTER].

Copying a Rectangular Block of Cells

Suppose you want to make copies of labels which run both across and down? You can use /Copy here as well. Suppose you have defined a worksheet with month labels JAN, FEB, MAR, APR, MAY, and JUNE across Row 1, from Columns B to G, and labels in Column A for SALES, UNIT PRICE, REVENUE, COSTS, and PROFIT, down Column A. You would like to copy this block of labels to another part of the worksheet.

To start copying this block, position the cell pointer at Cell A1 (the start of the block), and start /Copy, highlighting the FROM range, as follows:

```
G9:                                                              READY
Enter range to copy FROM: A1..G9

         A          B          C          D          E          F          G
 1                     JAN        FEB        MAR        APR        MAY       JUNE
 2                     ---        ---        ---        ---        ---        ---
 3
 4   SALES
 5   UNIT PRICE
 6   REVENUE
 7
 8   COSTS
 9   PROFIT
10
11
12
13
14
15
16
17
18
19
```

Figure 13.12 Copying a Block of Labels

Then, as with copying a row of labels, press [ENTER] to complete definition of the FROM range, position the cell pointer to the beginning of the TO range, and press `[ENTER]` again. If the block of labels is to be copied starting at Cell A12, the worksheet displays as follows:

```
A12:                                                            POINT
Enter range to copy FROM: A1..G9  Enter range to copy TO: A12

          A        B        C        D        E        F        G
  1                 JAN      FEB      MAR      APR      MAY      JUNE
  2                 ---      ---      ---      ---      ---      ---
  3
  4   SALES
  5   UNIT PRICE
  6   REVENUE
  7
  8   COSTS
  9   PROFIT
 10
 11
 12   [        ]
 13
 14
 15
 16
 17
 18
```

Figure 13.13 Pointing to TO Range

When when the copy is completed, the worksheet displays as shown in Figure 13.14.

BEWARE ***Avoid Overlapping TO and FROM Ranges***

If the FROM and TO ranges overlap, unpredictable results may occur. /Copy, even when it copies a block, copies cell by cell. If the FROM and TO ranges overlap, some cells may already have had their contents changed by /Copy. The *changed* cell, rather than the original, will be copied. If the FROM and TO ranges don't overlap, 1-2-3 will more likely perform the copying operation to your liking.

There is one exception to this rule: if both the FROM and TO ranges start at the same cell, the /Copy will avoid the overlap problem.

BEWARE ***You Cannot Copy to a Protected Part of the Worksheet***

If the TO range has even one protected cell, and global protection is enabled, 1-2-3 will not perform the copy. Instead, it will display the `Protected cell` error message. 1-2-3 will not tell you which cell caused the error. You

```
A1:                                                    READY
_

          A           B        C        D        E        F        G
  1                         JAN      FEB      MAR      APR      MAY     JUNE
  2                         ---      ---      ---      ---      ---      ---
  3
  4  SALES
  5  UNIT PRICE
  6  REVENUE
  7
  8  COSTS
  9  PROFIT
 10
 11
 12                         JAN      FEB      MAR      APR      MAY     JUNE
 13                         ---      ---      ---      ---      ---      ---
 14
 15  SALES
 16  UNIT PRICE
 17  REVENUE
 18
 19  COSTS
 20  PROFIT
```

Figure 13.14 Completing Copying a Block of Cells

must find that out for yourself. You could, of course, disable global protection with /Worksheet Global Protection Disable and redo the /Copy. This is potentially dangerous, because you may defeat the purpose of global protection and destroy worksheet formulas.

BEWARE `Worksheet Full` ***Message***

If you use /Copy to overflow the TO range into an invalid cell address, 1-2-3 displays the `Worksheet full` message. Try this one:

/CA1..D1[ENTER]	TO range is A1..D1
IV1	FROM range starts at IV1

Cell IV1 is at Column 256, Row 1. You are asking /Copy to start the TO range at Column 256, and continue to Columns 257, 258, and 259. Since these columns don't exist on the worksheet, 1-2-3 displays `Worksheet full`.

HOW TO: Use Named Ranges with /Copy

You can (and should!) use named ranges with /Copy. For example, if you named the block of cells in our worksheet displaying six months of data

SIXMONTHS, you could use the range name in **/Copy**. The range name SIXMONTHS is certainly clearer than the cell addresses A1..G9. You could have copied the block of cells as follows:

/RNCSIXMONTHS[ENTER]A1..G9[ENTER]	Create range name SIXMONTHS
/CSIXMONTHS[ENTER]	SIXMONTHS is FROM range
C12[ENTER]	Start TO range at C12

COPYING VALUES

You use the same process with copying numbers as you do with labels. You can copy a cell, a row or column of numbers, or a block of numbers to another part of the worksheet. The cell format and protection status of the cell is copied, along with the value.

If the values are input numbers (numbers you simply enter), you should observe the same BEWAREs as for copying labels. However, copying *formulas* is quite another matter. A thorough understanding of how 1-2-3 copies formulas is essential for producing effective worksheets. Copying formulas is discussed in the next section.

USING RELATIVE AND ABSOLUTE ADDRESSES IN FORMULAS

Copying Formulas with Relative Addresses

As you have seen in our discussion of formatted numbers, in 1-2-3, things aren't always what they seem. When you learned kabout formatted numbers, you saw that the appearance of a number can differ from how 1-2-3 stores the number.

With cell formulas, it's the cell *addresses* referenced in the formulas which aren't what they seem to be. When you are entering a number in Cell B1, 1-2-3 displays the address **B1** in the control panel, and you really are at address B1. However, when that same Cell B1 is referenced in a *formula* such as **@SUM(B1..D1)** Cell B1 means something different.

What does Cell B1 mean in the formula? That depends on which cell you are using to enter the formula. If you enter the **@SUM** formula in Cell E1, the reference to Cell B1 doesn't refer to Cell B1. Rather, it means the cell, in the same row in which the formula is entered, but 3 columns to the left. In the formula, Cell B1 is referenced *relative* to Cell E1 (i.e., the cell three columns to the left of it), and is called a *relative reference*. This idea of relative reference can be confusing at first, because in any context other than being referenced in a formula, when you identify a cell such as Cell B1, you really mean Cell B1.

Why did 1-2-3 introduce this somewhat puzzling idea of relative references? To make copying formulas easier! If you copy the @SUM formula down (from Cell E1 to Cell E2) the relativeness of the cell references is copied with it. The copied formula in Cell E2 will be @SUM(B2..D2). In other words, the position of Cell B2 relative to Cell E2 (three columns to the right) is the same as the position of Cell B1 relative to Cell E1.

In many situations, this is exactly what you want! For example, if you want to use @SUM to add 12 columns of monthly SALES, COSTS, and PROFIT, producing yearly SALES, COSTS, and PROFIT, you want to define the formula once (for yearly SALES) and copy it down the column. In the same worksheet, you might enter a formula which calculates NET PROFIT for January, and copy it across the row to get NET PROFIT for February, March, and so on. Since the cells in the formula are referenced relative to where the formula is entered, and /Copy preserves the relative reference, copying them makes the same formula apply in the copied cells. If this did not occur, you would be forced to enter each formula separately.

Copying Formulas with Absolute Addresses

Are there times in which, when you reference a cell in a formula, you mean precisely that cell address? Can you tell 1-2-3 that a particular cell is *not* a relative reference, but is rather an *absolute reference*? Yes to both questions!

In fact, you will find many cases when you will require absolute references in cell formulas. A common situation is calculating percent of a total. Suppose Acme Widget sells three types of widgets—Widget A, Widget B, and Widget C. You would like to sum sales for these three widgets in Column B, and compute sales of each widget as a percent of total sales, in Column C. The worksheet containing the labels and sales data as shown in Figure 13.15.

You need to enter the formulas. First, use @SUM to compute total sales in Cell B11. Enter, in Cell B11 the formula @SUM(B6..B9). The worksheet now displays as shown in Figure 13.16.

In Cell C6 compute Widget A Sales as a percent of total sales. If you enter the formula +B6/B11, you will, indeed, compute the correct percentage for Widget A.

But what happens when you copy this formula down to get the percentages for Widget B and Widget C? After the formula is copied, the worksheet displays as shown in Figure 13.17.

The numerators (Widget B Sales and Widget C Sales) are correct because they were copied relative to the formula in Cell C6. However, the result displayed as ERR because the denominator was *also* copied relative to the formula. (ERR is 1-2-3's way of telling you that it cannot calculate a formula.) For Widget B, instead of dividing by Total Sales, the formula divided by the cell *below* total sales. This cell is blank, which 1-2-3 assumes in a formula to be 0. Since division by zero is impossible to do, 1-2-3 displays ERR.

To get the calculation to proceed correctly, you must prevent 1-2-3 from

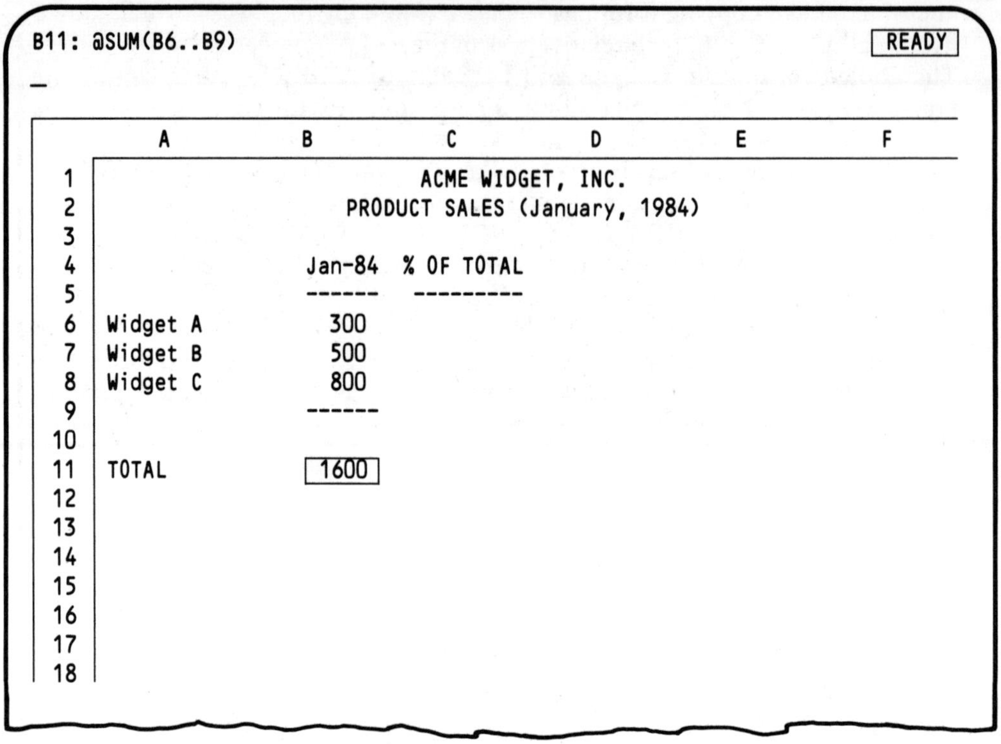

Figure 13.15 Computing the Total Sales

assuming that the total sales cell is a relative reference. To do this, make its reference *absolute*.

To define an absolute reference, simply insert dollar signs before the column letter and the row number. Define the formula in Cell C6 as **+B6/$B$11** rather than **+B6/B11**. With the presence of dollar signs, 1-2-3 assumes the cell is referenced by its address, and when the formula is copied, the reference to the cell does not change. Copying the formula in Cell C6 down the column will preserve the relative reference to the product sales number in Column A, but will divide it by the total sales number in B11. After the formula is copied, the worksheet displays as shown in Figure 13.18.

Using Mixed Addresses

You could also define a *mixed reference* (absolute on the row and relative on the column, or relative on the row and absolute on the column). Defining mixed references is a powerful tool in developing a worksheet.

Suppose Acme's Treasurer decides a loan of $100,000 is necessary to finance plant expansion. The banks offer several options for interest rate and term. You have been asked to build a table of monthly payments with interest rates varying from 9% to 15% (in increments of .5%), and yearly terms of 10,

```
C6: +B6/B11                                                    READY
_

          A           B          C          D          E          F
 1                              ACME WIDGET, INC.
 2                         PRODUCT SALES (January, 1984)
 3
 4                     Jan-84  % OF TOTAL
 5                     ------
 6   Widget A             300   0.1875
 7   Widget B             500
 8   Widget C             800
 9                     ------
10
11   TOTAL               1600
12
13
14
15
16
17
18
```

Figure 13.16 Computing Total January Sales

15, and 20 years. 1-2-3 provides a function called **@PMT** which calculates the payment for a loan. **@PMT** has the following arguments:

```
@PMT(principal,interest,term)
```

The Treasurer would like to build a table with interest rates down Column A, and terms across Row 4, as shown in Figure 13.19.

To have the formula copied correctly, the *principal* is constant and must be an absolute reference. The *interest*, however, changes in Column A and is a mixed reference (absolute on Column A, but relative on the row). Finally, the *term*, while constant in Row 4, changes in each column.

To reference the formula so that it can be copied correctly, enter the following in Cell C5 (the first cell of the range).

```
@PMT($C$1,$A5/12,C$4*12)
```

The **@PMT** formula in each cell will always reference Cell C1, the cell containing the $100,000 amount. Cell C1 is thus an absolute reference. The interest rate amounts start at Row 5 and reference Column A. The interest rate is thus

```
C7: +B7/B12                                                    READY
_

          A           B          C          D          E          F
  1                           ACME WIDGET, INC.
  2                      PRODUCT SALES (January, 1984)
  3
  4                      Jan-84  % OF TOTAL
  5                      ------  ----------
  6  Widget A               300      0.1875
  7  Widget B               500         ERR
  8  Widget C               800         ERR
  9                      ------
 10
 11  TOTAL                 1600
 12
 13
 14
 15
 16
 17
 18
```

Figure 13.17 Result After Formula Is Copied

a mixed reference in which the column (Column A) remains constant but the row reference changes. To get a monthly payment, you must divide the yearly interest rate by 12. On the other hand, the term is a mixed reference in which the row (Row 5) remains constant but the column reference changes. If you copy the formula from Cell C5 to the rest of the cells, you'll get the table shown in Figure 13.20.

This is a clever example of using absolute, and mixed references in formulas to build a table. Chapter 19 discusses another 1-2-3 command (/Data Table) which achieves the same result. 1-2-3 is so powerful that there is frequently more than one way to accomplish a task.

HOW TO: Use [F4/ABS] to Change a Cell Reference

If you are building a formula by referencing the cells in POINT mode, you can use a special key called [F4/ABS] to insert dollar signs into the formula. Using [F4/ABS] you can have 1-2-3 fill in the dollar signs, so that without typing can transform a relative reference into an absolute or a mixed reference.

[F4/ABS] toggles among four settings. When you're in POINT mode enter-

```
C6: +B6/$B$11                                                  READY

     A            B           C           D          E          F
 1                      ACME WIDGET, INC.
 2                  PRODUCT SALES (January, 1984)
 3
 4               Jan-84  % OF TOTAL
 5               ------  ---------
 6  Widget A        300     0.1875
 7  Widget B        500     0.3125
 8  Widget C        800        0.5
 9               ------  ---------
10
11  TOTAL          1600
12
13
14
15
16
```

Figure 13.18 Result if Copied Formula Contains Absolute Reference

ing a formula, and you are at Cell C1, if you:

press [F4/ABS] once,	the reference changes to $C$1 (absolute)
press [F4/ABS] again,	the reference changes to C$1 (relative on the column but absolute on the row)
press [F4/ABS] again,	the reference changes to $C1 (absolute on the column but relative on the row)
press [F4/ABS] again,	the reference changes to C1 (relative)

and so on.

[F4/ABS] works only in POINT mode, so if you're typing in the cell addresses, you must type in the dollar signs yourself.

HOW TO: Make a Range Name Absolute in a Formula

If you use a range name in a formula, you can make it an absolute reference by preceding it with a dollar sign. Thus, if you have defined a range name SALES, referencing B1..D1, then:

@SUM(SALES)	is the equivalent of @SUM(B1..D1)
@SUM($SALES)	is the equivalent of @SUM($B$1..$D$1)

There is, unfortunately, no way to make a range name a mixed reference.

```
C1: (C0) 100000                                              READY
_

        A         B         C         D         E         F         G
 1  PRINCIPAL:          $100,000
 2
 3                                  TERM (YEARS)
 4  INTEREST                  10        15        20
 5   9.0%
 6   9.5%
 7  10.0%
 8  10.5%
 9  11.0%
10  11.5%
11  12.0%
12  12.5%
13  13.0%
14  13.5%
15  14.0%
16  14.5%
17  15.0%
18
19
```

Figure 13.19 Acme Widget Monthly Payment Table

USING /MOVE

Moving Labels and Values

For labels and values /Move, instead of creating another copy of the data in the cells, moves the contents of the cells to the TO range and erases the FROM range. In addition to erasing the data from the FROM range, all cells in the FROM range become protected and all numeric formats are erased. In effect, the FROM range looks as it did when you started 1-2-3.

Effect of Moving Cells Referenced in Formulas

If you /Move a cell which is referenced in a formula, 1-2-3 adjusts the formula to refer to its new location. Thus, if your original formula is @SUM(B1..D1) and you use /Move to move the range to B2..D2, the new formula is @SUM(B2..D2).

```
C5: (C2) @PMT($C$1,$A5/12,C$4*12)                                  READY
_
```

	A	B	C	D	E	F	G
1	PRINCIPAL:		$100,000				
2							
3				TERM (YEARS)			
4	INTEREST		10	15	20		
5	9.0%		$1,266.76	$1,014.27	$899.73		
6	9.5%		$1,293.98	$1,044.22	$932.13		
7	10.0%		$1,321.51	$1,074.61	$965.02		
8	10.5%		$1,349.35	$1,105.40	$998.38		
9	11.0%		$1,377.50	$1,136.60	$1,032.19		
10	11.5%		$1,405.95	$1,168.19	$1,066.43		
11	12.0%		$1,434.71	$1,200.17	$1,101.09		
12	12.5%		$1,463.76	$1,232.52	$1,136.14		
13	13.0%		$1,493.11	$1,265.24	$1,171.58		
14	13.5%		$1,522.74	$1,298.32	$1,207.37		
15	14.0%		$1,552.66	$1,331.74	$1,243.52		
16	14.5%		$1,582.87	$1,365.50	$1,280.00		
17	15.0%		$1,613.35	$1,399.59	$1,316.79		
18							
19							

Figure 13.20 Completed Table Using Copied @PMT Formula.

/Move is designed so that you can move cells, even those containing formulas, freely. In most cases, your formulas will adjust for the moved cells.

BEWARE *You Can Destroy Formulas with /Move*

Most of the BEWAREs that apply to /Copy apply to /Move as well. As in /Copy, /Move overwrites the TO range. And the same principles of defining one-cell, one-row or one-column, or blocks of cells, apply to /Move.

Your worksheet can contain many complex formulas which depend on each other. It's not always possible to check the effects of /Move on all the formulas until (alas) you've done it (and then it is too late). Any formulas which depend on the contents of cells in the TO range will display ERR. You must then laboriously analyze your formulas to find out what caused the problem.

Practice copying different types of labels, values, and formulas. Also practice moving, paying particular attention to cell formulas. When you feel you understand copying and moving, proceed to Chapter 14, which discusses inserting and deleting rows and columns. These are other ways to change the display and meaning of the worksheet.

CHAPTER 14

Inserting and Deleting Rows and Columns

From time to time, you will want to add or delete entire columns and/or rows. Suppose, for example, Acme Widget decides to sell Widget D in addition to Widget A, Widget B, and Widget C. You have developed your revenue analysis worksheet to sum revenues only for the three products. You might need to insert a row for Widget D and have the formulas automatically include the revenue for Widget D into the calculations.

That is precisely what /Worksheet Insert Rows was designed for. You can insert a row for Widget D into the worksheet and (within certain rules) 1-2-3 will automatically adjust the formulas to include the data for the new product.

Suppose you had created a revenue analysis worksheet for six months, with each month's data stored in a column, and a year-to-date revenue column. You would now decide that you want to add revenue data for the other six months to create a worksheet for all 12 months. Here, you would use /Worksheet Insert Column to make room for the additional data.

In addition to inserting rows or columns, you may want to delete them. Acme Widget decides to discontinue a product, or you want to reduce the number of months of revenue data in the worksheet. To delete a row or rows, use /Worksheet Delete Rows; to delete a column or columns, use /Worksheet Delete Column.

INSERTING ROWS AND COLUMNS

Inserting Rows

To insert a row or rows, do the following, if you are in READY mode:

1. Position the cell pointer at the row at which you want the insertion to occur. If you want to insert more than one row, expand the cell pointer down a row for every additional row you want to insert. The cell pointer's column does not matter.
2. Type /WIR (for /Worksheet Insert Row). Row 1 to the row immediately above the cell pointer is left unchanged. 1-2-3 moves the worksheet data which started in the first row of the highlighted range, to start at the first row immediately below the highlighted range. Expand the cell pointer, if desired, and press [ENTER]. Cells in the inserted rows are erased, protected, and unformatted.

If any data would be lost by inserting (for example, if Row 2048 contained data before you tried to insert a row, inserting a row would cause data in that row to be lost) 1-2-3 does not insert the row(s) and instead issues the `Worksheet full` error message.

If rows are inserted within a cell-range, 1-2-3 automatically adjusts the range to include the inserted row(s). Thus, if in Cell B10, you had entered a formula **@SUM(B2..B9)**, and if you insert a row at Row 8, 1-2-3 adjusts the **@SUM** formula (now at Cell B11) to be **@SUM(B2..B10)**. This range adjustment also applies to named ranges—rows inserted within the rows of a named range automatically expand the range name.

BEWARE *Range Adjustment Does Not Occur if a Row Is Inserted at the Top or Bottom Corner of a Range*

Suppose your worksheet displays as follows:

```
B10: @SUM(B2..B9)                                                    READY
_

          A           B          C         D          E          F          G
  1                                    ACME WIDGET REVENUES
  2  Atlanta           200
  3  Los Angeles       300
  4  Boston            230
  5  Miami             175
  6  Chicago           260
  7  New York          324
  8  Home Office        85
  9  Unassigned          5
 10  TOTAL            1579
 11
 12
 13
 14
 15
 16
 17
 18
```

Figure 14.1

At Cell B10, the formula reads **@SUM(B2..B9)**. If you insert a row with the cell pointer positioned at Row 9, the worksheet displays as shown in Figure 14.2. The **@SUM** formula, which is relocated to Cell B11, *still* reads **@SUM(B2..B9)**! That's because you inserted a row at Row 9. (A similar non-adjustment would occur if you inserted a row at Row 2).

How can you avoid this problem? Try this!

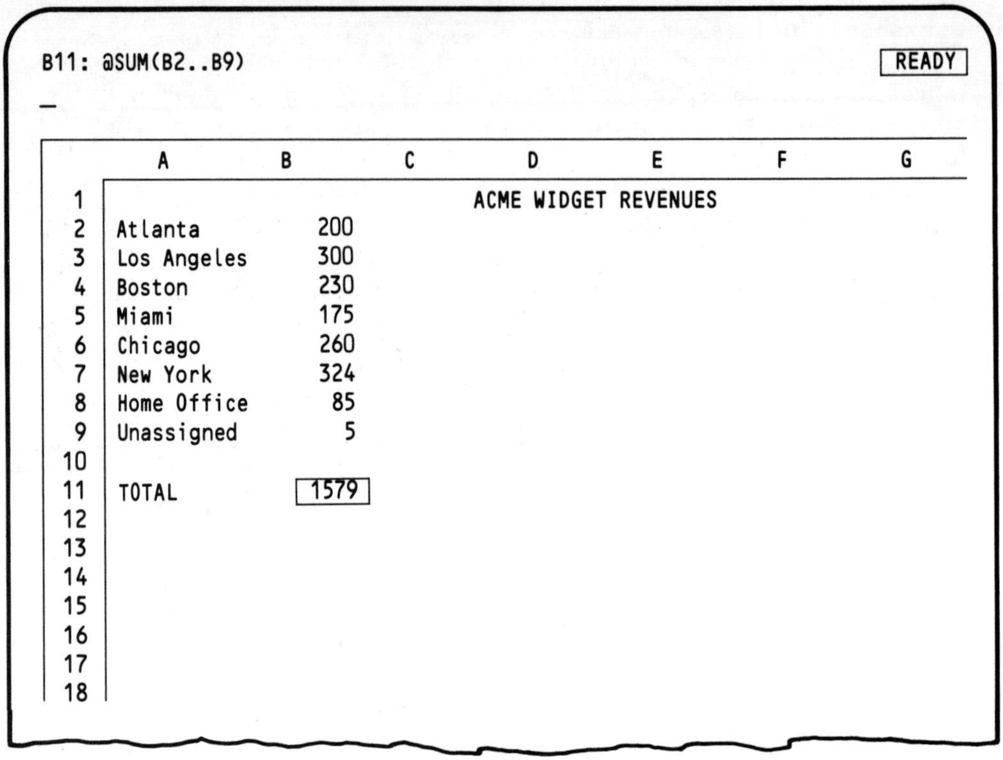

Figure 14.2

HOW TO: Make Sure an **@SUM** Formula Is Adjusted

To make sure an **@SUM** formula is adjusted, define a row of underlines (you probably want to underline the data anyway), as shown in the HOW TO in the last chapter. Once you have done this, include the row of underlines in the formula. Make the worksheet display shown in Figure 14.3. By making the row containing the underlines as the bottom row of the **@SUM** range argument, you can insert a row after the last product and have the range adjust automatically. This row is now within the **@SUM** range, where before, it was on the edge of the range.

Inserting Columns

What you've learned about inserting rows applies as well to columns. To insert a column or columns do the following, if you are in **READY** mode:

1. Position the cell pointer at the column at which you want the insertion to occur. If you want to insert more than one column, expand the cell pointer right one column for every additional column you want to insert. The cell pointer's row does not matter.

```
B11: @SUM(B2..B10)                                              READY
_

         A           B          C          D          E          F          G
  1                                        ACME WIDGET REVENUES
  2  Atlanta            200
  3  Los Angeles        300
  4  Boston             230
  5  Miami              175
  6  Chicago            260
  7  New York           324
  8  Home Office         85
  9  Unassigned           5
 10                    ----
 11  TOTAL             1579
 12
 13
 14
 15
 16
 17
 18
```

Figure 14.3

2. Type **/WIC** (for /**W**orksheet **I**nsert **C**olumn). Column A to the column immediately to the left of the the cell pointer is left unchanged. 1-2-3 moves the worksheet data which started in the column row of the highlighted range, to start at the the first column immediately to the right of the highlighted range. Cells in the inserted columns are erased, protected, and unformatted.

If any data would be lost by inserting (for example, if Column IV contained data before you tried to insert a column, inserting a column would cause data in that column to be lost) 1-2-3 does not insert the column(s) and instead issues the `Worksheet full` error message.

As with inserting rows, inserting columns within ranges automatically adjusts the ranges to include the inserted columns. Thus, if in Cell J10 you had entered a formula `@SUM(B10..I10)`, and if you had inserted a column at Column H, the `@SUM` formula (now at Cell K10) would be `@SUM(B10..J10)`. Also, as with inserting rows, inserting columns at a range boundary (at the leftmost or rightmost column of a range) does not adjust the range.

DELETING ROWS AND COLUMNS

BEWARE *You Can Delete More Than You See*

Deleting rows and columns (unlike inserting) can cause you to lose part of your worksheet data. Deleting is another all-or-none proposition. You delete an *entire* row or an *entire* column. The problem, of course, is that you cannot *see* an entire row or an entire column—you see only the part that displays. So, you may delete Column C, thinking you delete only Cells C1 to C20, and conveniently forget that you had some data in Cell C105 which (as a bonus) is also deleted. You cannot now restore the worksheet back to its state before you deleted the column.

Therefore, before you start deleting rows and columns, you should be sure that either (a) are quite sure there is no data that you will unintentionally delete, or (b) use /File Save before doing the deletion so that you can retrieve the file as it was, if you make a mess of it.

Deleting Rows

To delete a row or rows, do the following, if you are in READY mode:

1. Position the cell pointer at the row at which you want the deletion to occur. If you want to delete more than one row, expand the cell pointer down a row for every additional row you want to delete. The cell pointer's column does not matter.
2. Type /WDR (for /Worksheet Delete Row). Row 1 to the row immediately above the cell pointer is left unchanged. 1-2-3 deletes the rows in the highlighted range and moves the worksheet rows which started immediately below the highlighted range, to start at the first row of the highlighted range.

As with insertion, 1-2-3 adjusts ranges and named ranges. This time, however, the ranges are contracted if the deletion occurs within the range. Thus, if in Cell B10, you had entered a formula @SUM(B2..B9), if you delete Row 8, 1-2-3 adjusts the @SUM function (now at Cell B9) to be @SUM(B2..B8).

BEWARE *Deleting the First or Last Row of a Cell Range*

Deleting the first or last row of a cell range causes the meaning of the range to be destroyed. If you think about it, this is logical. By deleting a row, you have destroyed a boundary of the rectangle (it's a bit like erasing one of the sides of a rectangle). Any formulas (such as @SUM) which referred to this range will now contain ERR, indicating that 1-2-3 cannot evaluate it. The same BEWARE applies to command ranges, such as named print ranges.

Deleting Columns

To delete a column or columns, do the following, if you are in READY mode:

1. Position the cell pointer at the column at which you want the deletion to

occur. If you want to delete more than one column, expand the cell pointer to the right, one column for every additional column you want to delete. The cell pointer's row does not matter.

2. Type /WDC (for /Worksheet Delete Column). Columns from Column A, up to the column immediately to the left of the cell pointer, are unchanged. 1-2-3 deletes the columns in the highlighted range and moves the worksheet columns which started immediately to the right of the highlighted range, so as to start at the first column of the highlighted range.

As with deleting rows, deleted columns within cell ranges cause the range to contract. Thus, if in Cell J10, you had entered a formula @SUM(B10..I10), and you delete Column D, 1-2-3 adjusts the @SUM formula (now at Cell I10) to be @SUM(B10..H10).

Deleting the first or last column of a cell range has the same drastic effects as deleting its first or last row. So be careful!

HOW DELETING IS DIFFERENT FROM ERASING A CELL RANGE

You might think that deleting is the same as erasing a cell range. After all, both terms have nearly the same English meaning. They're not the same! Bear in mind the following differences:

- /Range Erase erases only cell contents, while preserving formats and protection status. Deleting gets rid of all cell settings.
- Formulas and ranges are not adjusted when you use /Range Erase. They are adjusted when you delete columns or rows.
- You can never invalidate ranges with /Range Erase. You can easily invalidate ranges by deleting rows and columns.

HOW TO: Shrink the Active Worksheet (Method Two)

When you delete rows or columns, you are on your way to shrinking the active worksheet. However, you're not quite there. Another way to shrink the active worksheet is to do the following:

1. Delete rows or columns.
2. Save the file, using /File Save.
3. When you retrieve the file with /File Retrieve, the active worksheet will have shrunk by the number of rows and columns deleted.

It's time to explore 1-2-3's recalculation options: how and when to recalculate the worksheet. As with controlling the worksheet display, there are some subtleties to controlling recalculation. This is the subject of the next chapter.

CHAPTER 15

Recalculating and Displaying Worksheet Status

This chapter covers the recalculation options available in 1-2-3, and the use of /Worksheet Status to display global worksheet information.

AUTOMATIC AND MANUAL RECALCULATION

You can see the recalculation options by using /Worksheet Global Recalculation. 1-2-3 displays the following recalculation options.

```
Natural Columnwise Rowwise Automatic Manual Iteration
```

With 1-2-3, you can control (a) whether or not you want the entire worksheet to be recalculated whenever you change an entry in a cell; and (b) what the recalculation order is.

If you do not specify differently, 1-2-3 recalculates the entire worksheet automatically whenever you change an entry. Remember when you entered the @SUM formula? When you changed the value in a cell which was referenced in the formula, 1-2-3 automatically recalculated the @SUM formula. This feature is called *automatic recalculation.*

Automatic recalculation is what you want most of the time. It's a jazzy feature—if you change January Revenue for Widget A, the yearly revenue is automatically recalculated. Automatic recalculation lets you play "what-if" games. You can change as many numbers as you want (sales units, advertising expenses, unit price) and see the formulas recalculate almost instantaneously. Before you make a decision, you can try different scenarios and see their effects.

There are situations, however, when you want to turn off automatic recalculation. One problem with automatic recalculation is that, when the worksheet is large enough (when it contains about 150 to 200 rows of data, and in some cases even less) you will notice a hesitation (the WAIT indicator may flash for five seconds or more) after you change each cell entry. This can be frustrating when you are entering large amounts of data (such as many individual monthly revenue numbers). 1-2-3 is recalculating the formulas most of the time. These formulas are meaningless until all of the data has been entered. In this situation, you would like to turn off automatic recalculation until you have entered all the numbers. After all the numbers are entered, you can press a button and have 1-2-3 recalculate the formulas.

To turn off automatic recalculation, use /Worksheet Global Recalculation Manual. With manual recalculation, the worksheet does not recalculate after you change an entry, thus speeding up data entry. The CALC indicator displays, indicating that the worksheet must be recalculated. After you have completed data entry, press [F9/CALC] and 1-2-3 recalculates the formulas.

HOW TO: Recalculate Part of the Worksheet

1-2-3 does not have an option to recalculate only a *part* of the worksheet. This option could be quite useful. For example, if you only changed three cells in a worksheet containing 2,000 cells, it might take considerable time to recalculate the entire worksheet. If you just want to recalculate a cell range while in manual recalculation, this HOW TO will recalculate just the cell range:

Copy the cell range to itself! For example, to recalculate the range from Cell A101 to X103, type the following:

```
/CA101..X103[ENTER]A101..X103[ENTER]
```

The CALC indicator will display, because 1-2-3 isn't sure that this recalculation didn't affect another part of the worksheet. You should be sure of that as well.

HOW TO: Recalculate the Formula Pointed to by the Cell Pointer

If the cell pointer is positioned at a cell containing a formula, and you are in manual recalculation mode and want to force 1-2-3 to recalculate just that cell, you can simply press [F2/EDIT], followed by [ENTER]. This will make that cell recalculate.

You can change back to automatic recalculation by using /Worksheet Global Recalculation Automatic. Then, every time a cell entry changes, the worksheet recalculates.

You might consider using manual recalculation in conjunction with /Range Input (where you are, after all, defining a form for entering data into many cells). After you enter the data and terminate /Range Input (by pressing [ESC], or pressing [ENTER] without entering anything), you should recalculate the worksheet. You can do so in one of two ways:

1. Press [F9/CALC]. The worksheet will recalculate, but you will stay in manual recalculation mode.
2. Use /Worksheet Global Recalculation Automatic. This will also cause the worksheet to recalculate, but you will return to automatic recalculation mode.

RECALCULATION METHODS

Rowwise and Columnwise Recalculation

In addition to whether a worksheet is to be recalculated, 1-2-3 lets you control the *order* of recalculation. For most worksheets, recalculation order isn't a problem.

Almost all first-generation automated spreadsheet packages recalculate in one of two ways, which are:

1. Row-by-row (or rowwise). You recalculate all the cells in Row 1 (from Cell A1), followed by all the cells in Row 2 (from Cell A2), followed by the cells in Row 3, and so on. To make 1-2-3 recalculate row-by-row, use /Worksheet Global Recalculation Rowwise.
2. Column-by-column (or columnwise). You recalculate all the cells in Column A (from Cell A1), followed by all the cells in Column B (from Cell B1), followed by the cells in Column C, and so on. To make 1-2-3 recalculate column-by-column, use /Worksheet Global Recalculation Columnwise. Rowwise recalculation almost always works for simple worksheets. All the calculations in a row usually relate to an item, such as a particular product or account. All of the formulas in a row are based on cells whose value is already known by the time the formula is ready to be recalculated.

There are, however, simple worksheets where rowwise recalculation will not work. For example, to track month-by-month inventory, typically February's beginning inventory is January's ending inventory. January's ending inventory is calculated by subtracting shipments from and adding receipts to January's beginning inventory. Recalculating the worksheet row by row will not work—the worksheet must be calculated column-by-column.

1-2-3 can recalculate the worksheet either row-by-row or column-by-column. It can calculate January's ending inventory, in its column, and then store the result as February's beginning inventory.

This type of situation, in which a cell depends on a cell below it, is called a *forward reference*. The February beginning inventory cell, references the January ending inventory cell, which is below it in the worksheet. This particular forward reference is simple to diagnose. Others are more complex. You can have complex worksheet interactions, such as calculations of cash reserves in a balance sheet and income statement, with many forward references. In this case, if the numbers aren't consistent, finding the problem (or problems!) may be very difficult. Whenever possible, you should design worksheets to contain the minimum number of forward references.

Natural Recalculation

1-2-3 uses a more innovative approach to recalculation, designed specifically to minimize difficulties in recalculating formulas with forward references. This is called *natural recalculation*.

With natural recalculation, 1-2-3 doesn't predetermine a recalculation order, rather, it looks at the formulas and determines which must be recalculated first, which next, and so on. Instead of recalculating row-by-row or column-by-column, 1-2-3 recalculates based on the formulas in the worksheet. Where the formulas are in the worksheet is unimportant. Thus, you could create forward references and, in most instances, 1-2-3 would recalculate the worksheet correctly. In fact, it is unnecessary to specify rowwise or columnwise recalculation in 1-2-3, since its natural recalculation order will automatically detect and resolve forward references.

If you want 1-2-3 to recalculate naturally, you need do nothing, since 1-2-3 assumes natural recalculation unless you tell it otherwise. If you specify another type of recalculation order and want to return to natural recalculation, use /Worksheet Global Recalculation Natural.

Circular References and How To Avoid Them

Forward references are not the only problem you can encounter in recalculation. You could define formulas which reference themselves. For example, if in Cell A1 you entered the formula +B1+2, and in Cell B1, you entered the formula +A1+2 you would have created two formulas which cannot be evaluated. Cell B1's formula must have been calculated before Cell A1's formula, and vice versa. This no-win situation is called a *circular reference.*

Like forward references, circular references can be hard to pinpoint. Your worksheet could contain many circular references. For example, consider the following case:

Cell A1 contains:	+B1+2
Cell B1 contains:	+C1+3
Cell C1 contains:	+A1+3

Here, you need to see all three equations to detect the circular reference. Having just one or two of them is not enough.

HOW TO: Troubleshoot Circular References

When 1-2-3 detects a circular reference, it displays a CIRC indicator in the bottom row. These are the three most common causes of circular references:

1. A formula cannot reference itself. If you enter in Cell A1 the formula +A1+2, you will have generated a circular reference.
2. Two formulas cannot reference each other. If your formula in Cell B1 references Cell A1, and your formula in Cell A1 references Cell B1, you will have generated a circular reference as well.
3. No formulas can form a chain. If the formula in Cell A1, references Cell B1, which in turn references Cell C1, which references Cell A1, you've created a chain of formulas, none of which can be evaluated correctly.

Once you have introduced a circular reference, you must look at all of the formulas and analyze them. One way is to display them (using /Range Format Text). The other way is to print them. You will learn about how to print formulas in the next chapter.

If you reenter a formula, eliminate the circular reference, and recalculate the worksheet, the CIRC indicator will disappear. Another way to eliminate the indicator—but not necessarily the problem—is to change to columnwise or rowwise recalculation. These recalculation methods will never produce a circular reference, since the order of recalculation is predetermined. You should check the values in the cells containing formulas, however, because they still may be inconsistent.

Using Iteration

Sometimes you can't get rid of the CIRC reference because the formulas really do depend on each other. You may never get the precise answer, but you can get a very close approximation to the answer.

As an example, suppose Acme Widget pays its salespeople a bonus of 10% of net profit. The bonus, as an expense item, must be known in order to calculate the profit. Unfortunately, the bonus cannot be calculated unless the profit is known beforehand. Here, there is no way around the circular reference. It's built into the worksheet.

By *iterating* (a fancy term for repeatedly recalculating the worksheet), you can get closer and closer to the answer. The more times you iterate, the closer to the answer you should get. For situations where you want to get as close as you can to the precise answer, you use /Worksheet Global Recalculation Iteration, specifying the number of times you want the worksheet to recalculate.

DISPLAYING THE WORKSHEET STATUS

You have seen the operation of global settings previously, in the discussion of numeric formats and label prefixes. Global settings are settings for the entire worksheet. For example, the type of recalculation (columnwise, rowwise, natural, or iterations) applies to the entire worksheet and is thus a global setting.

Another term you have seen previously is *default*. A default is a setting that 1-2-3 assumes unless you use a command to tell 1-2-3 to use a different setting. For example, the default recalculation type is natural.

The /Worksheet Status command lets you see the global worksheet settings in effect, and in addition displays the amount of memory available for expansion of the active worksheet. For an empty worksheet running 1-2-3 on an IBM PC with 512K of RAM, from the Lotus Access System, using PC-DOS Version 2.0, the /Worksheet Status settings are as follows:

RECALCULATION is AUTOMATIC (AUTO)—whenever a cell is changed, 1-2-3 automatically recalculates the worksheet. The recalculation order is NATURAL—1-2-3 recalculates formulas in their natural, hierarchical order. You can control these settings with /Worksheet Global Recalculation.

FORMAT is GENERAL—numbers entered into cells are displayed with General format, unless previously formatted with /Range Format. You can change this default global format with /Worksheet Global Format.

LABEL-PREFIX is LEFT—any labels which are subsequently to be entered will be left-aligned relative to the column width. You can change this default global label prefix with /Worksheet Global Label-prefix.

COLUMN WIDTH is 9—any column whose column width has not been set with /Worksheet Column-width Set will be given a column width of 9. You can change this default global column width with /Worksheet Global Column-width.

AVAILABLE MEMORY is 400700—the number of bytes available for the active worksheet. This number decreases as you expand the active worksheet. Since 1-2-3 needs memory to store the contents of cells within the active worksheet, you will see this number decrease as you enter data, even if you are not expanding the active worksheet. If your worksheet contains complex formulas, this number can decrease very fast.

You should check available memory frequently as you are entering information into the worksheet. 1-2-3 displays the `Memory full` error message when it has run out of memory. If this happens, consider the two methods discussed for decreasing the size of the active worksheet and thus increasing available memory. If these methods don't work, consider installing additional RAM in your PC.

PROTECTION is OFF—although all cells are initially protected, since global protection is off, you can enter information in any cell. If you turn global protection on, you can enter information only in unprotected cells (i.e., cells which you unprotected with **/Range Unprotect**). To control worksheet global protection use **/Worksheet Global Protection**.

You have now thoroughly explored the 1-2-3 worksheet. You should feel quite comfortable creating very sophisticated worksheet applications. In the next chapter, you will create fancy *printouts* to really make your worksheets come to life!

CHAPTER 16

All About Printing the Worksheet

FUNDAMENTALS

No-Frills Printing

It's easy to produce a simple report in 1-2-3. You have already done this if you did the exercises at the end of Chapter 10 to print the Acme Widget worksheet.

To start the process of printing a worksheet, you use /Print Printer. The main print menu displays, with the following options:

```
Range Line Page Options Clear Align Go Quit
```

This menu is an example of a sticky menu. The name comes from the fact that the menu sticks around until you Quit. (You can, of course, still use [ESC] to return to the previous menu, or [CTRL]-[BREAK] to go all the way back to READY mode.) To print a worksheet, you must select from several options, depending on how fancy you want the printout to be. Therefore, rather than forcing you to return to the main print menu after you have selected an option (which means you must type /Print Printer after selecting each option), 1-2-3 stays in the main print menu, ready for you to select another printing option.

To print the worksheet, simply define the range which you want to print, and then print it. The steps are as follows:

Step 1. Specify the print range. Specify a print range by selecting Range. Either type the cell addresses, or use a named range, a cell range you previously defined using /Range Name Create.

You may want to designate the entire active worksheet Use [END] and [HOME], as described in a HOW TO in Chapter 7.

If more columns are requested than fit on the printed page the additional columns are printed on subsequent pages. The rows which do not fit on the page are also printed on subsequent pages. 1-2-3 prints all the columns for one set of rows before printing the data for the next set.

Step 2. Print the worksheet. Use Go. Before issuing the command, make sure your printer is turned on. Then issue /Print Printer Go to start printing.

Step 3. Quit the main print menu. Use /Quit to quit the sticky menu and return to READY mode.

Stopping the Printout

What if, after printing three rows of a worksheet containing 1,000 rows of data, you suddenly remembered that a number was wrong and you wanted to stop the printout? Can you stop the printout? Sure! Press [CTRL]-[BREAK]. You may see the WAIT indicator flash for a while, but eventually the printout will stop and you will be returned to the main print menu.

To change a number, you must return to READY mode. You can do this either by (a) pressing Q to quit the print menu; (b) pressing [ESC] three times to go back to the menus you used before getting to the main print menu; or (c) pressing [CTRL]-[BREAK] once.

After you have changed the number, use /Print Printer Go. 1-2-3 remembers the print range, and the printout starts again from the beginning.

HOW TO: Print Whatever Is On The Screen

You can print the information which displays on the screen without using /Print. Simply press [SHIFT]-[PRTSC]. Remember to press both keys at the same time. Using this technique, you print out not only the worksheet, but also worksheet control information, such as the control panel, indicators, the column letters and row numbers, and any error messages. Using [SHIFT]-[PRTSC] is, in fact, the only way you can get the column letters and row numbers to print with the worksheet.

CONTROLLING THE PRINTER

Advancing One Line

To make the printer skip one line, use the Line option from the main print menu. Rather than wasting a row on the worksheet if you want to skip a line, say between the headings and the worksheet numbers themselves, you can use Line to skip a line.

Advancing to the Next Page

To advance the printer to the next page, use the Page option from the main print menu. The three most common situations in which to use Page are:

1. After printing a worksheet. 1-2-3 does not automatically skip to the next page after printing a worksheet. This lets you print more than one range on a page. If you have finished printing a worksheet and want the printer to be positioned correctly for other printouts, use Page.

2. To print more than one copy of a worksheet. Use Page to ready the printer for the next copy of the worksheet. If you are using page numbers in headers and footers, you might need to use Align as well to reset the page number. These topics are discussed later in this chapter.

3. To print the last footer of the last page. Use Page to position the printer to the top of the form after printing the last footer of the last page.

Changing the Margins

If you do not change them, 1-2-3 assumes the following values for your print margins:

- Left margin at 4.
- Right margin at 76.
- Top margin at 2 (the first two lines of the printed page are not used).
- Bottom margin at 2 (the last two lines of the printed page are used).

The top and bottom margins are for the entire printed page, from the header to the footer. 1-2-3 reserves 3 lines for the header and 3 for the footer. The printed worksheet thus starts 5 lines from the top of the page, and ends at 5 lines from the bottom of the page. These margins are geared to standard computer forms of 8 1/2" by 11".

You can change the margins from the main print menu, using Options Margins. For example, if your printer has a wider carriage than the Epson MX-80 printer, you can set the left and right margins accordingly. You can set the left or right margin to any value between 0 and 240. You can also set the top and bottom margins to any value between 0 and 10.

Changing the Page Length

In addition to resetting the margins, you can reset the page length. 1-2-3 assumes a page-length of 66 lines per page—again corresponding to the standard computer form. You may choose to print the worksheet on another form which has a different page length. From the main print menu, use Options Page-length. 1-2-3 accepts any number from 20 to 100 as a valid page-length. Additionally, if your printer supports compressed print, you can fit 88 lines on the standard page and you should change the page length accordingly.

Aligning the Printer to Agree with 1-2-3

Align causes you and 1-2-3 to agree that the paper is positioned at the top of the form.

You should use Align either (a) after you have interrupted printing the worksheet by pressing [CTRL]-[BREAK]; or (b) after you have reset the page-length to a different value (to use print forms with a different length, for example). After you have interrupted printing the worksheet, the printer may not stop immediately, because it is printing characters in its own memory, called the *print buffer*. To start afresh, you must clear the buffer and realign the paper. To accomplish this do the following:

1. Turn off the printer, thus erasing the buffer.

2. Turn the printer on again.
3. Position the paper at the top of the page.
4. Use **Align**.

In addition to aligning the printer, **Align** sets the page counter (which can be used to count page numbers in headers or footers) to 1.

HOW TO: Print Multiple Parts of the Worksheet

If you want to print different parts of the worksheet, the print ranges must be designated and printed one at a time. Use **/Print Printer Range** to specify each range, then **Go** to print the range, **Range** to specify the next range, **Go** to print it, and so on. To help make the meaning of the worksheet clear, use range names for each print range. Use **Align** as necessary to align the printer with the top of form. If you want to print three ranges (RANGE1, RANGE2, and RANGE3) and ensure that the page numbers are consecutively numbered, do the following:

/PPRRANGE1[ENTER]AGP	Print the first range
RRANGE2[ENTER]GP	Print the second range
RRANGE3[ENTER]GPQ	Print the third range and quit

Before the first range is printed, **Align** guarantees that 1-2-3 and the printer agree on top of page, the page counter is reset, and headers and footers print properly. If you are not sure of this, issue **Align** before printing. **Page** skips to the top of the next page before printing the next range. The last **Page** causes the footer to print on the last printed page.

BEWARE *A Print Line Wider than the Printer Destroys Alignment*

If your left and right margins are set so that the printer cannot print the data on one print line, the printer prints whatever doesn't fit on the next line, and continues until all the data is printed. For example, if your printer can only print 80 characters on a line, and your print line contains 200 characters, each row of data will occupy 3 print lines. For alignment and page-length purposes, this counts as only one line. Therefore, your page alignment will be destroyed.

FANCY PRINTING

So far, you have seen the basic steps for printing and controlling the printer. 1-2-3 lets you do some fancy printing as well! You can do the following:

Add headers and footers. A *header* is a line that prints at the top of each page of the report. A *footer* is a line that prints at the bottom of each page of the report. Typically, headers and footers contain identifying information such as the report title, date, and page number, which prints on each page of the report.

Specify border rows and/or columns. Borders are specific rows or columns which print on each page of the report. For example, if all the 13 columns of revenue for the Atlanta office cannot fit on a page, you would specify that the column containing the label Atlanta (typically Column A) is a border row. In this way, as all the revenue columns for Atlanta print on separate pages, they are labeled as Atlanta data. Border columns typically contain column headings, such as the column labels for each month. In this way, the column heading for each month (such as JAN) prints above the data for that month (the January revenue numbers).

Print cell formulas. For documentation purposes, or to check for circular references, 1-2-3 lets you print the cell formulas. Use Options Other Cell-formulas to enable this option. Then Quit the menu, and issue Go to get the formulas, as well as the values and labels in the worksheet, to print. While this doesn't qualify as fancy printing, it is certainly a useful feature!

Print the worksheet without headers, footers, or borders. Perhaps, after defining all the fancy additions, you decide that you would like to see just the worksheet data, the labels, values, and calculated formulas, without these additions. You'd like to check the numbers before printing them. You can do that by specifying that the printout be *unformatted* (two-cents plain). Specify Options Other Unformatted from the main print menu.

Use setup codes to get the most from your printer. 1-2-3 lets you send *setup codes* to the printer. Your printer probably has more features than you are aware of. For example, the Epson MX-80 printer used on many IBM PCs supports italics, boldface, compressed print (printing with smaller letters so you can fit more text on one line), expanded print (printing with larger letters for emphasis), and a host of others. Your printer might be even fancier! If you have a color printer attached to the PC, for example, you can produce a multicolor printout. The HOW TO in this chapter describes how to make the standard Epson MX-80 printer produce italics, boldface, compressed print, and any type of spacing (half, double, triple, etc.) you want.

Adding Headers and Footers

You can specify up to 240 characters of text as a header, and you can align the headers to the left, the center or the right. You use the vertical bar (|), the shifted key to the left of the Z, to separate left, centered, and right justified text in headers and footers. To define headers, use Options Header.

To create the following header:

```
Page 1                    Sales Summary                    Date
```

where the page number increments by 1 every time the worksheet prints on another page, and the date is the PC-DOS system date, enter the following (from READY mode):

Keystrokes	Result
/PPOH	Use /Print Printer Options Header
Page #	Page number is left-aligned
|Sales Summary	Sales Summary is centered
|@[ENTER]QQ	Date is right aligned; back to READY

Note the following special characters used in header text:

Automatically prints the page number and increments as each page is printed.

| Lets you separate left, center, and right justified text. You start at the left, use | to start centering, and use | again to start right justification.

@ Gives you the PC-DOS date (where March 23, 1974 prints as 03- Mar-74).

Note, in addition, the following:

1. 1-2-3 always skips two lines between the header and the first line of the print text. Where the header *itself* starts printing depends on the setting for the top margin.

2. If you use the # special character for page numbers and want to print the report again, you should use Align. If you don't do this, the page counter starts from its previous setting, rather than from Page 1.

You can also create a footer line using Options Footer. Like the header, you can separate the footer into three parts—left, center, and right-aligned. To create the following footer:

```
Page 1                         Footer Line                          Date
```

enter the following (from READY mode):

Keystrokes	Result
/PPOF	Use /Print Printer Options Footer
Page #	Page number is left-aligned
|Footer Line	Footer Line is centered
|@[ENTER]QQ	Date is right aligned; back to READY mode

1-2-3 prints the footer line two lines below the last line of the print text. Where the footer *itself* prints depends on the setting for the bottom margin.

Adding Border Columns or Rows

Frequently, you will have reports that span more than one page. You may want to print the column headings such as the title and the month labels at the top of each page, and the row identifiers, such as the label for each field office, along the side for all the pages. Use Options Borders from the main print menu to specify border columns and/or rows. Use Options Borders Columns to specify which columns are to repeat on each page. Use Options Borders Rows to specify which rows are to repeat on each page. There are two BEWAREs to bear in mind when using borders.

BEWARE ***Don't Put Borders in the Print Range***

If you put the border columns or rows in the print range, they are printed *twice*: once, as part of the borders; the other, as part of the print range. You probably don't want the column headings for the months to print out twice.

BEWARE ***If You Invoke the Borders Option By Mistake, You Define Blank Borders***

If you use Options Borders, and press [ENTER], you will have created a border column or row, even if previously there were no borders. If you want to remove the borders, press [ESC], which performs its usual function of telling 1-2-3 to forget about specifying that option.

Printing Cell Formulas

For documentation purposes, you may wish to print each cell formula. In this way, you know exactly what formulas were used and what information was entered directly. From the main print menu, use Options Other Cell formulas. To return to printing the calculated results of formulas instead of the formulas themselves, use Options Other As-displayed.

When cell formulas are printed, each non-empty cell prints on a separate line. The cell address is followed by a colon. On the same line, the entire label or value will print, along with the range format and protection status of the cell. The actual cell formula prints, rather than its current value. As-displayed returns to printing values in formula cells, rather than the formulas themselves.

Formatted and Unformatted Printouts

Formatted print includes headers, footers, and page breaks. You may want to see just the worksheet values themselves, without formatting. In this case, you would want *unformatted* print. Unformatted print will cause a line to print for each worksheet row in the print range. Use Options Other Unformatted to specify unformatted print; to return to formatting, use Options Other Formatted. Using unformatted printing for sharing data with other programs is discussed in Chapter 18.

BEWARE ***Unformatted Print Does Not Suppress the Margin Settings***

Margin settings are still in effect when you specify unformatted print. If you do not modify the default left margin setting of 4, for example, the first column is indented 4 spaces. If the row is too large to fit on the print line, the data will overflow onto the next line.

Using Setup Codes

You can pass special setup codes to your printer. The actual setup code values, and their function, depend on the characteristics of your printer. With setup codes, you can really make your printer do tricks! To define a setup code to your printer, use Options Setup from the main print menu.

A setup code is a backslash (\) followed by a 3-digit number, which represents a particular printer function. The number is the decimal form of the printer code. For example, for the Epson MX-80 printer, the setup code for compressed print (print smaller than regular size so that more information can fit on one line) is \015. Look up the setup codes in your printer manual. Compressed print may not be implemented on your printer, or it may be represented by some other code.

Here are some other setup codes for the Epson MX-80. (Note that some functions require more than one setup code. You can specify more than one code by starting the next code with a \.

\007	Sound the print buzzer
\018	Turn off compressed mode
\027\048	Print at 8 lines per inch (rather than 6)
\027\050	Print at 6 lines per inch
\027\052	Print worksheet in italics
\027\053	Turn off printing in italics
\027\069	Print in emphasized mode (for better print quality)
\027\070	Turn off emphasized mode
\027\071	Turn on double strike mode
\027\072	Turn off double strike mode

Since setup codes apply to the entire print operation (you can't, in one print operation, print the headers wide and in italics with the worksheet data in compressed print), you should experiment until you get the printed output you want.

You can even combine setup codes! For example, to sound the print buzzer and print the worksheet in compressed print style, at 8 lines to the inch, enter the following setup code sequence:

```
\007\015\027\048
```

HOW TO: Set Your Own Line Spacing with the Epson MX-80 Printer

Did you ever want to print your worksheet with double or triple spacing? If you have the Epson MX-80 printer, you can set the spacing to whatever you like! Here's how.

The standard line spacing is 1/6". However, a special setup code sequence \027\051 lets you set line spacing to N/216", where N is a number you supply. The standard line spacing is 36/216" (or 1/6"). So to get double spacing, set the spacing to 72/216" (or 1/3"). To get triple spacing, set the spacing to

108/216", (or 1/2"), and so on. Three setup codes are required. The first two codes are \027\051. The following setup codes change line spacing:

\027\051\036	Sets printer to single spacing
\027\051\072	Sets printer to double spacing
\027\051\108	Sets printer to triple spacing
\027\051\054	Sets printer to 1 1/2 spaces

You should remember that when you use setup codes, the 1-2-3 commands which control the printer, such as Page or Line, will work according to your setup code settings. You may have to use a setup code to cancel the effect of another setup code. The page length and margins may be affected by the setup code, for example.

If you want to return to single spacing after you have set double spacing, use the single spacing setup codes, align the paper to the top of form, and use Align. Experiment with setup codes until they work as you want them to.

THE GLOBAL DEFAULT PRINTER SETTINGS

Displaying and Changing the Settings

You have seen how 1-2-3 uses global settings (for example, in defining cell formats) to provide default values, which 1-2-3 uses if you don't change them. 1-2-3 uses global settings for printouts as well.

To see the current global settings, use /Worksheet Global Default Status. To change the settings, use /Worksheet Global Default Printer. The initial global default printer settings are as follows:

```
Interface: Parallel
Auto Line-Feed: No
Left Margin: 76
Right margin: 4
Top margin: 2
Bottom margin: 2
Page length: 66
Pause at end of page: No
Setup string: none
```

The global printer defaults are:

1. INTERFACE. You can attach a printer to the parallel port, a serial port, or a second parallel or serial port. 1-2-3 initially assumes that you are attaching your printer to the parallel port which is provided as standard equipment on the PC. If you are attaching your printer to a different port, you must change this default setting and use /Worksheet Global Default Update to change the interface.

2. AUTO-LF. Some printers automatically add a line feed (the equivalent of skipping to the next line) after a carriage return; most do not. 1-2-3's initial global default is not to add a line feed after a carriage return. If your printer does add a line feed after a carriage return, your printouts will be double-spaced. You must change Auto-LF to Yes from its initial default of No, and then use /Worksheet Global Default Update to get the printer to space correctly.

3. LEFT MARGIN. The initial global default left margin is 4, to indent 4 spaces before printing.

4. RIGHT MARGIN. The initial global default right margin is 76, to go to the next line after printing to column 76 of the print line.

5. TOP MARGIN. The initial global default top margin is 2, to skip two lines from the top of the page before printing.

6. BOTTOM MARGIN. The initial global default bottom margin is 2, to print the last worksheet row on the page two lines before the bottom.

7. PAGE-LENGTH. The initial global default page-length is 66 lines per page.

8. WAIT. 1-2-3 assumes initially that you do not want the printer to pause after printing a page. Rather, you want the printing to continue to the next page. You might be printing your worksheet on a letter-quality printer where you must insert each page individually. In this case, you must change Wait to Yes from its initial setting of No, and then use /Worksheet Global Default Update.

9. SETUP. 1-2-3 does not assume any printer setup string. To use a print option which is special to your printer, you can supply a setup string which will be used before printing, and then use /Worksheet Global Default Update to save it.

Saving the Printer Settings

After you have changed the global default printer settings with /Worksheet Global Default Printer, use /Worksheet Global Default Update to save them permanently. 1-2-3 stores the global default settings in a file called 123.CNF. When you start 1-2-3, 1-2-3 uses the settings stored in 123.CNF for global settings. This is only required if you want to save the changed settings permanently. If you want to change the global settings for this session only, you need not update the 123.CNF file.

CLEARING PRINT OPTIONS

You may wish to clear some or all of the printer options you have specified. If you wish to clear print options, select Clear from the main print menu. You can clear the following:

All	Clears print range, border columns and rows, and sets margins, page-length, and setup string to worksheet global default settings.
Range	Clears the print range, leaving other settings intact.

Borders	Clears border columns and rows, leaving other settings intact.
Format	Resets margins, page-length, and setup string to worksheet global default settings.

You have a great deal of flexibility to clear all or some of the print settings. Clear is useful when you want to generate differently formatted reports from the same worksheet.

HOW TO: Save the Print Options

Simple! Just use /File Save. 1-2-3 remembers all print settings when you save the file. Here's another instance where 1-2-3 makes it easy for you. If you want to rerun the report, just retrieve the file, and use /Print Printer Go. The report will print with the same print options which were in effect when you saved the file.

CREATING A PRINT FILE

You might want to incorporate the worksheet into a word processing document such as a memo to field office managers. You can create a print file on disk, which can be accessed by virtually any word processing document, and which contains the information that would otherwise be printed.

To create a print file, use /Print File, rather than /Print Printer. You specify the filename; 1-2-3 adds the .PRN extension. If a print file with the name you specify already exists, 1-2-3 asks you whether you want to replace the file with the new file. If you replace the file, the old file's contents are lost. You can keep the old print file by simply specifying a name that does not exist.

You can display the names of all print files in your current directory with /File List Printer. You can also erase a print file, or several of them, by using the wild-card feature with /File Erase Printer. Chapter 18 discusses using print files to share data with other programs, in more detail.

Exercises

Practice the fancy print options with the Acme Widget worksheet. Try adding border rows and columns, setting the margins, adding headers and footers, and the setup codes for your printer. You'll be quite surprised at how much you can do!

You now know the basics: how to use the worksheet. Everything else in 1-2-3 is built on the worksheet. Since you know your way around it, you're already halfway towards being able to use the advanced worksheet commands, and to create graphs, databases, and macros. Read on!

PART IV

Making Your Worksheet Hum

You now know the basics. You can use 1-2-3 productively. You can enter labels, values, and formulas. You can copy and move data in cell ranges. You can manage your worksheet files on disk, and you can produce printouts ranging from the simple, just printing the contents of a cell range, to the complex, such as adding headers and footers, printing with border rows and columns, using setup codes, and controlling page-length, margins, and alignment. You understand how to control the worksheet display by using cell formats, changing column-widths, and protecting and unprotecting cell ranges. Finally, you can control how and when 1-2-3 recalculates the worksheet. Along the way, you have picked up valuable HOW TO tips and understand potential dangers which you should BEWARE of.

That's quite a bit. In these two chapters, you will go even further—probably further than you thought you could go! You will learn how to enter complex formulas and functions in your worksheet. You will discover how to use dates in calculations. In Chapter 18, you will learn how to share 1-2-3 files with other IBM PC applications, such as word processing and database programs, and how to share 1-2-3 files with mainframe databases and systems written in programming languages such as COBOL or FORTRAN. you will learn how to build "what-if" tables, to evaluate many possibilities at once by using /Data Table; how to calculate statistical distributions by using /Data Distribution; and how to write a simple memorandum by using /Range Justify. After you have completed this part of the book, you should feel comfortable implementing virtually any spreadsheet application required in your business.

CHAPTER 17

Advanced Formulas and Functions

WRITING COMPLICATED FORMULAS

Using 1-2-3 As A Calculator

Although you are probably going to use 1-2-3 for more sophisticated applications than your calculator, it's nice to know that you can use 1-2-3 as a powerful calculator. The following table shows the types of calculations you can perform in 1-2-3.

Calculation	Symbol	Example
Exponentiation	^	2^3 (2*2*2, or 8)
Negative number	-	-3 (negative 3)
Positive number	+	+3 (positive 3)
Multiplication	*	2*3 (6)
Division	/	2/3 (.667)
Addition	+	2+3 (5)
Subtraction	-	2-3 (negative 1)

These calculations are performed in the following order:

1. Exponentiation.
2. Making a number negative or positive.
3. Multiplication and division.
4. Addition and subtraction.

A complex calculation is sometimes called an *expression*. For example, the expression *2^3−3*2-3* is evaluated as follows:

1. The exponentiation (2^3) is calculated, giving the following result:

   *8−3*2-3*

2. The numbers are made negative or positive. The (−3) is resolved into a +3, giving the following result:

   *8+3*2-3*

3. The multiplication (3*2) is calculated, giving the following result:

   8+6-3

4. The addition and subtraction is done, giving the final answer of *11*.

You can use parentheses to change the order of operations. Parentheses separate the expression into groups. Before the entire expression is evaluated, the expression in each group is evaluated. For example:

`3+2*5`	evaluates as 3+10 or 13 (multiplication done first)
`(3+2)*5`	evaluates to 5*5 or 25 (addition done first)

You can use *logical expressions* to evaluate whether a condition is true or false. If a condition is true, the expression is evaluated to 1; if it is false, the expression is evaluated to 0. For example, if you want to know whether the value, such as the quantity, in Cell B1 is greater than 100, you could code the following in Cell C1:

```
+B1>100
```

If the value in Cell B1 is greater than 100, Cell C1 will contain a 1; otherwise, Cell C1 will contain a 0.

You can use the following symbols in logical expressions:

=	equal to
<	less than
>	greater than
<=	less than or equal to
>=	greater than or equal to
<>	not equal to

HOW TO: Use Range Names with Expressions

You can use range names to make the meaning of expressions clearer. For example, if you created a range name called QUANTITY, at Cell B1, by typing the following:

```
/RNCQUANTITY[ENTER]B1[ENTER]
```

The formula in Cell C1 would display `+QUANTITY>100`. In formulas, the upper-left corner of the cell range is used—even if QUANTITY were B1..E2, the value in Cell B1 would be used in the formula. Expressing the formula this way shows exactly what you are testing and makes the meaning of the worksheet clearer.

Complex Logical Expressions

1-2-3 lets you get even fancier. Suppose you want to find out if QUANTITY is between 101 and 200. You could code the following in Cell C1.

```
+QUANTITY>100#AND#QUANTITY<=200
```

The #AND# means *both conditions must be true.* QUANTITY must be both greater than 100 and less than or equal to 200 for the expression to be true (and

Cell C1 to contain a value of 1). If either of these conditions is false, (QUANTITY less than or equal to 100, or QUANTITY greater than 200), Cell C1 will contain a value of 0 (for false).

In addition to #AND#, you can use #OR# which means *either condition must be true*. You can also use #NOT# which means *the condition must be false*. Here are some other examples: **#NOT#(+QUANTITY>100)** Quantity must NOT be greater than 100

+QUANTITY=200#OR#QUANTITY=0 Quantity must be 200 OR 0

FUNCTIONS AND ARGUMENTS

A *function* is simply a short-cut formula. 1-2-3 has many of the commonly used formulas already done for you. You have already used the **@SUM** function several times in previous chapters. Rather than having to reinvent the wheel, you can use these functions to speed up development of your worksheet.

1-2-3 functions have the following rules:

Functions are used like formulas. Anything that applies to formulas applies equally to functions. You can use /Copy or /Move to copy and move cells containing functions to other functions. 1-2-3's natural recalculation order automatically takes into account cells containing functions, and so on.

Functions all start with @, followed by the function name. In addition, the names of the 1-2-3 functions are meaningful and easy to remember. As examples, the function to compute the sum of values in a cell range is called **@SUM**, while the function to calculate internal rate of return of a series of cash flows is @IRR.

Most functions require arguments, which are used in calculating the function's value. Arguments give 1-2-3 the information it needs to evaluate the function. The number and meaning of the arguments vary with the function. For certain functions, arguments refer to cell ranges. For example, before **@SUM** can be calculated, you must tell **@SUM** what cell range is to be summed. In fact, **@SUM** can sum any number of cell ranges.

For other functions, arguments refer to a value. For example, the **@PMT** function, which calculates a loan payment, requires the principal, interest rate, and term as values. When a function requires a value, you can either specify the value directly, or specify the cell which contains the value.

There are even functions which take no arguments. If the meaning of the function is self-evident, no arguments are required. For example, the function @PI is a shorthand way of using the number pi in a formula. Since @PI does not need a cell range or a value, (it, in fact, is shorthand for a value), no arguments are required.

If a function takes arguments, they are enclosed in parentheses. If more than one argument is required, they are separated by commas. For some functions, the order of the arguments is important. For example, **@PMT** requires the following arguments:

```
@PMT(principal,interest-rate,term)
```

You must specify the principal first, the interest rate second, and the term of the loan last to get @PMT to calculate the loan payment properly.

Most functions require that the arguments be in a specific order. There are certain exceptions. For example, @SUM takes any number of arguments. The order of the arguments is not important. For example:

```
@SUM(A1..D1,D5..F8,C9)
```

produces the same result as:

```
@SUM(C9,D5..F8,A1..D1)
```

This chapter explores all of the 1-2-3 functions, with the exception of the database statistical functions. (These, which are used with 1-2-3 databases, are discussed with 1-2-3 databases.) I will describe the arguments (if any) to each function, and show you some nifty HOW TOs. There are also some occasional BEWAREs.

LOGICAL FUNCTIONS

@IF and Logical Expressions

Logical functions let you perform *if tests.* @IF is the most commonly used logical function. @IF requires the following arguments:

```
@IF(logical-expression,value-if-true,value-if-false)
```

All arguments must evaluate to a value. The logical-expression can be simple or complicated. A common use of @IF is in calculating quantity discounts. For example, suppose you give a 10% discount for quantities greater than 100. You could code an @IF function to calculate the discount as follows:

```
@IF(+QUANTITY>100,+PRICE*10%,0)
```

In other words, if the quantity is greater than 100 (the logical-expression), the discount is +PRICE*10%. If the quantity is 100 or less (i.e., the logical expression is false), the discount is 0."

HOW TO: Code a Table in an @IF Function

Suppose your discount schedule was a bit more complex, as follows:

10% for quantities between 101 and 200.
20% for quantities over 200.

You could use one @IF function to code this discount schedule as well.

How? By using another @IF as an argument of the @IF! Remember that a function evaluates to a value. Therefore, a function rather than a value or a formula can be used within @IF. The following @IF function would fill the bill:

```
@IF((+QUANTITY>100#AND#QUANTITY<=200),+PRICE*10%,@IF
(+QUANTITY>200),+PRICE*20%,0)
```

This one may look complex but it's really simple. The first logical expression +QUANTITY>100#AND#QUANTITY<=200 checks if the quantity is between 101 and 200. If it is, the discount is the value-if-true (PRICE*10%). If it isn't, use another @IF function to test whether the QUANTITY is greater than 200. If it is, the discount is PRICE*20%. If the quantity passes *neither* of the @IF tests, it must be less than 101, and thus, no discount applies.

You could extend this concept to incorporate a larger discount table in the @IF function. With large tables (greater than 4 or 5 entries), the function would become quite cumbersome. Although the principle would hold, there are easier ways to code table lookups. The special table handling functions @CHOOSE, @VLOOKUP, and @HLOOKUP, are more convenient than @IF. These will be discussed later in this chapter.

BEWARE ***You Cannot Use Labels as Arguments to @IF***

This means that you *cannot* code an expression such as:

```
@IF(+PRICE>40,"BUY","SELL")
```

in a stock portfolio analysis worksheet to enter a label to indicate whether to buy or sell a stock based on its price. This inability to use labels in @IF may be the most serious limitation of 1-2-3.

HOW TO: Use @TRUE and @FALSE with @IF

Although you cannot use @IF to enter a label, you can use the special functions @TRUE and @FALSE to indicate whether the expression was true or false.

@TRUE is a function which takes no arguments and which returns the value 1, the value 1-2-3 takes if an expression is true. @FALSE returns the value 0, the value 1-2-3 takes if an expression is false. You could re-code the stock portfolio expression as follows:

```
@IF(+PRICE>40,@TRUE,@FALSE)
```

If this @IF function were in a column with the heading of BUY?, you would see a 1, to indicate a buy, for all stocks with a price greater than 40, and a 0, to indicate a sell, for all stocks with a price less than or equal to 40.

You might try substituting an @IF for the @FALSE to identify a HOLD situation. In that case, since you cannot enter the label "HOLD", you could invent a code (say, 2) to indicate a hold when the price stays at 40. The expression might be coded as follows:

```
@IF(+PRICE>40,@TRUE,@IF(+PRICE<40,@FALSE,2))
```

Using @ERR, @NA, @ISERR, and @ISNA

You have seen, in the discussion of absolute references and copying formulas, that when 1-2-3 cannot calculate a formula, it displays ERR. ERR is actually the result of the @ERR function. @ERR takes no arguments.

You can use @ERR in formulas. Let's suppose that you don't want the ERR indicator to display if a formula which causes a division by zero occurs. Rather, you would like the worksheet to display a zero.

If Cell A1 contains a 1, and Cell A2 contains a 0, entering the following in Cell A3:

```
+A1/A2
```

will cause ERR to display in Cell A3. However, if you code the following @IF function in Cell A3:

```
@IF(A1/A2=@ERR,0,A1/A2)
```

Cell A3 displays A1/A2 only if the division does not produce an error.

You might consider another special function @NA in this case. @NA, another function which takes no arguments, stands for *not available*. Your worksheet might not include all input numbers from which you can calculate the formulas. If you enter @NA for all cells where you don't have the number, the following happens:

1. The cell displays NA for not available.
2. All formulas or functions which reference the cell also display NA. This is what you want. It means that you don't have enough information to calculate the formula, or the formula is meaningless given these numbers.

If you recoded the formula in Cell A3 as follows:

```
@IF(A1/A2=@ERR,@NA,A1/A2)
```

then division by 0 would produce NA rather than 0. This would separate the case where Cell A1 is 0 and the division is meaningful, from the case where Cell A2 is 0 and the division is meaningless.

Finally, you can use @ISERR and @ISNA to test whether a particular cell is displaying ERR or NA. For example, if you code the formula in Cell A3 as follows:

```
@IF(@ISERR(A2),@NA,A1/A2)
```

it means if Cell A2 has the value ERR (perhaps it also contains a formula which could not be evaluated correctly), display NA in this cell; if Cell A2 has a valid value, do the division.

MATHEMATICAL FUNCTIONS

In addition to using 1-2-3 as a calculator, you can use 1-2-3 to do most of your children's math homework! Many arithmetic and trigonometric functions are included. The following table shows the format of these functions:

Function	Format
Absolute value of a number	@ABS(value)
Arccosine of a number (radians)	@ACOS(value)
Arcsine of a number (radians)	@ASIN(value)
Arctangent of a number (radians)	@ATAN(value)
4-quadrant arctangent	@ATAN2(value1,value2)
Cosine of an angle	@COS(angle-in-radians)
Exponential function	@EXP(value)
Integer part of a number	@INT(value)
Natural logarithm	@LN(value)
Common logarithm	@LOG(value)
Remainder modulo function	@MOD(value1,value2)
The value PI	@PI
Random number between 0 and 1	@RAND
Rounded number	@ROUND(value,digits-to-round)
Sine of an angle	@SIN(angle-in-radians)
Square root of a number	@SQRT(value)
Tangent of an angle	@TAN(angle-in-radians)

Unless you are using highly complex mathematics in your worksheet, you will not use most of these formulas in common business applications.

The functions you may use are:

@INT. If you would like to store a number without its decimal value, storing whole dollars and forgetting about cents, you can use @INT.

@ROUND. If you would like to store a number rounded to a specific number of decimal places, use @ROUND. For example, @ROUND(123.4567,2) stores the value 123.46. You can also round a number to hundreds or thousands by using a negative number as the second argument. For example, @ROUND (123.4567,-2) stores the value 100. Unlike /Range Format Fixed, which displays the number rounded but stores the number to its full precision, @ROUND stores the number rounded.

@MOD. To test periodic occurrences, you could use @MOD. You will see @MOD in action, checking for leap years, later in this chapter.

STATISTICAL FUNCTIONS

The statistical functions let you analyze lists of numbers to get a pattern. Suppose, as Acme Widget's sales manager, you were given the sales results for five salespeople in the worksheet as follows:

```
A1:                                                          READY
_

      A              B          C          D          E          F          G
 1                                   ACME WIDGET SALES RESULTS
 2
 3  SALESPERSON      SALES
 4  Jones         $100,000
 5  Brown         $150,000
 6  Smith         $125,000
 7  Adams         $235,000
 8  Franklin      $137,500
 9
10
11
12
13
14
15
16
17
18
```

Figure 17.1 Acme Widget Sales Results

You would like to analyze these numbers to see:

- the number of salespeople
- the highest and lowest sales
- the average amount of sales
- the star salespeople, and those who need more help

You could enter the functions and display the worksheet shown below:
This worksheet in Figure 17.2 answers the questions above!

@COUNT was used to count the number of salespeople. @COUNT counts the number of values or labels in a range. There are 5 values in the SALES range C4..C8.

@MAX (for maximum) found the highest sales ($235,000) in the range. @MIN (for minimum) found the lowest sales ($100,000).

@AVG (for average) found the average sales ($149,500).

```
A1:                                                          READY
_

        A         B         C         D         E         F         G
 1                              ACME WIDGET SALES RESULTS
 2
 3   SALESPERSON              SALES
 4   Jones                 $100,000
 5   Brown                 $150,000
 6   Smith                 $125,000
 7   Adams                 $235,000
 8   Franklin              $137,500
 9
10
11
12   @COUNT(SALES)                5
13   @MAX(SALES)           $235,000
14   @AVG(SALES)           $149,500
15   @MIN(SALES)           $100,000
16   @STD(SALES)            $45,857
17   @VAR(SALES)           2.10E+09
18
19
```

Figure 17.2 Analysis of Sales Results

@STD (for standard deviation) and @VAR (for variance) measure the statistical distribution of the salespeople's performance. If you had a large number of salespeople, you could measure from the standard deviation whether these particular salespeople were producing comparable results with all the company's salespeople. If everything else is equal, a typical salesperson should have sales within one standard deviation of the average. Since the average is $149,500, and the standard deviation is $45,837, salespeople whose sales were under $104,663 ($149,500 - $45,847) are problems; sales over $195,337, however, are extraordinary. The variance, @VAR, is the square of the standard deviation. Probably, you would not use @VAR too often.

BEWARE *Rules to Remember When Using Statistical Functions*

Bear in mind the following rules when using these functions. If you forget them, you can easily produce invalid results.

If a cell contains a label, it is given a value of 0. However, if a cell is erased, it is ignored. Here's where the difference between a cell containing a label-prefix with spaces (which is a label), and an erased cell (which never contained any label or was erased with /Range Erase) comes into play.

For example, if you use **@MIN** to calculate the minimum value in a cell-range, **@MIN** returns 0 if there is any label at all in the cell range. However, if the cell is erased (i.e., there is no label in it), **@MIN** ignores the cell.

As another example, **@AVG** includes a cell with a label; it gives the cell a value of zero and counts it in the average. **@AVG** does not include erased cells.

@COUNT always returns 1 for one-cell ranges. @COUNT(A1) always returns the value 1. It doesn't matter whether Cell A1 is erased, has a label, or has a value. This is inconsistent, because @COUNT(A1..A2) returns 0 if both Cell A1 and Cell A2 are erased.

FINANCIAL FUNCTIONS

1-2-3's financial functions are designed for helping to make investment decisions. The following financial functions are provided by 1-2-3:

@NPV	Calculate Net Present Value of cash flows
@IRR	Calculate Internal Rate of Return of cash flows
@FV	Calculate Future Value of an annuity stream
@PV	Calculate Present Value of cash flows
@PMT	Calculate Loan Payment

Net Present Value and Internal Rate of Return

The **@NPV** function, to calculate net present value, has the following format:

```
@NPV(interest-rate,cash-flow-range)
```

@NPV is used for making investment decisions.

@NPV and **@IRR** are used to analyze investment alternatives. Typically, you make an investment and then expect a return on your investment. Should you make the investment?

Whether or not you make the investment depends on future interest rates, which are of course unpredictable. With **@NPV**, you input an interest rate and a range of *cash flows*, your initial investment, entered as a negative number, and expected payback amounts, entered as positive numbers. **@NPV** tells you how much money, invested (say, in a bank), this cash flow is equivalent to, at the interest rate you specify.

The **@IRR** function, to calculate internal rate of return, answers the investment question in a slightly different way. With **@IRR**, you supply the cash flow and a guess of the interest rate, and **@IRR** tells you what interest rate you would need to find to get the same return on your investment. The format of **@IRR** is as follows:

```
@IRR(interest-rate-guess,cash-flow-range)
```

Figure 17.3 illustrates the use of **@NPV** and **@IRR** to analyze an investment of $100,000 today, with expected returns of $45,000, $55,000, $65,000, $70,000, and $75,000 over the next five years.

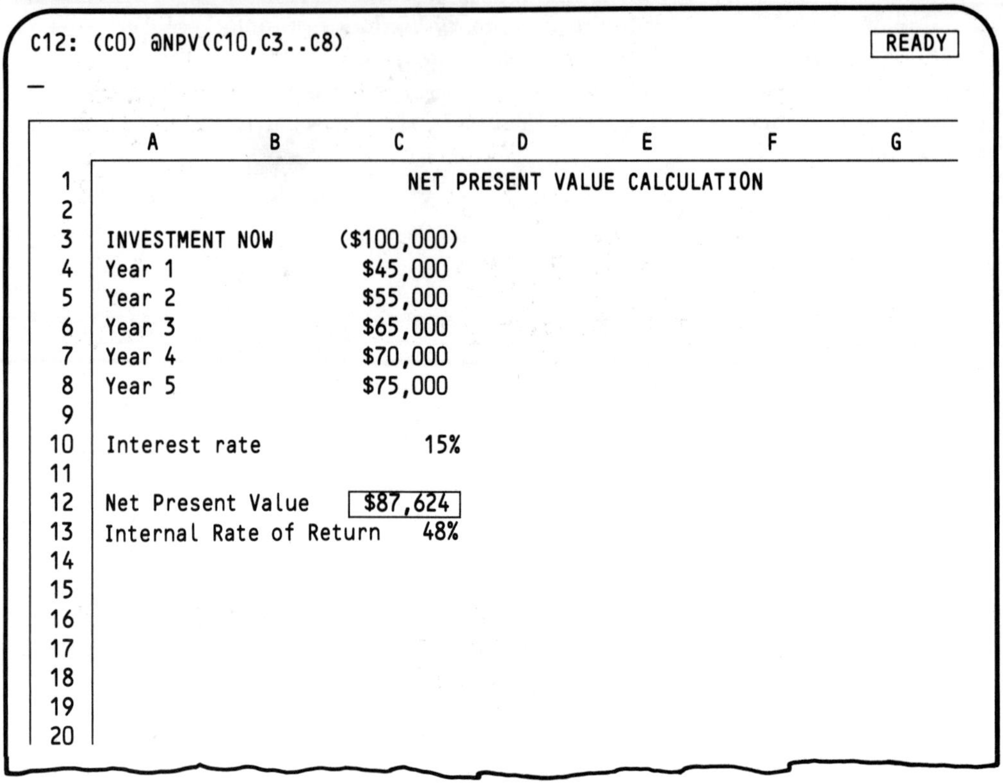

Figure 17.3 @NPV Calculation

At 15% interest, this investment is the equivalent of depositing $87,624 in the bank. With a 48% internal rate of return, it certainly seems attractive! You could use the same worksheet to evaluate other investments. All other things being equal, choose the one with the best internal rate of return.

Future Value, Present Value, and Loan Payment Functions

Future value (**@FV**), present value (**@PV**), and loan payment (**@PMT**) functions are also used for investment decisions. The formats are as follows:

```
@FV(payment,interest-rate,term)
@PV(payment,interest-rate
@PMT(payment,interest-rate,term)
```

These three functions have identical arguments!

Suppose you are investing $2,000 in an Individual Retirement Account, at a rate of 10% per year. How much money will you have in 30 years? You can use @FV to find out. Figure 17.4 tells you the answer:

```
D9: (C0) @FV(D3,D4,D5)                                          READY
_

        A         B         C         D         E         F         G
 1                                   FUTURE VALUE CALCULATION
 2
 3   YEARLY PAYMENT TO IRA              $2,000
 4   INTEREST RATE                         10%
 5   NUMBER OF YEARS                        30
 6
 7
 8
 9   AMOUNT ACCUMULATED               $328,988
10
11
12
13
14
15
16
17
18
19
20
```

Figure 17.4 @FV Calculation

You would have $328,988 at the end of 30 years. You might try 1-2-3's "what-if" capability to see how much you would have if you could get 11% or 12% on your investment. You may be surprised at how much more money you would have.

The present value (@PV) function is used to calculate annuity premiums. In an annuity, you give a financial institution a certain amount of money, in return for income over a period of time. Suppose you wanted to get a check for $2,000 every year for 30 years, and you assumed that interest rates over this time would average 10%. How much should you spend for this annuity? Figure 17.5 gives you the answer: using @PV, 1-2-3 calculated that you should spend $18,854.

The loan payment (@PMT) function is used to calculate payments for a loan or mortgage. If you wanted to borrow $10,000 at an annual interest rate of 15% for 1 year, what would your monthly payment be? Figure 17.6 gives you the answer: Using @PMT, 1-2-3 calculated a monthly payment of $902.58. Note: since you assumed a yearly interest rate, you had to divide the rate by 12 to

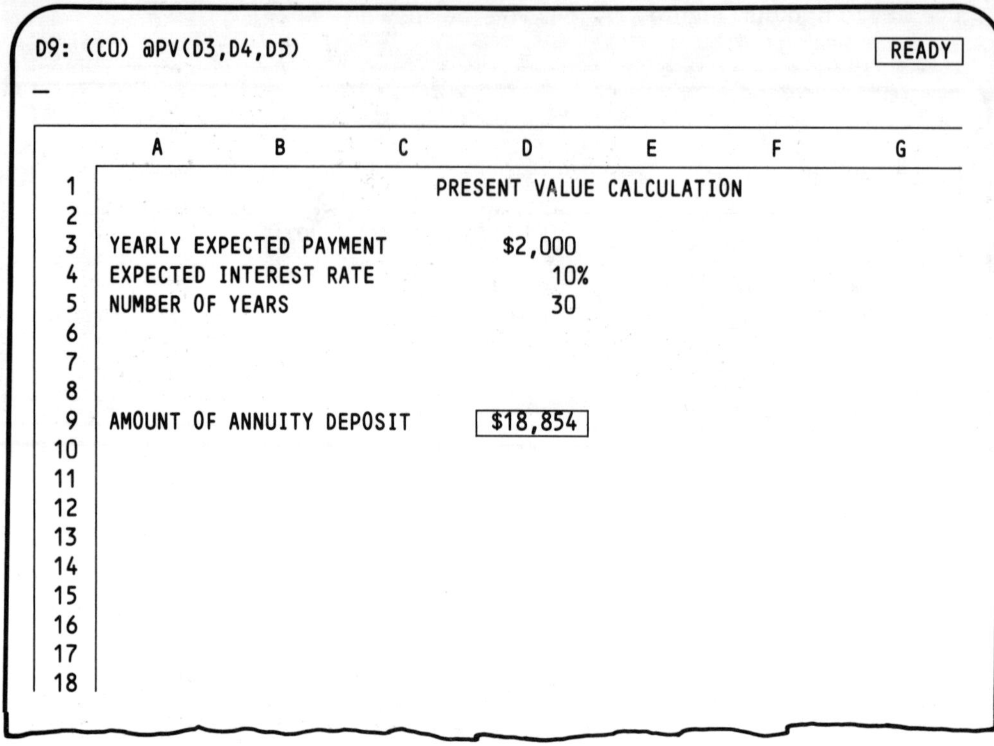

Figure 17.5 @PV Calculation

get a monthly rate. Since you supplied a number in years, you had to multiply it by 12 to get the number of monthly payments.

Although these functions are adequate for standard investment analysis, you may find that you need more sophisticated calculations. For example, if you are a bank manager offering variable rate mortgages with balloon payments, with interest credited in the middle of a period, you may have trouble calculating a true payment using 1-2-3's financial functions.

DATE FUNCTIONS AND FORMATS

Entering and Displaying Dates

1-2-3 stores dates as numbers—the number of days between December 31, 1899 and the specified date. This is very useful, because *the dates can be used in calculations.* You can age your receivables, calculate when to pay bills, find out how many days are left to the end of the year, calculate your life insurance

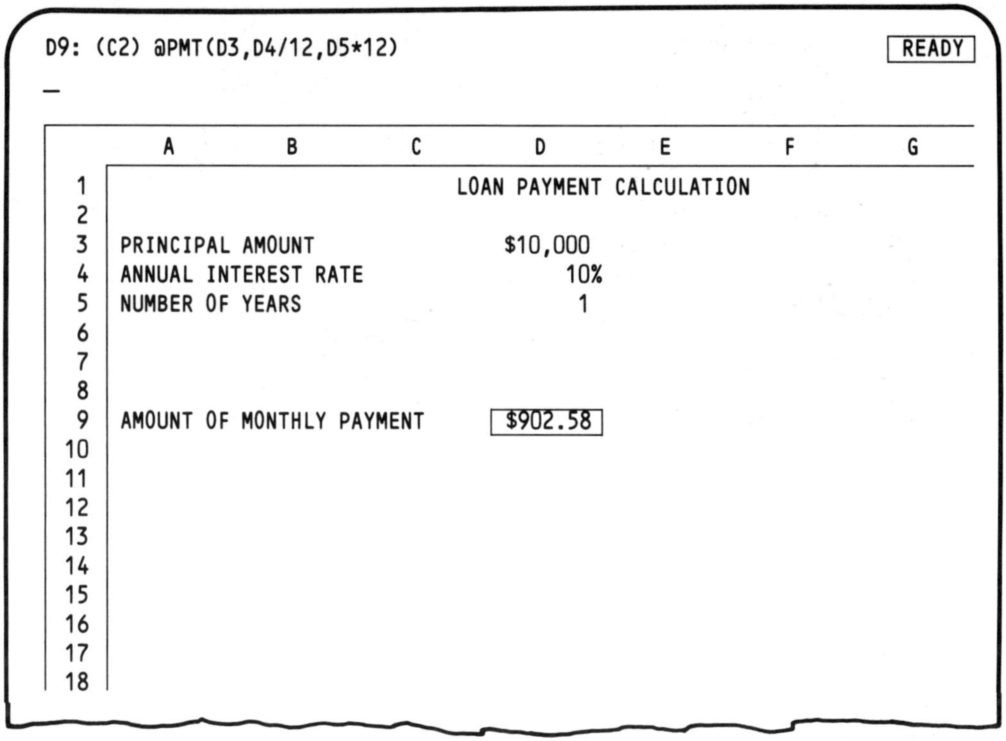

Figure 17.6 Loan Payment Calculation

premium—these are just a small sample of the variety of applications of date calculations.

How do you enter the date? You use the **@DATE** function, which has the following format:

```
@DATE(year-number,month-number,day-number)
```

Year-number is a number from 0 to 199. Any year from 1900 to 2099 can be entered. Subtract 1900 from the year you want to enter to get the year-number. For this century, use the last two digits of the year; for dates in the 21st century, use the last two digits of the year and add 100.
Month-number is a number from 1 representing January, to 12 representing December.
Day-number is a number from 1 to 31, representing the day. 1-2-3 checks that the day-number is consistent with the month-number. It even adjusts for leap year for days in February! You can enter any date from January 1, 1900 to December 31, 2099 (that's the last day of the next century).

1-2-3 uses the numbers in **@DATE** to store a date-number. When you use **@DATE** you see a number in the cell. For example, to enter January 15, 1983 as a date, you code **@DATE(83,1,15)**. The cell contains the following value:

```
30331
```

There are 30,331 days between December 31, 1899 and January 15, 1983.

To *display* the date, you must *format* the cell, using /Range Format Date. There are three possible date formats: Date-1, Date-2, and Date-3, which let you display the date in one of three different ways. January 15, 1983 displays as follows:

(Date-1 Format) 15-Jan-83
(Date-2 Format) 15-Jan
(Date-3 Format) Jan-83

Here's where there's a world of difference between how the date is stored (as a number), and how the date displays (with day, month, and/or year).

BEWARE ***You May Have to Widen Your Column Width***

If you want Date-1 format, you must use /Worksheet Column-width Set or /Worksheet Global Column-width to widen the column. That's because dates in the 21st century display with the entire year. In Date-1 format, January 15, 2083 displays as 15-Jan-2083. That's too large for the default column-width of 9. You could, of course, use Date-2 or Date-3 format if you like. You will probably need dates in the 21st century if you are calculating payments for long-term debts, such as mortgages.

Special Date Manipulation Functions

1-2-3 provides additional date manipulation functions to increase your date handling capabilities. These are the following:

```
@TODAY
@YEAR(date-value)
@MONTH(date-value)
@DAY(date-value)
```

@TODAY returns the PC-DOS system date. @YEAR, @MONTH, and @DAY return to year number, month number, and day number, respectively, of the cell containing a date value. For example, if you start the PC with a date of January 15, 1984, the following would be the values returned from these formulas:

@TODAY	returns 15-Jan-84 if cell in Date-1 format
@YEAR(@TODAY)	returns 84
@MONTH(@TODAY)	returns 1
@DAY(@TODAY)	returns 15

You can use these in formulas. For example, @TODAY+30 returns the date 30 days from today, which is useful if you want to take advantage of Net/30 terms in paying invoices. On the other hand, you might want to use it in a spreadsheet to determine which customers are 30 days overdue with their payment!

BEWARE ***If You Use Date Arithmetic, Set the Date Before Entering 1-2-3***

If the correct PC-DOS date is not set, @TODAY will return erroneous results. @TODAY will be set at January 1, 1980, the default PC-DOS date. Any calculations involving @TODAY, and any saved files, will use that date.

If you set the date correctly, however, you won't run into this trouble. When you retrieve a file (provided it was saved with automatic recalculation set), a cell containing the @TODAY function will be updated with the current date, and all calculations will be based on that date.

SELECTING FROM LISTS OR TABLES

1-2-3 provides three powerful list or table lookup functions. These functions are:

@CHOOSE	Choose a value from a list
@HLOOKUP	Look up a value from a horizontal table
@VLOOKUP	Look up a value from a vertical table

Although you cannot use these functions to lookup labels based on values (you cannot use them to look up the department name from a department code, for example), nevertheless they can be very useful. You can create a table of tax rates or discount rates and use these lookup functions to get the correct value.

@CHOOSE

You can use these functions, in combination with the date functions, to calculate the number of days in a month, referencing a cell containing a date. There are many applications for this calculation, notably in accounts payable and accounts receivable worksheets where you want to know when to pay or when an invoice becomes overdue.

Suppose you received a bill on February 3, 1984 and have until the end of the month to pay it. How many days can you wait until the bill must be paid? Your worksheet contains, in the column labeled DATE BILLED, a cell (say, Cell B3) entered with the @DATE function, as

```
@DATE(84,2,3)
```

If Cell B3 is formatted as Date-1 (dd-mmm-yy format), Cell B3 displays as follows:

```
03-Feb-84
```

You can use @CHOOSE to select from a list of arguments, based on a value you supply. @CHOOSE has the following format:

```
@CHOOSE(indexvalue,argument-0,argument-1,...,argument-n)
```

Based on the integer portion of the index-value, @CHOOSE selects from the arguments in the list. Index-value must be positive. If index-value is negative, @CHOOSE calculates the value ERR. If the integer part of index-value is 0, @CHOOSE chooses argument-0. If it is 1, @CHOOSE chooses argument-1, if 2 argument-2, and so on. You can use @MONTH to get the month number of the date, and use that to lookup the corresponding number of days in the month. The following formula will get the correct number of days for 1984, given any date value in Cell B3.

```
@CHOOSE(@MONTH(B3)-1,31,29,31,30,31,30,31,31,30,31,30,31)
```

@MONTH(B3) gets the month number of the date. For February 3, this month number is 2. Since @CHOOSE starts counting arguments from 0, month number 2 will actually get the third value (31), rather than the second value (29). You therefore must subtract 1 from the index-value, to make it @MONTH(B3)-1. The index value will then be 2-1 (or 1), making @CHOOSE choose the second value, or 29.

The formula above works for 1984, but it does not work for 1985 because 1985 is not a leap year. One way of changing the formula is to modify the @CHOOSE function for 1985, substituting 28 for 29 as the number of days in February.

But what if your worksheet contains dates in both leap years and non-leap years? Is there a way to code one @CHOOSE function which takes both into account? You bet! All leap years are divisible by 4. You can use the @YEAR and @MOD functions to add this to the @CHOOSE function for February, and code the following:

```
@CHOOSE(@MONTH(B3)-1,31,@IF(@MOD(@YEAR(B3),4)=0,29,28),
 31,30,31,30,31,31,30,31,30,31)
```

The function @IF(@MOD(@YEAR(B3),4)=0,29,28) was substituted to calculate the number of days in February. The @IF function calculates as follows: If the year in Cell B3 is divisible by 4, enter 29; otherwise, enter 28.

You can take advantage of the fact that you can use a function within a function. 1-2-3 can calculate the answer, as long as it can turn every argument into a number.

Table Lookup Functions

If the @CHOOSE coding becomes too complicated, 1-2-3 provides you with a simpler alternative. You can create a table in the worksheet and use one of the table lookup functions (either @HLOOKUP or @VLOOKUP) to look up the value in the table. Create a table in the cell range A136..B147, as follows:

	A	B
136	1	31
137	2	29
138	3	31
139	4	30
140	5	31
141	6	30
142	7	31
143	8	31
144	9	30
145	10	31
146	11	30
147	12	31

Figure 17.7

Column A contains the month number; Column B contains the number of days in that month. You can use @VLOOKUP (the vertical table lookup function) to look up the number of days in the month, given the month number. @VLOOKUP has the following format:

```
@VLOOKUP(index-value,table-range,column-offset)
```

@VLOOKUP looks up the index-value in the first column of the table-range. Unlike @CHOOSE, which automatically chooses the value based on the integer portion of the index-value, @VLOOKUP goes down the first column of the table-range. As soon as it finds a value which is greater than index-value, @VLOOKUP turns right the number of columns specified in column-offset and chooses that value. If the value in the first column exceeds the index-value, @VLOOKUP returns the value ERR.

You can use @VLOOKUP to find the number of days in the month, as follows:

```
@VLOOKUP(@MONTH(B3)-1,A136..B147,1)
```

Again, you must be careful to subtract 1 from the month. Remember: you start from zero. @VLOOKUP gets the month number in the date (2) and subtracts 1. The value 1 is the index-value. @VLOOKUP scans Column A (starting from A136) until it finds a value greater than 1 (the 2 in Cell A137). It travels right one column (column-offset is 1) to find the number 29 in Cell B137.

Can you change the @VLOOKUP table to account for both leap years and non leap years? Sure! Substitute the @IF function in Cell B137, as follows:

	A	B
136	1	31
137	2	@IF(@MOD(@YEAR(B3),4)=0,29,28)
138	3	31
139	4	30
140	5	31
141	6	30
142	7	31
143	8	31
144	9	30
145	10	31
146	11	30
147	12	31

Figure 17.8

Before returning the number of days in February, @VLOOKUP will do the @IF calculation and return to correct number of days.

@VLOOKUP assumes you are building the table down the rows of the worksheet. You can also build the table across by using @HLOOKUP. The format of @HLOOKUP is:

```
@HLOOKUP(index-value,table-range,row-offset)
```

@HLOOKUP operates exactly like @VLOOKUP except that instead of traveling *down* the rows, you travel *across* the columns from left to right. When you find a value greater than index-value, instead of traveling to the right, you travel *down* the number of rows specified in row-offset.

BEWARE ***The Comparison Values Must Be in Increasing Order***

If the values in the first column (for @VLOOKUP) or the first row (for @HLOOKUP) are not in increasing order, you will get erroneous results. For example, if the month number and number of days in December are the first entry in the table, the lookup functions will return ERR for *all* months *except* December. It will return the correct number of days in December, however.

You will also run into problems if the comparison values contain duplicates. The lookup functions will always look up on the first column or row containing the duplicate values. They will never look up on rows containing any subsequent duplicate values.

The next chapter discusses how to incorporate information stored in other 1-2-3 data files into the worksheet, and how to incorporate non-1-2-3 data files into the worksheet as well. In this way, you can make 1-2-3 participate in your company's total information processing.

CHAPTER 18

Sharing Your 1-2-3 Data Files

In this chapter, you will learn how to:

- Transfer information between different 1-2-3 worksheets.
- Import and export information stored in 1-2-3 worksheets to external systems, such as mainframe databases or other IBM PC software.

THE INPORTANCE OF SHARING DATA FILES

Incorporating Other 1-2-3 Data Files

There are many situations in which you might want to access 1-2-3 data files, incorporating the data into your worksheet. One common use is for *budget consolidations*. Suppose several departments in a division use the same budget worksheet. The Division Manager gives each Department Manager a quarterly budget; at the end of the quarter, the Division Manager would like to see which departments stayed within the budget and which overspent their budget.

The Department Managers and the Division Manager use the same budget worksheet format. The difference is that, while each Department Manager has a budget for her (or his) particular department, the Division Manager wants to see the *combined* budget—the total for all departments. The information requirements are as shown in Figure 18.1.

You can use /File Combine and /File Xtract (for *extract*) to produce the consolidated budget for the Division Manager (the total divisional budget) based on the departmental budget worksheet files. /File Combine *combines* data from another 1-2-3 file (either the entire file or a named range in the file) into your worksheet in memory. /File Xtract goes the other way—it *extracts* data from your worksheet in memory (either the entire worksheet or a named range) and creates a 1-2-3 data file from the information.

In addition to budget consolidations, you can combine and extract data for other purposes. Suppose your revenue comes from various product lines. You might have individual worksheets which track *each* product line. You could use the same consolidation techniques to find your *total* revenue for *all* product lines. The number of applications of these techniques is almost as many as the number of types of businesses which use 1-2-3!

Incorporating Data Files Produced by Other Programs

If you are using more than one program in your business, chances are that data used in one program can be used in another. For example, suppose your

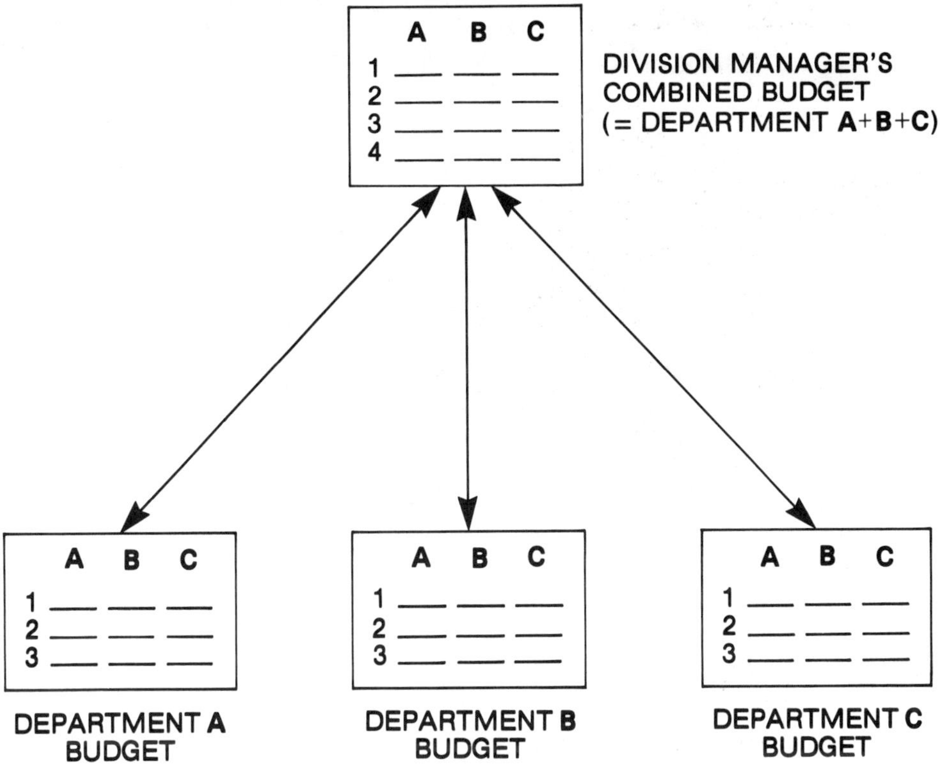

Figure 18.1

accounting system was developed in a database management system, such as dBASEII or a mainframe database. You could use 1-2-3 for "what-if" analysis based on the data stored in the database files. For another example, suppose you are using a word processing program and want to send a form letter to each customer whose names and addresses are stored in a 1-2-3 worksheet. You would want to send the data stored in the 1-2-3 file to the word processing program, for use in this mail merge application.

So there is a need both to use data files created by other programs in 1-2-3 and to use data created by 1-2-3 in other programs. If you cannot share the data in these different programs, you wind up duplicating the data. Figure 18.2 illustrates this situation. You have two major problems.

Inconsistent data. Suppose you use 1-2-3 to try different "what-if" scenarios based on your accounting information. The data in your database program probably is not consistent with the data for which you are doing the "what-if" analysis. It may contain recent transactions which are not reflected in the 1-2-3 files, for example.

Duplicate data. If you cannot use the database files in 1-2-3, you must recreate the data in 1-2-3. You thus have duplicate copies of the data and you must also go through the trouble of re-keying the information.

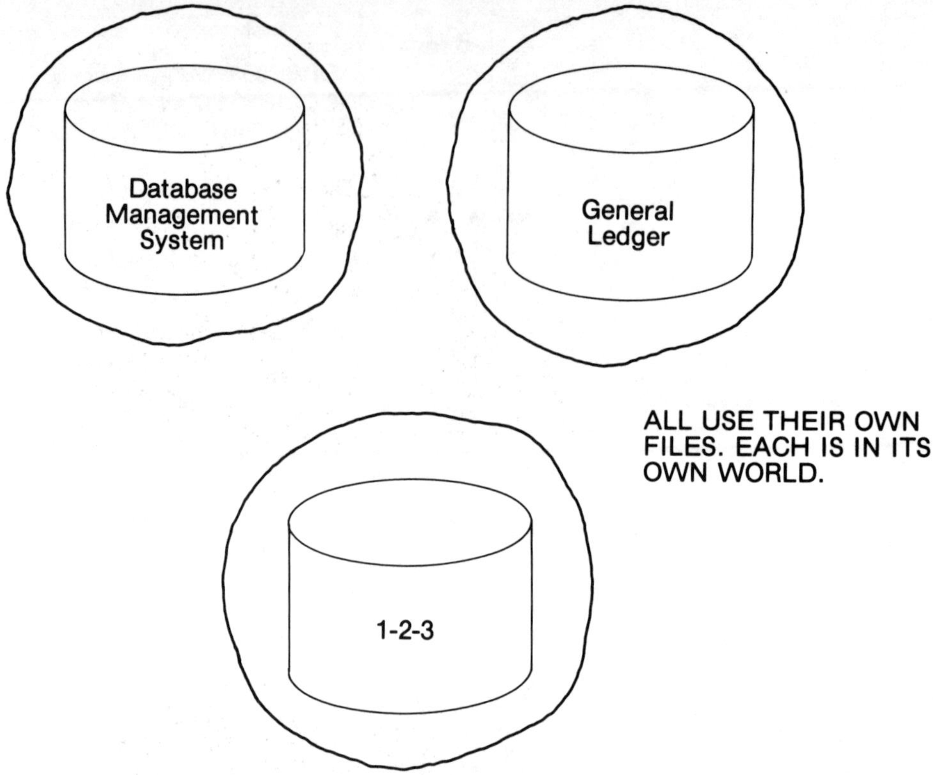

Figure 18.2

If your 1-2-3 worksheets could share the files created by your database, both these problems would be solved. Figure 18.3 illustrates this situation. Here, you have a truly integrated system, based on common data. Your "what-ifs" are based on the most up-to-date data stored in the database, and you don't have to re-key the data which is already in the database file.

You can use several techniques to share data files from other programs in 1-2-3. You can use /Print File to create a text (ASCII) file from your 1-2-3 worksheet. This file can then be used by many other programs—particularly mainframe database and accounting software. You can use /File Import to read ASCII files which have been created by other programs, directly into 1-2-3. 1-2-3, through its Translate menu, lets you convert files created by VisiCalc, dBASEII, and programs which use the DIF file format. Altogether, there is a rich variety of options for sharing data between 1-2-3 and other programs.

EXTRACTING AND COMBINING 1-2-3 FILES

Extracting

Use /File Xtract to create a 1-2-3 worksheet file which consists of a cell

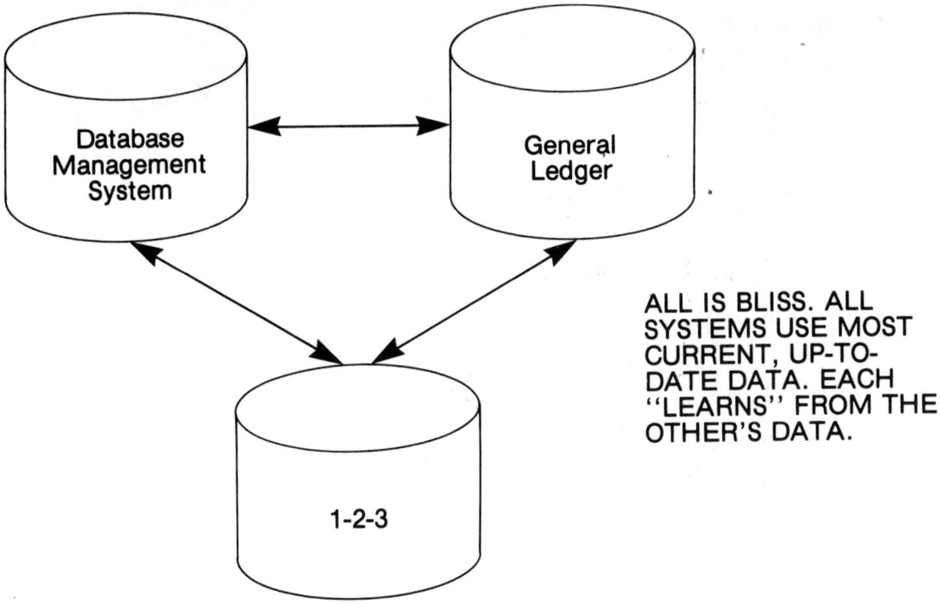

Figure 18.3

range in your worksheet. Unlike /File Save where you *must* save the entire worksheet, you can save just a *part* of the worksheet with /File Xtract.

/File Xtract gives you even more flexibility! As with /File Save, you can save the cell formulas and values by using /File Xtract Formulas. If you want, however, *you can save just the values, without saving the formulas* by using /File Xtract Values. This capability is handy in producing consolidations, as you will see later in this chapter.

Combining

Use /File Combine to combine information from another 1-2-3 worksheet disk file, into your worksheet in memory. Rather than erasing the worksheet as /File Retrieve does, /File Combine combines data from the file with the data in your worksheet.

/File Combine differs from /File Retrieve in several other respects. /File Combine does not bring cell ranges, global settings, or command ranges into the worksheet. Labels in the file overwrite labels in the worksheet. With values, however, you can control how the combining occurs, as follows:

You can copy the value in the file to the cell. If you use /File Combine Copy, values in the file overwrite values in the worksheet. Use this command if you want the values in the data file to replace the values in the worksheet.

You can add the value in the file to the value in the cell. If you use /File Combine Add, values in the file are added to the values in the worksheet. Use this command to produce a consolidated budget worksheet based on individually added files.

You can subtract the value in the file from the value in the cell. You might have a file for budget adjustments. This file contains information which must be subtracted from the consolidated budget worksheet to produce the final worksheet. Use /File Combine Subtract to do this.

You can combine an entire file or a named cell range. When 1-2-3 asks for a cell range, you can usually specify the actual cell range or a range name. /File Combine is the only command which *requires* a named cell range. The reason is that you don't see the file which you are combining and it's easy to mistype the cell addresses. In that case, your worksheet will probably not look anything like what you intended.

BEWARE ***Check the Position of the Cell Pointer Before Using /File Combine***

/File Combine starts combining the file into your worksheet at the cell pointer. If the cell pointer is at Cell A1, the file is combined starting at Cell A1; if the cell pointer is at C1, the combining starts at Cell C1; and so on. Cell contents, even if the cells are protected and worksheet global protection is enabled, are replaced by the contents of the combined file. If the cell pointer is in the wrong place, your worksheet can really get messed up.

HOW TO: Produce a Consolidated Worksheet

It's simple to consolidate worksheets with the same format (i.e., worksheets with the same labels, values, and formulas). Suppose you want to consolidate four department budget worksheets called DEPT1.WKS, DEPT2.WKS, DEPT3.WKS, and DEPT4.WKS, and produce a consolidated divisional budget worksheet file called DIVISION.WKS. First, retrieve DEPT1.WKS. Type the following:

```
/FRDEPT1[ENTER]              retrieve DEPT1.WKS
```

Now, use /File Combine Add to add the other three worksheets. *Be sure the cursor is at Cell A1 before using the command!* Type the following:

```
[HOME]/FCAEDEPT2[ENTER]      add DEPT2.WKS
[HOME]/FCAEDEPT3[ENTER]      add DEPT3.WKS
[HOME]/FCAEDEPT4[ENTER]      add DEPT4.WKS
```

You now have the total division's budget. Save the file. Type the following:

```
/FSDIVISION[ENTER]           save as DIVISION.WKS
```

You can refine this technique by combining named ranges in situations where you only want to combine parts of data files.

HOW TO: Change Formulas in a Cell Range Into Values

Remember how [F2/EDIT] [F9/CALC] is used to change a formula in one cell into its current value? You can use /File Xtract Values to convert an entire cell range (say a column or a row) containing values. How? Suppose you want to convert the formulas in the cell range E1..E100 into their values. Type the following:

/RNCSALES[ENTER]E1..E100[ENTER]	Create range name SALES
/FXVSALES[ENTER]SALES[ENTER]	Extract this range to SALES.WKS

You now have a file containing the values in the SALES range name in a file called SALES.WKS. You can now use /File Combine to incorporate the values into the worksheet. Type the following, making sure the cell pointer is at E1.

/FCCNSALES[ENTER]SALES[ENTER]	Combine the range name into the worksheet

The sales values are in the worksheet, but not the formulas.

INCORPORATING DATA FILES NOT PRODUCED BY 1-2-3

Reading Standard Text Files

Almost all systems written in standard business programming languages, such as COBOL, RPGII, FORTRAN, BASIC, or PL/I, can produce standard text files. The most common text files use the ASCII (American Standard Code for Information Interchange) format. ASCII text files are so widely used that they are virtually a computer industry standard. When you want one program to read another program's data files, using the ASCII format is the most convenient way.

With /File Import, 1-2-3 can read ASCII files into the worksheet. You might, for example, read an ASCII file containing selected accounting transactions from your mainframe general ledger system. As long as the data file is in ASCII format, it doesn't matter what language or database system the file was written in. /File Import has the following rules:

The file must be on the IBM PC, accessible to 1-2-3. The filename must have the .PRN extension. If your file is on another computer, you need to transfer it to the PC. You may need a communications program with the ability to *download* (to copy files from another computer to your PC).

You can import text or text and numbers. If you use /File Import Text, you create a column of labels based on the position of the cell pointer. The contents of the first record become a left-aligned label (up to 240 characters) in the cell where the cell pointer is positioned. The contents of the next record becomes a left-aligned label in the cell immediately below the cell pointer, and so on for each record. Any data in these cells before you issued the command is lost.

/File Import Text, while importing the data from an ASCII file, does not separate text from numbers. For example, suppose the ASCII file contains the following record containing three months of sales data:

```
SALES 100 200 300
```

if the cell pointer is at Cell A1, /File Import Text creates the following label in Cell A1:

```
'SALES 100 200 300
```

The *numbers* are still part of the *label*. You probably want the label SALES to be in Cell A1, the number 100 to be in Cell B1, 200 to be in C1, and 300 in D1 because while Column A contains the labels for your accounts, Columns B, C, and D contain the actual sales values.

Use /File Import Numbers to separate labels from values. /File Import Numbers separates labels, enclosed in double quotes, from numbers. If the ASCII file contained a record in the following format:

```
"SALES" 100 200 300
```

/File Import Numbers would place SALES (enclosed in double-quotes) in Cell A1, followed by the values 100, 200, and 300 in Cells B1, C1, and D1. /File Import Numbers looks for the double-quotes, assuming that the text enclosed in double-quotes is part of a label, and then places the next information in the cell to the right. You probably want to use /File Import Numbers because you need to import numbers into the worksheet. Remember the following rules:

All labels must be enclosed with double quotes.

Numbers must be imported in General format. There must be no commas or dollar signs embedded in the numbers, and minus signs must lead (not trail). Thus, -100 will be imported successfully, while 100- will not.

Writing Standard Text Files

Can you send data created by 1-2-3 to another system by creating an ASCII file? Yes! Most programs cannot read 1-2-3 worksheet files directly. However, if you use /Print File to create standard ASCII files from your worksheet data, chances are the other program can read them.

Use the following procedure to create the ASCII file:

1. Use */Print File, specifying a filename.* Specify a filename of up to 8 characters. 1-2-3 adds the extension .PRN to it.
2. Make the print range correspond to the range of rows you want to send. Use Range to specify the cell range you want to export.
3. Specify unformatted output. Use Options Other Unformatted so that you do not export headers, footers, or page breaks. You just want the data in the worksheet to be transferred to the ASCII file.
4. Set the left margin to 0. Specifying unformatted printing does not affect margins. Since 1-2-3's default left margin is 4, your first column of numbers will be indented 4 spaces to the right. If you set the left margin to 0, this will not happen.
5. Write the data. Use Go to write the worksheet data to the print file.

Each record in the .PRN file corresponds to a row in the worksheet. Since the size of each field is determined by the column-width, you can use Worksheet Column-width or /Worksheet Global Column-width to adjust the column width to change the size of each field, if necessary. This ASCII file should be easily readable by most computer systems.

SHARING DATA WITH OTHER IBM PC PROGRAMS

Using the Translate option, from the Lotus Access System, you can convert data files created by VisiCalc, dBASEII, and programs which use the Data Interchange Format (DIF), into 1-2-3 worksheet (.WKS) files. You can also convert .WKS files into a format directly readable by these programs. In this way, many of the most popular IBM PC programs can share the same information.

VisiCalc

VisiCalc worksheet (.VC) files can be translated almost entirely into .WKS files. When you use Translate, the VisiCalc formulas (with the exception of @CHOOSE, @NOT, @OR, and @AND) are translated along with their values. If Translate cannot translate the VisiCalc formulas, it will produce a Formula error message.

Once the VisiCalc files are converted, you must re-enter any formulas which didn't translate. In addition, the 1-2-3 worksheet may not display or calculate the same way as the VisiCalc worksheet. VisiCalc and 1-2-3 have slightly different methods for formatting numbers, displaying labels, and using column widths, making the display of the worksheets differ. In addition, VisiCalc supports calculation only by row or by column. Since 1-2-3 defaults to natural recalculation, it is possible that VisiCalc worksheets will not produce the same results in 1-2-3. If this happens, use /Worksheet Global Recalculation to force the worksheet to recalculate either by row or by column, rather than naturally.

Lotus Development Corporation provided this automatic transfer of VisiCalc worksheets into 1-2-3 because they wanted to encourage VisiCalc users to upgrade to 1-2-3 without losing their work. Since 1-2-3 is much more powerful than VisiCalc, there really is no reason to make the conversion from VisiCalc to 1-2-3 more than once. Once in 1-2-3, the idea is to stay there.

DIF Files

Can you transfer 1-2-3 worksheets into VisiCalc? Yes, but the process is not nearly as easy. VisiCalc is one of many PC programs which can read DIF (or Data Interchange Format) files. You can create DIF files from 1-2-3 worksheet files using Translate.

DIF is designed to transfer labels and values from one program to another. DIF has a major drawback—*it will not translate formulas.* So unlike the VisiCalc to 1-2-3 conversion, (which for the most part translates formulas) the 1-2-3 to VisiCalc conversion does not translate them. So, when VisiCalc receives a number from 1-2-3, it cannot tell whether it is a value or a formula.

You can use Translate to convert DIF files to .WKS files. Many PC programs, which perform functions such as project scheduling or equation processing, which cannot easily be done in 1-2-3, use the DIF format. You can create a DIF data file in the program after managing the project or solving the equations, and bring the data into 1-2-3. Again, this is another aid in developing an integrated system, where all your programs share the same data.

DBASEII

If you are using a database management system on the IBM PC, it may very well be dBASEII. Using Translate, you can convert dBASEII files (.DBF files) into 1-2-3 .WKS files, and vice versa. There are several rules to bear in mind as you are doing the conversion.

When you use Translate to convert .DBF files into .WKS files, remember the following rules:

The dBASEII field names are converted to 1-2-3 labels on the top row of the worksheet. Each field name in the dBASEII STRUCTURE (the definition of the database) becomes a label in columns of the first row. Each record is stored in its own row, starting from the second row.

You cannot translate more than 2,047 dBASEII records into 1-2-3. The 1-2-3 spreadsheet contains a maximum of 2,048 rows. Since the top row contains the field names, and each succeeding row contains a translated record, this means that the maximum number of dBASEII records which can be read into a 1-2-3 spreadsheet is 2,047.

In practice, you probably cannot import that many records. The translated records must fit in the active worksheet. Depending on the RAM capacity of your PC, you may not have enough memory to store 2,047 records.

You cannot pre-select, or filter, dBASEII records with Translate. Translate translates an entire dBASEII file into a 1-2-3 worksheet. You cannot specify selecting records based on a criterion. To circumvent this, use dBASEII to extract the records before you translate them into a 1-2-3 worksheet.

You may unintentionally erase a 1-2-3 worksheet. Translate creates a .WKS file with the same name as the .DBF file. If your dBASEII file is called SALES.DBF, it is translated into the 1-2-3 file SALES.WKS. If a file called SALES.WKS already exists, Translate erases it with no warning message. You will therefore lose the contents of the old file.

The column widths correspond to the field sizes. Translate sets the column width to correspond to the field size in the dBASEII STRUCTURE. For example, if a dBASEII field called CUSTOMER is defined as being 20 characters long, the column width for the column containing the CUSTOMER field is adjusted to 20 characters in the worksheet.

If a dBASEII field contains n decimal places, the format is adjusted to (Fn) format. For example, suppose a dBASEII field is called SALARY and has two decimal places. The cells in the column containing SALARY are adjusted to (F2) format, to display the cents.

Logical fields are not always converted. BASEII lets you define a true /false field called a *logical field*. You could, for example, store whether a customer is active or inactive by creating a logical field called ACTIVE. If the customer is active, dBASEII stores the value .T. for true; if the customer is inactive, dBASEII stores the value .F. for false. Although the dBASEII field name is converted, the .T. or .F. values may not be. In dBASEII, you can enter a true value as either Y or T and a false value as either N or F. Only those fields in which T or F were entered are translated. Translate translates the T into @TRUE, or 1 and the F into @FALSE or 0. It ignores any Y or N entries. So be careful in translating logical fields.

Deleted records are not converted. When you use the DELETE command in dBASEII, the record is flagged for deletion. These flagged records are not converted to 1-2-3. If you want the deleted records to be converted, you must use the DBASEII RECALL command, which removes the deletion flag, before doing the conversion.

Once you have done the conversion, enter 1-2-3. Since 1-2-3 created a .WKS file with the same filename as the .DBF file you translated, use /File Combine to bring the records into the worksheet.

When you use Translate to convert .WKS files into .DBF files, remember the following rules:

The labels in the first row of the worksheet must correspond to the dBASEII field names. A dBASEII field name can contain a maximum of 10 characters. The first 10 characters of each field name must correspond exactly to the dBASEII field name. Otherwise, you could seriously damage the dBASEII data file.

The column widths must correspond to the dBASEII field sizes. Translate assumes that the 1-2-3 column-width is the dBASEII field size. Adjust the column-widths before you do the translation. If the column-widths don't match the dBASEII STRUCTURE, you will either transfer too little information (labels may be *truncated*, for example), or too much (labels may be *padded* with blanks). Numbers may also not transfer properly.

You are limited to 32 fields. Although 1-2-3 databases can have up to 256 columns, dBASEII contains a limit of 32 fields. You can create a .DBF file containing a maximum of 32 fields.

Translate does not check for valid field contents. If you put non-numeric data, such as a label, into a field which dBASEII has defined as numeric, zeroes are placed in that field. This could mean, for example, that the SALARY field, which was valid when it was translated into 1-2-3, becomes zero when translated back into dBASEII because you placed a label in the field in 1-2-3.

Translate uses the cell format to determine the number of decimal places in the field. If cells containing SALARY are in (F2) format, the cents will be transferred; however, if they are in (F0) format, the cents will not be transferred. If you change the format with /Range Format, you could lose data when you translate the data in the column back to dBASEII.

1-2-3 Date fields cannot be translated easily. 1-2-3 stores dates as numbers. 1-2-3 stores the date January 15, 1983 as the number 30331. Since dBASEII doesn't treat dates in this manner, you cannot simply take the date and transfer it into dBASEII. An alternative is to create the formatted date into a label. However, dBASEII doesn't recognize 15-Jan-83 as a date, but as text. In either case, although you can write a dBASEII program, and a fairly involved one at that, to get around the problem, you should be aware that the problem exists and cannot be solved unless you know (or are) an experienced dBASEII programmer.

You may unintentionally destroy a dBASEII file. Since Translate creates a .DBF file with the same filename as the .WKS file, you can erase a .DBF file with that name. If a file named SALES.DBF existed prior to translation, its contents are lost when you translate a file named SALES.WKS into dBASEII format. Translate does not warn you that SALES.DBF already exists.

You can either translate an entire worksheet, or a named range within the worksheet, into a dBASEII file.

Word Processing Programs

If you are using a word processing program, you might want to interchange data between the program and 1-2-3. Like most programmed systems, most word processors can read and write ASCII text files. Remember the following rules:

Use /File Import Text to read a word processing document into 1-2-3. /File Import Text will convert the document into a column of labels.

Use /Print File to create a document which can be read by the word processing program. /Print File creates an ASCII text file which can be read by most word processing programs. The file created by 1-2-3 has an extension of .PRN. You might use /Print File to create a mailmerge document, consisting of names and address which you are storing in a 1-2-3 worksheet.

With the information you have learned in this chapter, you can create an environment in which, rather than 1-2-3 being isolated from the other programs you may be using, 1-2-3 can use information residing in other programs. Other programs can use the information you generate in 1-2-3, as well. The next chapter discusses several powerful 1-2-3 commands which are not as widely understood as they should be.

CHAPTER 19

/Data Table, /Data Fill, /Data Distribution and /Range Justify

This chapter discusses several powerful 1-2-3 commands which are not generally available in other automated spreadsheet packages and which significantly enhance your ability to create sophisticated worksheets. These commands are:

/Data Table. /Data Table allows you to do "what-if" analysis, letting you create a table based on substituted values in one (or two) input cells.

Suppose you need to borrow $100,000 for a mortgage on a house. Since banks have different interest rates, and you want to compare your monthly payment based on the different interest rates, you might want to construct a table of monthly payments based on the different interest rates. Using /Data Table 1, you could construct this table easily.

/Data Table also lets you vary *two* input cells. Suppose the banks vary *both* in their interest rate *and* term. With /Data Table 2, you could construct a two-dimensional table, varying both the interest rate and the term.

You can use /Data Table for a wide variety of applications; in fact, anywhere you need to construct a table based on changes in one or two input values. For example, you could construct a table which shows the effect of changes in inflation rates on profit margin, or of a change in oil prices on raw material costs.

/Data Fill. With /Data Fill, you fill a range with numbers which are in arithmetical sequence. You can use /Data Fill, for example, to create headings of years (1981, 1982, 1983, and so on) for columns of a worksheet showing five-year growth projections. You can use /Data Fill to generate a column of increasing or decreasing interest rates, which can then be used by /Data Table. You have already used /Data Fill in earlier chapters. It's a convenient shortcut to entering each number in sequence by hand.

/Data Distribution. /Data Distribution is a handy way of creating a frequency distribution to analyze your data. Suppose you have received all the product sales unit numbers from each of your field offices, and you want to group them. How many had sales greater than 50,000 units? How many between 51,001 and 100,000? How many over 100,000? By using /Data Distribution, you can count the number of field offices which fit into each category. You can add, if you like, statistical functions such as @SUM, @AVG, and @STD to refine the analysis. In addition, you can graph the result. You could create a pie chart showing percentage of field offices in each category using the /Graph commands, which are covered in Chapter 20. Altogether, /Data Distribution is a powerful command which can be used in a wide variety of situations.

/Range Justify. Although 1-2-3 was not designed for word processing, you can use /Range Justify to create small documents. /Range Justify is ideal for creating a memorandum of several paragraphs which includes parts of the worksheet—for example, a letter from the home office to each field office showing sales results for each office.

CREATING "WHAT-IF" TABLES WITH DATA TABLE

Suppose you want to calculate the monthly payment for a mortgage of $100,000, at 13% yearly interest, for 30 years. If you create three cell ranges called PRINCIPAL, INTEREST, and TERM, you could use the @PMT function by typing the following:

```
@PMT(PRINCIPAL,INTEREST/12,TERM*12)
```

to calculate the monthly payment as $1,106.20.

But what if you want to shop around for interest rates? How would your monthly payment vary with the interest rate? What if the term can vary? To answer these questions, you can develop a table of monthly payments based on variations in both interest rate and term using /Data Table.

Changing One Cell

Let's first create a table based on interest rate changes, using /Data Table 1 to can create a table showing the payment based on these interest rates. Proceed as follows:

1. *Define the table range.* The result of /Data Table will be stored in the table range. Down the first column, enter each interest rate you wish to change. After /Data Table completes, the corresponding monthly payment rate will be stored in the second column.
2. *Reference the formulas to recalculate.* In Cell B4, reference the cell containing the @PMT formula (Cell D2), which is recalculated for each value of the interest rate and stored in the column. Although in this case you recalculate only one formula, you could recalculate other formulas by including additional columns and referencing the cells containing the formulas in the top row of each column.
3. *Use /Data Table 1.* Use the cell containing the interest rate (Cell B2) as the input cell, the cell for which /Data Table 1 will substitute values. The table range is A4..B10. The interest rates are entered in A5..A10. The contents of Cell A4 are not used by /Data Table. Type the following to specify the table range and the input cell:

/DT1	Use /Data Table 1
A4..B10[ENTER]	Specify the table range
B2	Specify the input cell

Your worksheet should display as follows:

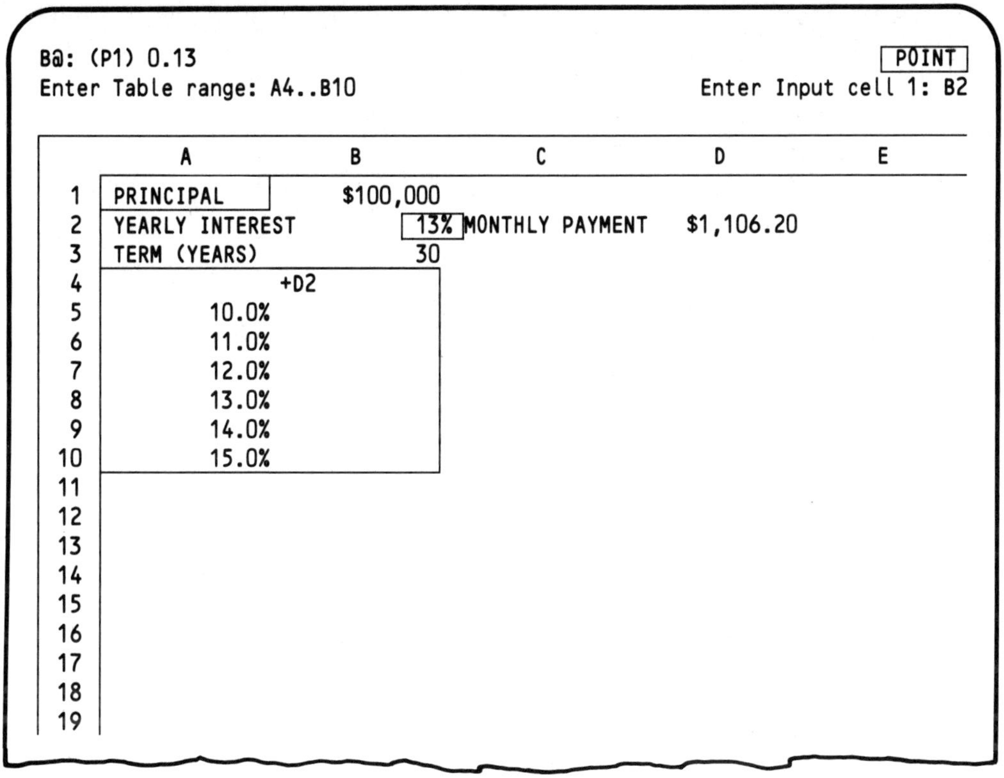

Figure 19.1 Table Range

Press [ENTER] to complete the table. Your worksheet should display as shown in Figure 19.2 after the table has been formatted to (C2) format:

/Data Table actually recalculates the worksheet for each value of the interest rate. If your table is large, and your worksheet contains many formulas, you may have to wait awhile before the command completes. The resulting table, I think, is well worth the wait.

BEWARE ***/Data Table First Erases the Table Range, Except for the First Column***

Before calculating the table, /Data Table erases the table range, except for the first column. The first column of the table range, of course, is used for the values to substitute in the input cell. Be sure the table range is in an area of the worksheet which either (a) is empty, or (b) contains information you don't need. Additionally, be sure the table range is in an area of the worksheet you will not overwrite with another 1-2-3 command such as /Copy or /Move.

```
A1: 'PRINCIPAL                                                    READY
_

          A              B              C              D            E
 1  PRINCIPAL        $100,000
 2  YEARLY INTEREST          13% MONTHLY PAYMENT    $1,106.20
 3  TERM (YEARS)             30
 4                  +D2
 5            10.0%    $877.57
 6            11.0%    $952.32
 7            12.0%  $1,028.61
 8            13.0%  $1,106.20
 9            14.0%  $1,184.87
10            15.0%  $1,264.44
11
12
13
14
15
16
17
18
19
```

Figure 19.2

After it completes the table, 1-2-3 returns the worksheet to its state before you used /Data Table, by recalculating the worksheet with the original value in the Input Cell. /Data Table will not destroy any other calculations you have done in the worksheet.

Using [F8/TABLE]

Once you have defined a table, you can change values and re-use it without re-issuing the /Data Table command. How? By using the [F8/TABLE] key.

Suppose you want to create a table using a different set of interest rates (say 15%, 16%, 17%, 18%, 19% and 20%). You can change the values in the first column of the table range and press [F8/TABLE]. The table will be re-calculated with the new interest rates, as shown below:
1-2-3 remembers the table range and the input cell, using them to recalculate the table. This automates the "what if" process an additional step. You can, if you wish, cause 1-2-3 to forget the table range by using /Data Table Reset.

In addition to remembering the table range for [F8/TABLE], 1-2-3 remembers the range when you save the worksheet with /File Save. So to recompute

```
A5: (P1) 0.15                                                    READY
_

         A              B            C                D             E
 1  PRINCIPAL         $100,000
 2  YEARLY INTEREST        13% MONTHLY PAYMENT    $1,106.20
 3  TERM (YEARS)           30
 4                   +D2
 5           15.0%   $1,264.44
 6           16.0%   $1,344.76
 7           17.0%   $1,425.68
 8           18.0%   $1,507.09
 9           19.0%   $1,588.89
10           20.0%   $1,671.02
11
12
13
14
15
16
17
18
19
```

Figure 19.3

a table on a worksheet you have previously saved, retrieve the file with /File Retrieve and then simply press [F8/TABLE].

Changing Two Cells

Suppose, however, that you want to vary the term *in addition to* the interest rate. You can produce a table based on varying 2 cells. To do this, use /Data Table 2, using the following steps:

1. *Specify the table range.* The table range contains the same interest rate values down Column A. However, it will be wider. Each column has, in its first row, the particular term to calculate. You want to produce a table based on terms of 10, 20, and 30 year terms. The table range contains more columns (A4..D10, instead of A4..B10). As with /Data Table 1, the interest rates are *down* Column A. However, the *terms* are *across* Row 4.
2. *Enter the reference to the formula to calculate in the top-left corner of the table range.* Unlike /Data Table 1 where you can see the "what-if" effect on as many formulas as specified, you can only recalculate *one* formula with /Data

Table 2. Enter the formula reference in Cell A4, the top-left corner of the table range. This tells /Data Table 2 what formula is to be recalculated.

3. *Use /Data Table 2, specifying the first input cell.* As with /Data Table 1 the cell containing the interest rate (Cell B2) is the first input cell.

4. *Specify the second input cell.* The term (Cell B3) is the second input cell. After entering the correct information in the table range, type the following to define the ranges for the two-dimensional table:

/DT2A4..D10[ENTER]	Use /Data Table 2; specify table range
B2[ENTER]	Input Cell 1 is Interest (Cell B2)
B3[ENTER]	Input Cell 2 is Term (Cell B3)

Your worksheet should display as follows:

```
B3: 30                                                          POINT
Enter Table range: A4..D10Enter Input cell 1: B2      Enter Input cell 2: B3

             A              B              C              D              E
 1   PRINCIPAL         $100,000
 2   YEARLY INTEREST        13%  MONTHLY PAYMENT    $1,106.20
 3   TERM (YEARS)            30
 4   +D2                     10             15             20
 5             15.0% $1,264.44
 6             16.0% $1,344.76
 7             17.0% $1,425.68
 8             18.0% $1,507.09
 9             19.0% $1,588.89
10             20.0% $1,671.02
11
12
13
14
15
16
17
18
19
20
```

Figure 19.4

Press [ENTER] to complete the table. Your worksheet should display as shown below after the table has been formatted to (C2) format. The table for interest rates of 15-20%, for terms of 10, 15, and 20 years, has been filled in.

A5: (P1) 0.15 READY

_

	A	B	C	D	E
1	PRINCIPAL	$100,000			
2	YEARLY INTEREST	13%	MONTHLY PAYMENT	$1,106.20	
3	TERM (YEARS)	30			
4	+D2	10	15	20	
5	15.0%	$1,613.35	$1,399.59	$1,316.79	
6	16.0%	$1,675.13	$1,468.70	$1,391.26	
7	17.0%	$1,737.98	$1,539.00	$1,466.80	
8	18.0%	$1,801.85	$1,610.42	$1,543.31	
9	19.0%	$1,866.72	$1,682.88	$1,620.68	
10	20.0%	$1,932.56	$1,756.30	$1,698.82	
11					
12					
13					
14					
15					
16					
17					
18					
19					

Figure 19.5

/Data Table 2 erases the table range except for the top row and leftmost column. However, in the use of [F8/TABLE] and remembering and resetting ranges, /Data Table 2 operates exactly like /Data Table 1.

FILLING A RANGE WITH NUMBERS

/Data Fill lets you fill in values in a cell range with numbers which differ by a constant. /Data Fill was used in a HOW TO, in Chapter 7, to count the number of cells in the active worksheet.

A common use of /Data Fill is to create successive years (1981, 1982, 1983, and so on) as column headings. To specify the numbers 1981 to 1990 as the headings for the cell range B3..K3, do the following:

/DFB3..K3[ENTER]	Use /Data Fill; specify fill range
1981[ENTER]	Start value is 1981
1[ENTER]	Step value is 1
1990[ENTER]	Stop value is 1990

/Data Fill fills the fill range, starting with the start value. It continues filling until it reaches either (a) the end of the fill range, or (b) the stop value. You can fill the range with headings for every other year (1981, 1983, 1985) by specifying a step value of 2, although in this case, the stop value must be at least 1999 to fill the entire range. The step value can be a negative number. You can therefore start with 1990, step by -1, and stop with 1981.

BEWARE ***/Data Fill Erases the Contents of the Fill Range***

Even if /Data Fill doesn't fill the range (it could reach the stop value before it finishes filling the range), the unfilled part of the fill range is erased. Be sure there is no information in the fill range that you need before using /Data Fill.

HOW TO: Fill a Range with Monthly Dates

Suppose you want to fill a cell range with dates (such as Jan-84, Feb-84, Mar-84, and so on). Since @DATE calculates a number, you can use it as a start value. After you have filled the range with calculated dates, you can then use /Range Format to format the cell-range to (D3) format, which displays the month and the year. Type the following to fill a cell range with monthly dates:

`/DFB3..K3[ENTER]`	Use /Data Fill; specify fill range
`@DATE(84,1,1)[ENTER]`	Start date is January 1, 1984
`31[ENTER]`	Step value is 31 (get to next month)
`99999[ENTER]`	Stop value is 99999 (make sure number is large enough)

This fills the cell range with the numeric equivalents of the dates. The step value of 31 is used to guarantee incrementing to the following month in filling the next column. Though this is approximate, it will work for any date range that can display with 1-2-3. To make the date display properly, format the cells to (D3) format. Type the following:

`/RFD3B3..K3[ENTER]`	Format the cells to (D3) format

The column headings now display as desired.

CREATING A FREQUENCY DISTRIBUTION

Using /Data Distribution, you can create a frequency distribution of values, as an analytical aid.

As Sales Manager for Acme Widget, you would like to count the number of salespeople with SALES greater than $100,000, the number with SALES between $100,001 and $200,000, and the number with SALES greater than $200,000. With /Data Distribution, you count these groups by first setting up *bins.* Think of bins as similar to slots at the Post Office, where letters are grouped by zip code. The values themselves, the sales numbers, are defined in the *value range.* The values associated with each bin are stored in the leftmost column of the *bin range.* The rightmost column stores the result of the distribution.

If the bin range values differ by a constant, you could use /Data Fill to fill in the values. /Data Distribution will count the number in each group.

Type the following to define the ranges:

`/DDC24..C29[ENTER]`	Define the values range for /DD
`A32..B33`	Define the two-column bin range

The worksheet displays as follows:

```
B33:                                                                   POINT
Enter Values range: C24..C29               Enter Bin range: A32..B33

          A           B           C           D           E           F
21                           ACME WIDGET SALES RESULTS
22
23   SALESPERSON                SALES
24   Jones                   $100,000
25   Brown                   $150,000
26   Smith                   $125,000
27   Adams                   $235,000  ← Values range
28   Franklin                $137,500
29   Brown                    $91,000
30
31   DISTRIBUTION OF SALES (BINS):
32   $100,000
                                    ←Bin range
33   $200,000
34
35
36
37
38
39
40
```

Figure 19.6 /Data Distribution Ranges

Press [ENTER] to distribute the sales values. The worksheet displays as follows:

```
B33:                                                              POINT
Enter Values range: C24..C29          Enter Bin range: A32..B33

         A          B          C          D          E          F
21                       ACME WIDGET SALES RESULTS
22
23  SALESPERSON                 SALES
24  Jones                    $100,000
25  Brown                    $150,000
26  Smith                    $125,000
27  Adams                    $235,000
28  Franklin                 $137,500
29  Brown                     $91,000
30
31  DISTRIBUTION OF SALES (BINS):
32  $100,000           2
33  $200,000           3
34                     1
35
36
37
38
39
40
```

Figure 19.7 After Completion of /Data Distribution

The result, in the second column of the bin range, displays the distribution of the number of salespeople with SALES less than or equal to $100,000. The cell below counts the number of salespeople with SALES greater than $100,000, but less than or equal to $200,000. Finally, salespeople with SALES greater than $200,000 are counted in the last cell of the second column.

You might want to enhance the analysis by using the statistical functions @SUM, @MAX, @MIN, @AVG, and @STD to show the statistical distribution of sales. Additionally, you could create a graph to illustrate the distribution. A pie chart showing the percentage and number of salespeople in each category would be a powerful reinforcement of the worksheet data.

BEWARE ***The Values in the Bin Range Must Be in Increasing Order***

Since /Data Distribution uses each value and the one below it to define a lower and upper limit to the bin, you will not get a proper distribution unless the values in the bin range are in increasing order. If they were in descending order, for example, all the values would be counted in the first bin.

BEWARE ***The Second Column of the Bin Range, Plus One More Cell, Is Erased***

/Data Distribution erases the part of the bin range where it will count the values. This means that the second column of the bin range is erased. Additionally, the cell immediately below the bottom-right corner of the bin range is used to count all values greater than the last value in the bin range, and is erased.

WRITING A SIMPLE MEMO

Although 1-2-3 was not designed as a word processing program, you can create a multi-paragraph or multi-page document using /Range Justify.

To use /Range Justify, define a range, called the *justify range*, which defines the width of the paragraph you are creating. There are two types of justify ranges:

The one-row justify range. Suppose you wanted to create a paragraph from the labels in Figure 19.8. If the justify range consists of the range A41..C41, the paragraph would be created by aligning the text down the leftmost column, for the width of the justify range row, as shown in Figure 19.9. The paragraph would be aligned, according to the column width.

The multi-row justify range. If the justify range consists of more than one row, no cells move down. Justification does not take place unless there is enough room in the justify range. If there is not enough room, the error message `Justify range is full` displays. Unfortunately, the labels are not returned to the state they were in before you issued the command, so your worksheet will probably display differently than before you issued the command. Since 1-2-3 has no undo command, you must manually reconstruct the worksheet.

BEWARE ***You May Move Some Worksheet Cells Down***

When the justify range consists of one row, the justification can force the cells in the leftmost column to be relocated down.

Once you have justified the text, you can print the memo using /Print. However you should be careful. Because of the potential problems, you should use /Range Justify with care. You should get the feel of it before you use the command seriously.

```
A41: 'Below are the Acme Widget Sales Results for 1984. I would like to     READY
_

        A           B           C           D           E           F
41  Below are the  Acme Widget Sales Results for 1984. I would like to
42  congratulate all of you on a job well done! We have been especially
43  gratified at the public's enthusiastic response to our new Widget D
44  product. Additionally, we have expanded sales on our other product
45  lines.
46
47
48
49
50
51
52
53
54
55
56
57
58
59
60
```

Figure 19.8

A Memorandum Incorporating Worksheet Data

Try incorporating the memorandum to Field Office Managers, shown in Figure 1.10 at the beginning of the book, above the Acme Widget worksheet. First, use /Worksheet Insert Rows to insert rows at the top of the worksheet. Then type the memorandum as long labels. Finally, experiment with /Range Justify. Try it first with a one-row justify range, and then with a multi-row justify range. Compare the results.

You now can use all of the 1-2-3 worksheet commands (the *1* of 1-2-3). You're ready to expand your horizons, to learn about graphics (the *2*), database management (the *3*), and macros. If you have thoroughly mastered the worksheet, you should find these additional features easy to understand and use.

```
A41: 'Below are the Acme Widget Sales                                  READY
            A          B          C          D          E          F
 41   Below are the Acme Widget Sales
 42   Results for 1984. I would like to
 43   congratulate all of you on a job
 44   well done! We have been especially
 45   gratified at the public's
 46   enthusiastic response to our new
 47   Widget D product. Additionally,
 48   we have expanded sales on our other
 49   product lines.
 50
 51
 52
 53
 54
 55
 56
 57
 58
 59
 60
```

Figure 19.9.

PART V

Using Graphs

Once you have designed your worksheet, graphs are powerful communicators. With 1-2-3, you can produce effective graphs which reinforce the numbers on the worksheet. The next two chapters discuss the variety of graphics capabilities available with 1-2-3. Chapter 20 discusses *displaying* graphs; Chapter 21 discusses *printing* them.

The functions of displaying and printing graphs are separate programs. You can display graphs in 1-2-3 by defining graph settings and then viewing the graph. You cannot, however, print the graph from 1-2-3. To print a graph that you have already specified, you must do the following:

1. Save the graph in a .PIC file. Use **/Graph Save** to save the graph to a disk file, called a *graph picture file*. This file has the .PIC extension. This file contains a snapshot of the graph, to be used when you print the graph.

2. Quit 1-2-3. Use **/Quit Yes** to quit 1-2-3.

3. Enter the PrintGraph program. The program to print graphs (GRAPH.EXE) is on the PrintGraph disk. If you are in the Lotus Access System, you can select **PrintGraph** to start the process of entering the PrintGraph program. If the program is not accessible, you will be prompted to insert the PrintGraph disk into the A-drive. After you enter PrintGraph, you can print any graph picture files you have saved in 1-2-3.

In addition to the separation of displaying and printing graphs, the way that 1-2-3 graphs are displayed differs, depending on the type of display monitor you are using. One of the major steps in the installation process is to install the correct *device driver* for the display monitor(s) you are using. You should be aware of the following variations:

If you are using the IBM PC monochrome monitor, you cannot display graphs. If you use the **/Graph** commands, and then attempt to display the graph, 1-2-3 will beep. You *can* save the graph to a .PIC file and then use PrintGraph to print the graph. However, printing graphs is much slower than displaying them. If the graph is not to your liking, you must re-enter 1-2-3, make the changes, save to the .PIC file, and print the graph again.

If you are using a monitor which supports non-color graphics, you can display the graphs without color variations. If your monitor can display in non-color graphics mode, the 1-2-3 graphs will display without color variations. However, 1-2-3 uses different cross-hatchings to distinguish between different items which are being graphed.

1-2-3 supports the addition of a hardware card, called the *Hercules card* or

Hercules board, which enables the IBM PC monochrome monitor to display non-color graphics. In addition, 1-2-3 can display graphs on the Compaq computer.

If you are using a monitor which supports color graphics, you can display graphs in color or without color variations. With a color monitor, you can display graphs either with cross-hatchings as with non-color graphics, or with up to 3 colors using /Graph Options Color. 1-2-3 selects the colors based on the type of graph you are displaying.

If you are using a monochrome monitor and a graphics monitor, the worksheet displays on the monochrome monitor and the graph on the graphics monitor. With two monitors, you can actually see "what if" changes. For example, if you make a change to the worksheet, you can press a function key ([F10/GRAPH]) and see how the pie chart associated with this worksheet changes.

Since the choice of display monitor(s) affects how the graphs display, be aware of your configuration before you read the chapters on graphs.

CHAPTER 20

Displaying Graphs

THE SIMPLE STEPS TO PRODUCING A GRAPH

Graphing in 1-2-3 is simple. You use the /Graph command to specify graph settings. The /Graph command menu has the following options:

```
Type X A B C D E F Reset View Save Options Name Quit
```

Like the /Print menu, the /Graph menu is a sticky menu. You must specify more than one option before producing a graph. You therefore select from the menu choices, and when you are finished, you use Quit to quit the menu, returning to READY mode.

To produce a minimal graph, you need only specify two things:

The type of graph. 1-2-3 lets you define line graphs, bar charts, stacked-bar charts, XY (or scatter) graphs, and pie charts. Select Type to specify which type of graph you want to define.

The cell ranges you are graphing. Depending on the type of graph, you can graph up to six groups of data. These groups are typically the rows or columns in a cell range, and are labelled from A through F. The A-range is the first range to graph, the B-range the second, and so on. Additionally, for all graph types except pie charts, you define the X-range to contain labels or values to be graphed along the X-axis.

You can then display the graph, either by invoking View, or quitting the /Graph menu (by using Quit) and pressing [F10/GRAPH].

You graph directly from the worksheet. Thus, if you change the worksheet numbers, the graph values are changed as well. The graph is thus *integrated* with the worksheet. In first generation automated spreadsheets, such as VisiCalc, this was not the case. To display a graph from a spreadsheet, you must create a file from the spreadsheet, which can be read by a separate graphics program. This is a time-consuming process, requiring switching between two programs and data files. You can display only one graph at a time; you cannot overlay a line graph with a bar chart, for example. However, you can print as many graphs as you want at once.

THE DATA RANGES

The data ranges to graph are typically either rows or columns of cells. Suppose you would like to graph Acme Widget's product sales, for each of six widgets, for four quarters of 1984, based on the following worksheet:

	A	B	C	D	E	F
1				ACME WIDGET SALES SUMMARY (1984)		
2						
3						
4		QTR1	QTR2	QTR3	QTR4	TOTAL
5		----	----	----	----	----
6	Widget A	125	150	275	300	850
7	Widget B	300	275	240	200	1015
8	Widget C	450	500	535	600	2085
9	Widget D	300	325	356	478	1459
10	Widget E	400	430	450	500	1780
11	Widget F	200	225	267	308	1000
12		----	----	----	----	----
13	TOTAL	1775	1905	2123	2386	8189
14						
15						

Figure 20.1

You would like to produce a bar graph which illustrates sales for Widget A through Widget F for each of these quarters. How would you do it? Just follow these steps!

Step 1. *Specify a bar graph.* Use **/Graph Type Bar** to specify a bar graph.

Step 2. *Specify each range.* The X-range (B4..E4) contains the labels to display on the X-axis (QTR1, QTR2, QTR3, and QTR4). The A-range through the F-range are the sales for each of the widgets for each quarter. The ranges are as follows:

The A-range (for Widget A):	B6..E6
The B-range (for Widget B):	B7..E7
The C-range (for Widget C):	B8..E8
The D-range (for Widget D):	B9..E9
The E-range (for Widget E):	B10..E10
The F-range (for Widget F):	B11..E11

You specify the ranges by selecting **A** through **F**.

Step 3. *View the graph.* By pressing **View**, the graph (Fig. 20.2) displays:

You are halfway home! You have displayed a bar graph showing the sales values. Later on in this chapter you will see how to enhance the display with the many options 1-2-3 provides to produce a really meaningful graph.

If the ranges are a block of cells containing multiple rows and columns, the values are graphed column by column. The values are graphed down the first column, then down the second column, and so on. Blank cells and cells containing the values **@NA** or **@ERR** are ignored. Cells containing labels are given a

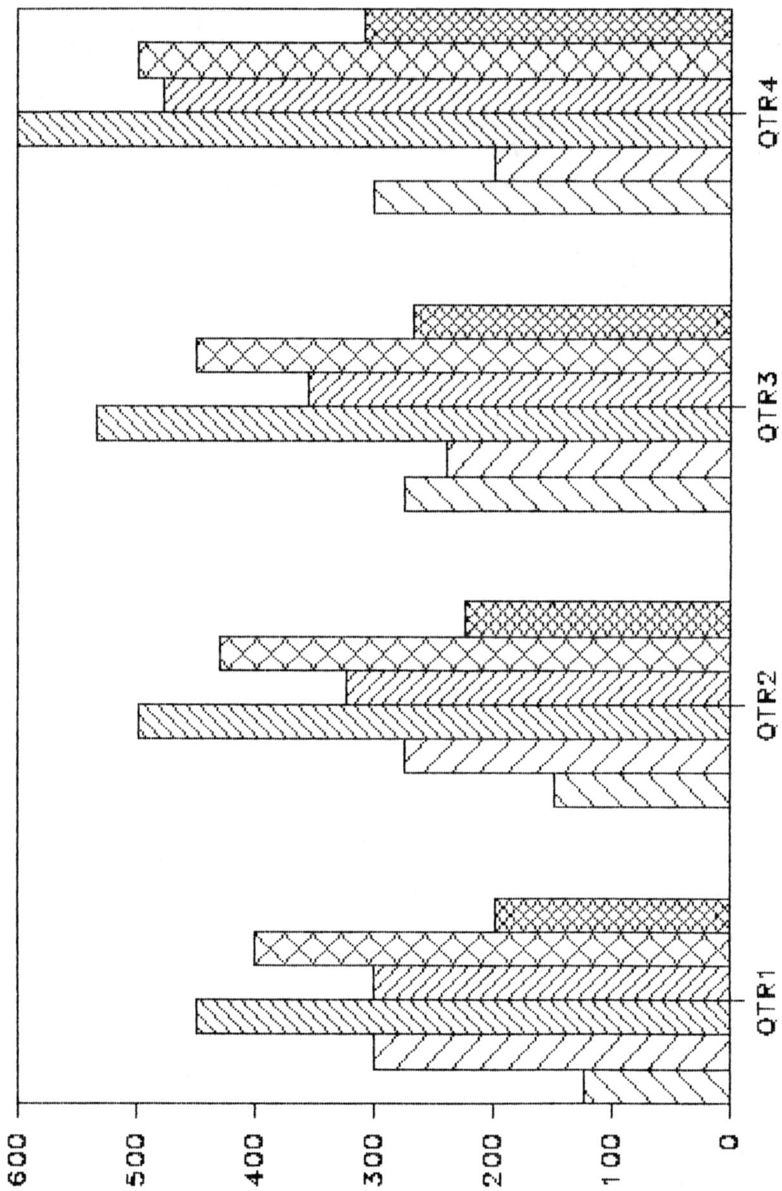

Figure 20.2

value of 0. Here's another instance of the difference between a blank cell and a label containing a space entry.

BEWARE ***If Ranges Vary Widely the Graph May Not Display Well***

If the values in the ranges you are graphing vary widely, perhaps showing exponential growth, the values may not all display. 1-2-3 automatically scales the Y-axis according to the values in the A- through F-ranges. If the values are numbers like 1, 10, 1000, and 1000000, the bars with the small numbers will not display. 1-2-3 cannot scale the Y-axis values logarithmically.

TYPES OF GRAPHS

Here are examples of the types of graphs you can produce with 1-2-3. To make the explanation clearer, titles and legends have been added.

Bar Graph

A bar graph produces groups of bars, arranged adjacent to each other, for each cell range. A bar graph comparing sales for four quarters displays as shown in Figure 20.2. 1-2-3 adjusts the width of each bar to fit the display. Thus, if you graph fewer ranges, each bar would be wider. Figure 20.4 is a bar graph for only Widget A sales.

Line Graph

You can also graph six ranges with a line graph. Because line graphs connect the data points, it's easier to spot trends than with bar graphs. A sales comparison using a line graph is shown in Figure 20.5.

Stacked-bar Chart

With a stacked-bar chart, instead of the bars displaying adjacent to each other, they display stacked on top of each other. Stacked-bar charts are useful for displaying the part each value contributes to the whole. For example, if you wanted to compare contribution of each widget's sales for each quarter, to the total company sales, you could use a stacked-bar chart. Figure 20.6 is a stacked-bar chart illustrating the same information.

The bars in the A-range through the F-range are stacked. You could use stacked-bar charts as well to display cost components, or to compare sales performance for field offices.

BEWARE ***Don't Use Stacked-bar Charts with Negative Numbers***

If any of the values in the ranges are negative, the stacked-bar will not dis-

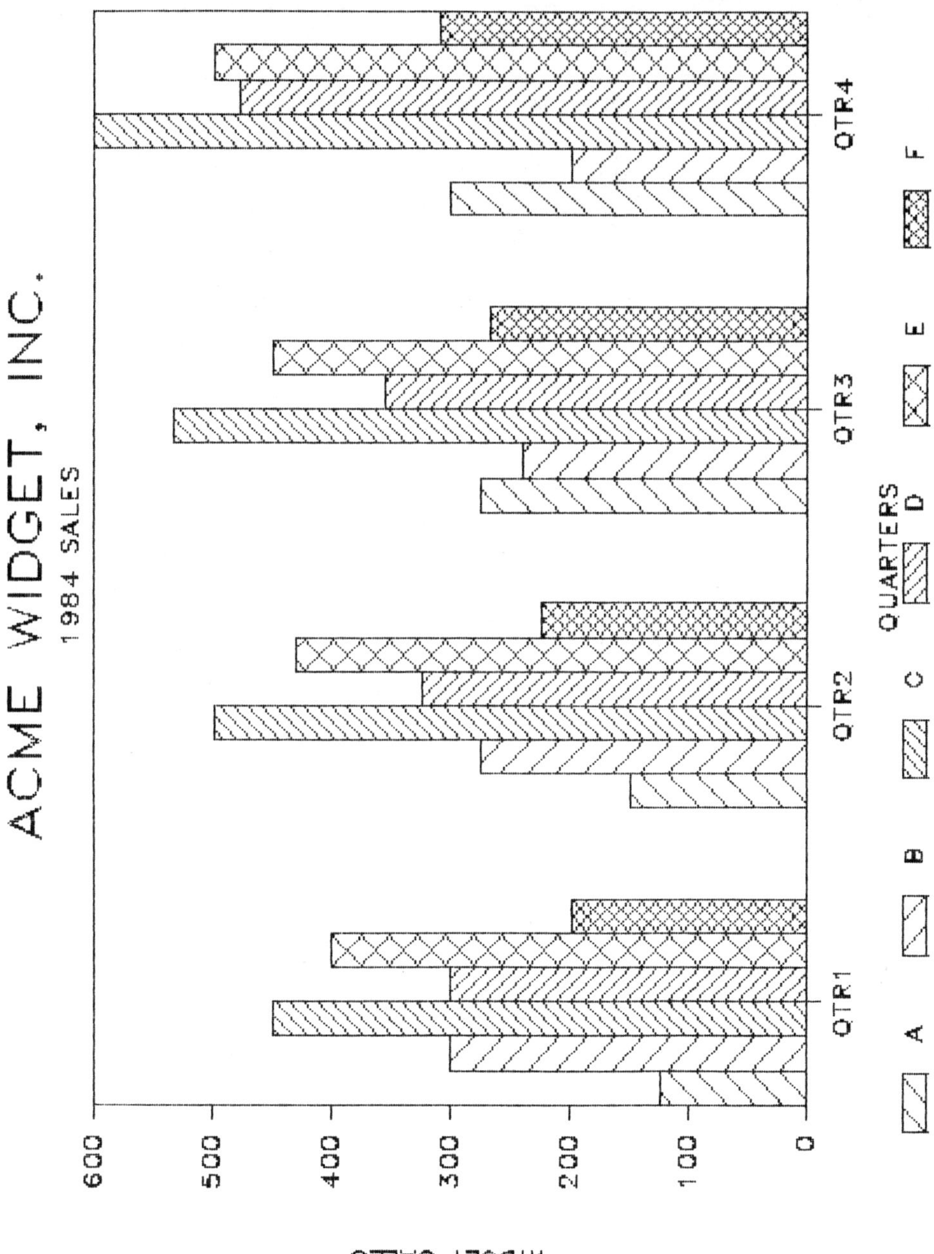
ACME WIDGET, INC.
1984 SALES
WIDGET SALES
0
100
200
300
400
500
600
QTR1
QTR2
QTR3
QTR4
QUARTERS
A
B
C
D
E
F

Figure 20.3

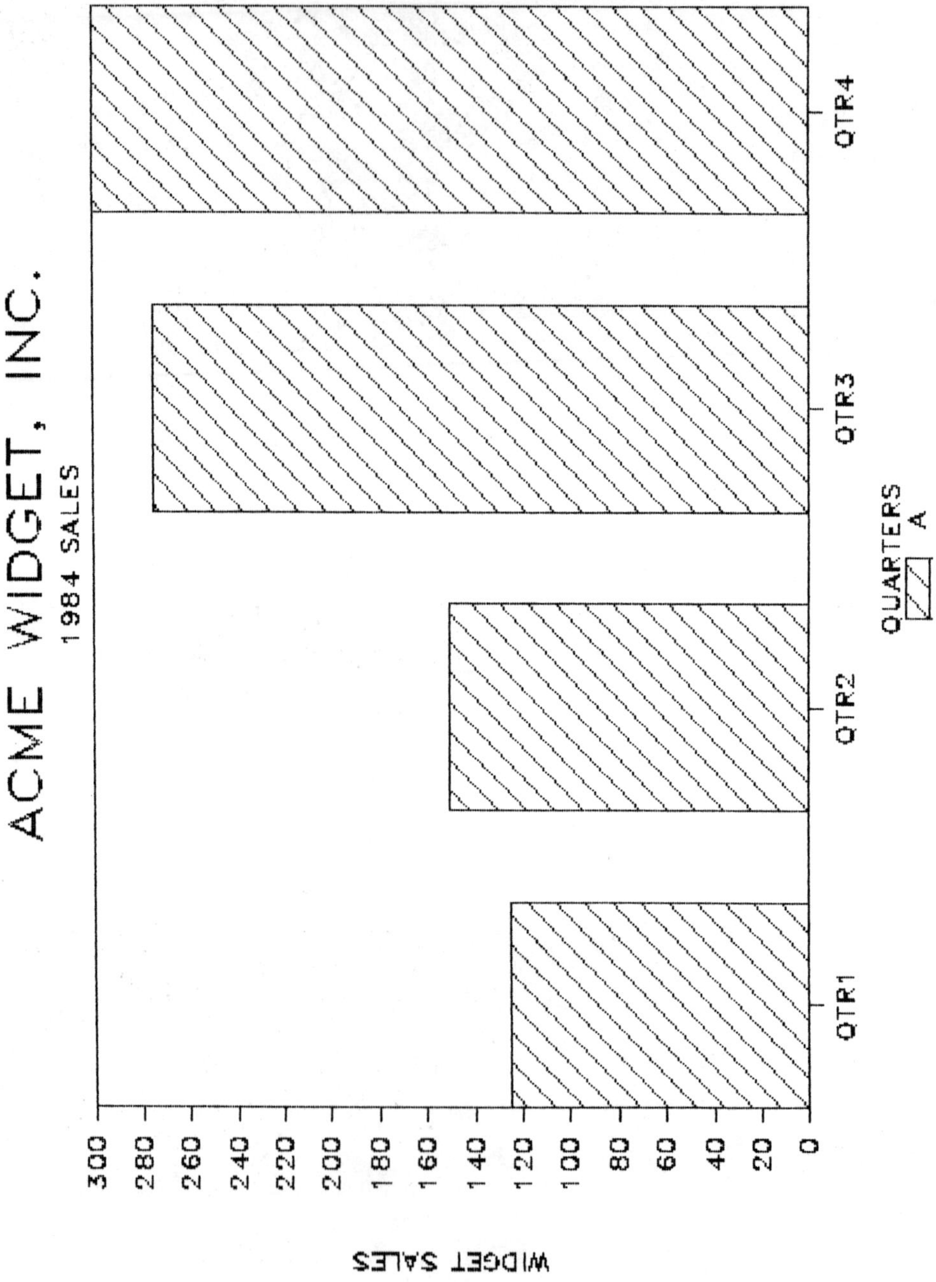
ACME WIDGET, INC.
1984 SALES
WIDGET SALES
300
280
260
240
220
200
180
160
140
120
100
80
60
40
20
0
QTR1
QTR2
QTR3
QTR4
QUARTERS
A

Figure 20.4

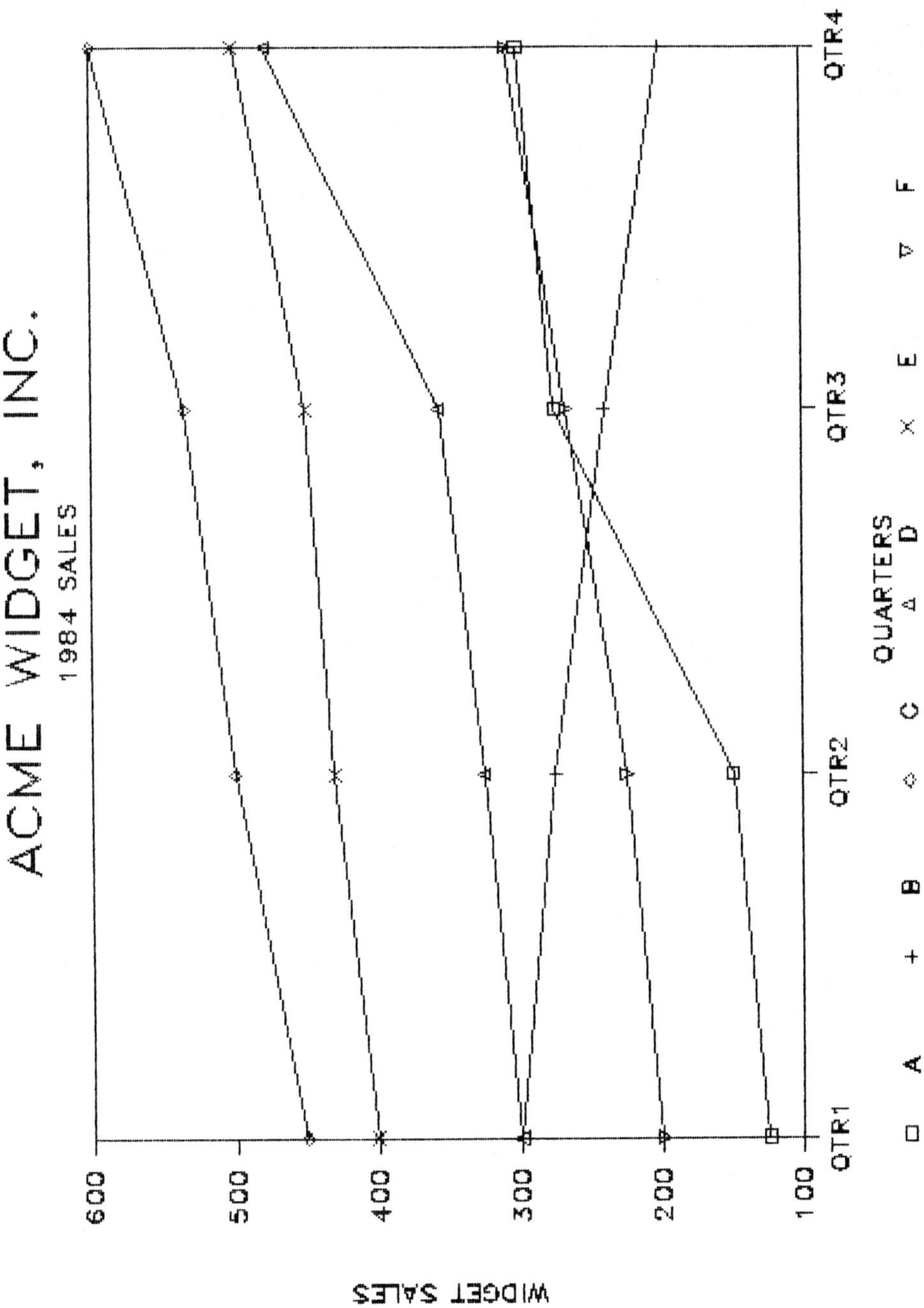
ACME WIDGET, INC.
1984 SALES
WIDGET SALES
600
500
400
300
200
100
QTR1
QTR2
QTR3
QTR4
QUARTERS
A
B
C
D
E
F

Figure 20.5

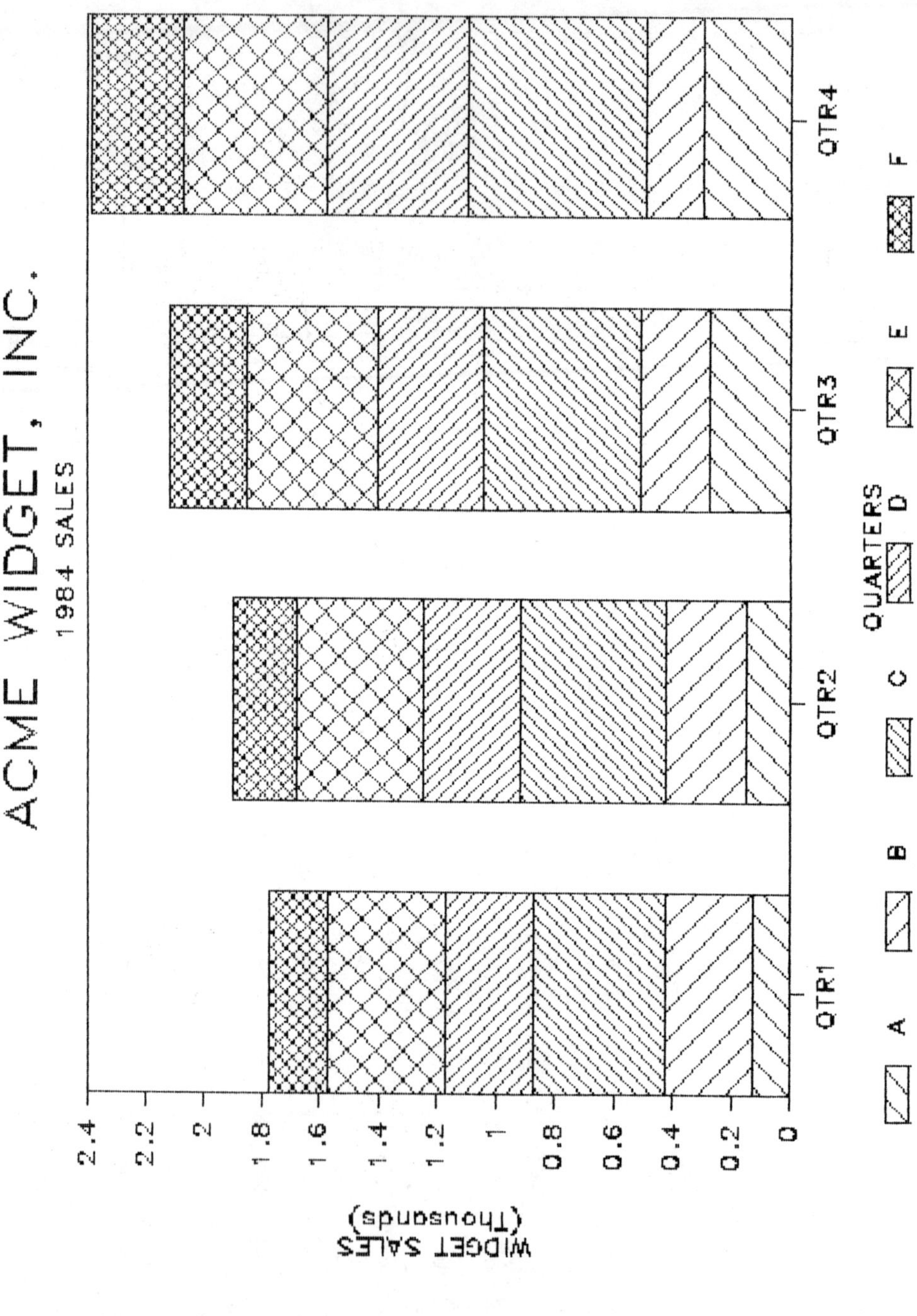
ACME WIDGET, INC.
1984 SALES
WIDGET SALES
(Thousands)
2.4
2.2
2
1.8
1.6
1.4
1.2
1
0.8
0.6
0.4
0.2
0
QTR1
QTR2
QTR3
QTR4
QUARTERS
A
B
C
D
E
F

Figure 20.6

negative value from the other values—the result would probably not be what you want. If you are graphing negative numbers, use a bar graph or a line graph instead.

Pie Chart

A pie chart is useful if you want to compare sales for a particular quarter. A pie chart uses only two ranges: the X-range and the A-range.

The X-range contains the titles for each part of the pie. Since the X-range contains titles, it typically references a cell range containing labels. In this case, the X-range references the range A6..A11, which contains the labels Widget A, Widget B, and so on.

The A-range contains the values to be used to generate the pie slices. 1-2-3 automatically (a) sums the values in the A-range, (b) computes the percentage of the value in each cell, as a percent of the total, and (c) displays the pie slices and the percentages. Figure 20.7 is an illustration of a pie chart based on a comparison of first quarter's sales.

You can have an unlimited number of pie slices. However, as you divide the pie into more and more slices, the resulting pie chart will become more and more crowded. The meaning of each of the slices will become less and less clear. In my experience, using up to 6 pie slices will produce a readable pie chart.

BEWARE ***Don't Use a Pie Chart with Negative Numbers***

Like stacked-bar charts, where 1-2-3 is basing the display on a calculated total of values in a cell range, you will get strange results if the values in the A-range contain negative numbers. 1-2-3 will subtract the negative numbers from the positive numbers, to calculate a total, and the pie chart will not display correctly as a result of this.

XY Chart

An XY chart or scatter plot can be used to display a trend. Do you think that Widget A sales correlate with Widget B sales? Are the widgets being sold in the same market, or in different markets? Displaying an XY chart could help you spot such a trend.

Like a pie chart, an XY chart also uses just the X-range and the A-range. However, the meanings of these ranges differ. Whereas the X-range for all other graphs represent *labels*, in the XY chart they represent *values*. An XY chart compares the *values* in the X-range with the *values* in the A-range. An XY chart is illustrated in Figure 20.8. As sales for Widget A increase, you can see that sales for Widget B decrease. Could that mean that Widget A sales is at the expense of Widget B? Perhaps. But before making any rash decisions, look for

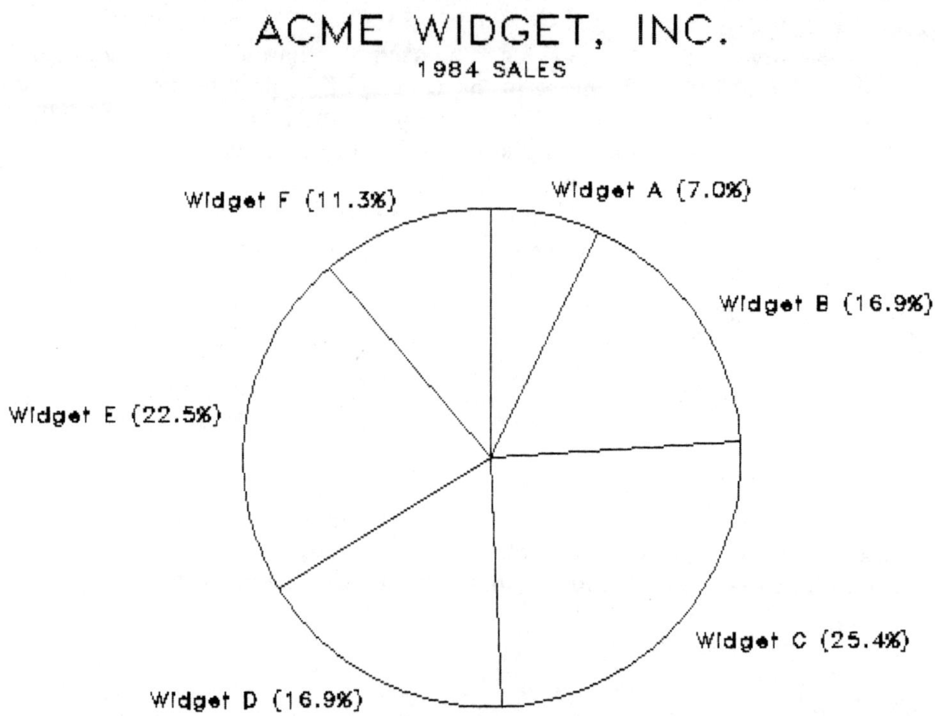
ACME WIDGET, INC.
1984 SALES
Widget F (11.3%)
Widget A (7.0%)
Widget B (16.9%)
Widget E (22.5%)
Widget C (25.4%)
Widget D (16.9%)

Figure 20.7

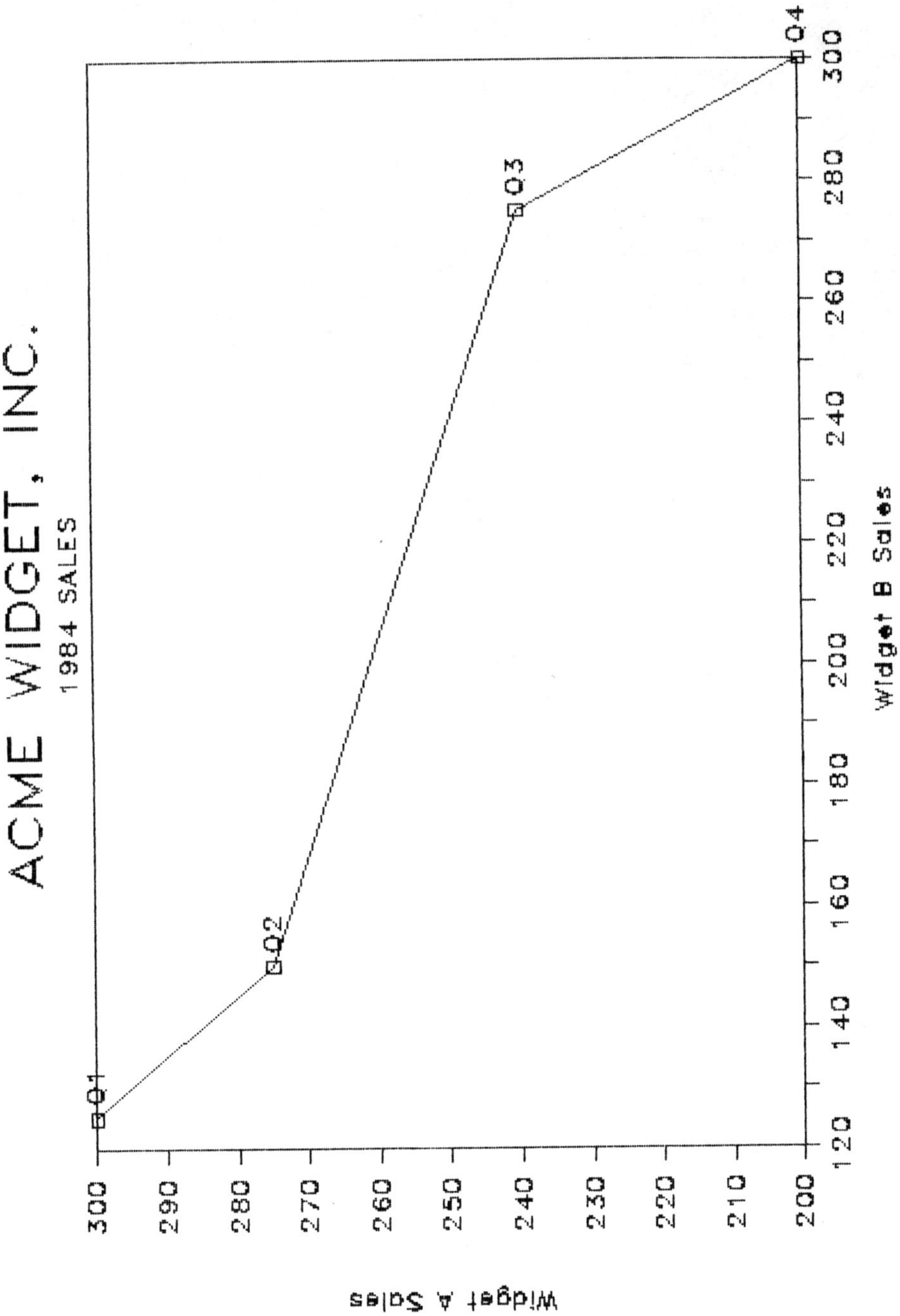
ACME WIDGET, INC.
1984 SALES
Q1
Q2
Q3
Q4
300
290
280
270
260
250
240
230
220
210
200
120
140
160
180
200
220
240
260
280
300
Widget B Sales
Widget A Sales

Figure 20.8

other factors such as decreasing market acceptance or less effective advertising that could have affected the Widget B sales decrease.

FANCY DISPLAY OPTIONS

1-2-3 provides a wealth of options for making the graph display and print meaningfully. You can add titles, legends, and data labels to enhance readablity. Although 1-2-3 automatically scales the axes to the values in the ranges to be graphed, you can define your own scaling and, optionally, the format of the numbers on the scale. If your monitor allows it, you can add color to the graph. You can create a line graph with or without symbols. You can add horizontal and/or vertical grid lines to the graph. Altogether, you can enhance the graph display so that it effectively communicates the meaning of the worksheet data. When you see how to print graphs in the next chapter, you will see that your options are even greater when you print.

This section discusses these options. The keys to be pressed are described assuming that you are at the Graph menu.

Titles

Use Options Titles to add titles to the graph. You can add titles up to 39 characters long. You can specify a separate title for the first line and for the second line. You can also specify a title for the X-axis and the Y-axis. When the titles display, 1-2-3 centers them automatically.

HOW TO: Specify a Cell Reference Containing a Title

Instead of specifying a title directly, you can reference a cell which contains the title by starting the reference with \. For example, by specifying \A15 as the title, 1-2-3 uses the contents of Cell A15 as the title. You can also use named ranges. If you create a range name called TITLE, whose top-right corner is at Cell A15, by specifying \TITLE, 1-2-3 takes the title from Cell A15. If you change the contents of Cell A15, you automatically change the title. You can use this technique for any of the four title options—the first line, the second line, the X-axis, or the Y-axis.

When you reference a cell, 1-2-3 centers the title just as it would if you enter the title directly, ignoring the label-prefix. So a label will display the same, regardless of whether it is stored as a left-aligned, centered, or right-aligned label.

BEWARE ***Unless You Use Range Names, the Cell Reference May Not Adjust***

This cell reference is not relocated as a result of a /Move or a /Worksheet Insert or a /Worksheet Delete. For example, if you insert a row at Row 14, the contents of Cell A15 will relocate to Cell A16. However, the title will still reference Cell A15. So be careful.

If you use a range name, 1-2-3 adjusts the reference if you move, insert or delete. Here is yet another example of the benefits of using cell ranges.

Legends

Use Options Legend to add legends to your graph. A legend pairs a label of up to 19 characters to a particular symbol for a line or XY graph, a cross-hatching for bar graphs or stacked-bar graphs without color variations, or color for bar graphs or stacked-bar graphs with color. The labels associated with the legend display in a row below the graph itself.

You can specify a cell or a named range to contain the legend label. Since the same BEWARE applies here as with titles, use a range name to avoid losing the legend when you change the worksheet around.

BEWARE ***Make the Legends Short to Fit in the Row***

The row must fit not only the label, but also the symbol or cross-hatching or color associated with the label. If you define six legends for a bar graph, for example, each legend must be only one character long for it to fit entirely in the row. If you have fewer ranges in your graph, your legends can, of course, be larger.

Data Labels

Use Options Data-labels to add data labels to your graph. Data labels are labels which 1-2-3 places above positive bars and below negative bars for bar graphs and stacked-bar charts, or to the left, right, above, below, or centered relative to the data points for line graphs and XY graphs. Data-labels are not used for pie charts. This is another aid to clarifying the meaning of the graph.

Like legends, data labels must be short. In fact, for most graphs, data labels over two characters long will probably make the graph unreadable because the data label will either overflow into the next data label, or obscure the data points, or both.

Controlling the Scaling

Use Options Scale to control scaling of the X-axis and/or Y-axis. 1-2-3 automatically scales the axes based on data values. However, you might like to define different scales, perhaps because you want to either accentuate or level the peaks and valleys of a line graph. For line graphs, bar graphs, and stacked-bar charts, only the Y-axis can be scaled. For XY graphs, both the X-axis and the Y-axis can be scaled. For pie charts, scaling is ignored.

To specify your own scaling, first specify Options Scale Manual to make

1-2-3 forget about automatic scaling. Then, specify an Upper limit and a Lower limit. You can also optionally use Format to format the numbers on the scale. Your options are identical to /Range Format for formatting numbers.

For bar graphs and Stacked-bar graphs, 1-2-3 ignores a positive lower limit or a negative upper limit on the Y-axis to ensure that the scale includes a 0. This ensures that 1-2-3 can draw the bars from the origin.

If you have specified manual scaling and want 1-2-3 to return to automatic scaling, use Options Scale Automatic.

You may find that your X-axis labels overflow into each other. Again, this can easily happen if your labels are too long. You can use Options Scale Skip to have 1-2-3 skip display of some labels. For example, if you tell 1-2-3 a skip value of 2, 1-2-3 displays every other label. This may cure the label overflow problem.

Color vs. Black-and-White Display

With black-and-white display, the graph ranges display (for bar graphs and stacked-bar charts) with different cross-hatchings. If you have a color monitor, use Options Color to activate color display. The colors display as follows:

A-range WHITE	B-range RED	C-range BLUE
D-range WHITE	E-range RED	F-range BLUE

You have no choice of colors for these ranges. This is a curious oversight, since the PC color monitor supports 8 colors. The only type of graph where you can make any change is a bar graph. Here, 1-2-3 does not display colors for undefined ranges. Therefore, if you were comparing two ranges and wanted both to display in blue, you could define the first range as the C-range and the second as the F-range. The spacing between the bars, in this case, would be wider than if adjacent ranges were used.

If you have a color printer or plotter which is supported by 1-2-3, your choice of colors is much more extensive. The colors in which you print graphs are independent of the colors in which you display them. And you can choose your color.

To return to black-and-white graphics display, use Options B&W.

Using Symbols with Line Graphs

With Options Format, you can display a line graph or XY graph with symbols only, symbols with lines connecting the symbols together, both, or neither. If you use neither, you must define data-labels, using Options Data-labels, that will be displayed on the graph. In this way, you can define a graph consisting of points, or of lines, or of points connected by lines.

Adding Horizontal and/or Vertical Grid Lines

With Options Grid, you can define horizontal and/or vertical grid lines. This option is available for all graph types except pie charts. Grids are useful in cases where the exact location of the bars or data points is unclear. When you display the graph with grids, the grids provide the coordinates, making the graph easier to read.

VIEWING THE GRAPH

Once you have added these display options to the graph, you are ready to display it. There are two ways to display it.

1. From the /Graph Menu. If you want to stay in the /Graph menu, you can useView to display the graph. In this way, you can modify the graph settings without having to re-enter the /Graph menu.

2. From READY *Mode.* If you are in the worksheet and you press [F10/GRAPH], you redisplay the graph. This is useful for "what-if" graphics. You change a number in one of the graph ranges and press [F10/GRAPH] to redisplay the graph. The operation of [F10/GRAPH] is similar to [F8/TABLE]: in both cases, the command does not have to be respecified after the worksheet is changed. Simply press a function key.

If you are using a graphics monitor, the graph *replaces* the worksheet. 1-2-3 remembers the worksheet contents; it just doesn't display them. If you are using both the monochrome monitor and a graphics monitor, the graph displays on the graphics monitor while the worksheet remains on the monochrome monitor. You cannot display more than one graph at a time in 1-2-3.

NAMING GRAPH SETTINGS

You can create names for graph settings that you define. 1-2-3 will associate these settings with a name. From the /Graph menu, use Name Create to create a name for your graph settings.

1-2-3 does not remember the graph itself; it remembers the commands that you used to create the graph. You can, in fact, create as many graph names, within the limits of 1-2-3's memory, as you wish. For example, suppose you want to create a pie chart, a stacked-bar chart, an XY chart, and two bar charts from the same worksheet information. It does not matter that the titles, data ranges, legends, or everything else, differs with each graph. Simply create a different graph name for each set of commands which produce the graph.

When you save the file using /File Save 1-2-3 saves the graph names associated with the worksheet, as well as any unnamed graph settings. When you retrieve the worksheet using /File Retrieve, and press [F10/GRAPH], 1-2-3 displays the graph according to the settings when the worksheet was previously saved. If you have named a set of graph settings, you can use /Graph Name Use to make these settings current. In this way, you do not have to reenter the graph specifications.

HOW TO: Create a Graphics Slide Show

If you want to display several graphs which are derived from the same worksheet as a slide show, do the following:

Create graph names for each graph. After you have displayed each graph to your liking, use /Graph Name Create to save these settings. Create meaningful names.

Save the worksheet to a file. Use /File Save to save the worksheet file, and the graph names associated with it.

To run the show, retrieve the file, and use /Graph Name Use. With /Graph Name Use, 1-2-3 recalls graph settings. Press [F10/GRAPH] to display the graph. When you are ready to display the next graph, use the next graph name and display the graph based on those settings.

As with range names, you can delete a particular graph name, or you can reset all graph names.

BEWARE *Graph Name Reset Resets All Graph Names, Without Warning*

Unfortunately, this BEWARE is similar to the problem with /Range Name Reset. 1-2-3 gives you no warning when it resets graph names. It simply resets them. You also cannot restore the old settings unless you have saved the worksheet with the graph names earlier.

RESETTING RANGES

You can reset all graph settings from the /Graph menu with Reset Graph. You can also cancel individual graph ranges (the X-, A-, B-, C-, D-, E-, and F-ranges) with Reset. When you reset a graph range, legends and formats associated with that range are still remembered. They are not used, however, until you respecify the range. This is a handy convenience when you are defining multiple graphs.

SAVING GRAPHS FOR PRINTING

To save a graph so that you can use PrintGraph, use Save. 1-2-3 creates a .PIC file. You can list all .PIC files in your directory using /File List Graph. You can also erase some or all graph picture files in your directory by using /File Erase Graph. As with worksheet files and print files, you can manage graph picture files from within 1-2-3.

Having learned how to define and display the graph, you are ready to learn how to print graphs. This is the subject of the next chapter.

CHAPTER 21

Printing Graphs

After reading the last chapter, you should be convinced that 1-2-3 offers a wide variety of graphics display options. When you print a graph, you have even greater flexibility!

After you have used the **/Graph Save** command to create your graph picture (.PIC) files, you can use the programs and data on the PrintGraph disk to print the graph based on these files. To run the PrintGraph program, either (a) type **GRAPH[ENTER]** at the A> prompt, or (b) select **Graph** from the Lotus Access System. Your options are as follows:

```
Select Options Go Configure Align Page Quit
```

The PrintGraph menus operate like the other Lotus Access System menus (such as the File-Manager or Disk-Manager menus). If you need additional information for an option, you can press **[F1/HELP]**. You select from the menu choices by either typing the first letter of the choice, or positioning using **[LEFT]**, **[RIGHT]**, **[HOME]**, and **[END]**, and pressing **[ENTER]** when the choice is highlighted. If you are selecting from a list such as a list of printers or a list of .PIC files to print, you can use **[DOWN]**, **[UP]**, **[HOME]**, and **[END]** to position to the selection, and then press **[SPACE]** to select the choice. When you print graphs, you can:

- Print many graphs at once
- Preview (display) a graph before you print it
- Print many graphs on a page by controlling the margins
- Print on any size paper
- Control the placement of the X-axis and Y-axis
- If your printer or plotter permits, print in color
- Print two title lines with one of eight fonts
- Control pausing, page ejecting, and alignment of the printer

You also can easily configure PrintGraph to support different printers or plotters. In fact, your choice of printer is the main criterion determining the quality of the printout. This chapter first discusses configuring PrintGraph for your printer or plotter, and then the options you can control when you actually print graphs.

CONFIGURING PRINTGRAPH

From the main PrintGraph menu, select **Configure** to start the configuring process. Your options are as follows:

```
File Device Page Interface Save Reset Quit
```

Here is another sticky menu. You do not leave this menu unless you select Quit, or press [ESC] for a quick exit. This section discusses PrintGraph configuration options.

Locating Picture and Font Files

If you select File, you can control the location of the graph picture (.PIC) files and the font (.FON) files. PrintGraph assumes that the .PIC files are stored in the current directory in the disk on the B-drive, and that the font files, which contain fonts to print text on the graph in fancy style, are stored in the disk on the A-drive. If your disk configuration is different, and/or your .PIC or .FON files are in different directories, you can change them here.

Selecting the Printer or Plotter Device

If you select Device, you select the printer or plotter which you are going to use to print the graph. PrintGraph uses this in deciding what choices you have. For example, if your printer does not print in color, you will not be able to choose any color except black. As Henry Ford once said about the Model T, "you can choose any color, so long as it is black".

New printers and plotters which can print 1-2-3 graphs are constantly being added. Make sure your printer is on the list, and select it. You select it by using the arrow keys to point to the selection, and pressing [SPACE]. A number-sign (#) will display next to your selection. Pressing [SPACE] again removes the number sign, letting you choose another device.

You'll notice that, for certain printers, you have a choice of single density, double density, or quad density. The higher the density, the better the print quality of the graph. A graph printed in quad density mode will print out much more precisely than a graph printed in single density mode. The problem, though, is that quad density printouts print out approximately four times slower than single density printouts. So in return for better quality printouts, you must wait. If you have a printer or plotter with density options, you should experiment and see whether the finer quality printout is worth the extra time.

PrintGraph initially assumes that you are using the Epson FX-80 printer in single density mode.

Controlling the Page Size

By selecting Page, you can control the page size. PrintGraph assumes a page length of 11 inches and a page width of 8 inches. If your graphs print on this standard size paper, don't change the page size. Otherwise, change the page size, specifying the number of inches of page length and width.

Changing the Interface

By selecting Interface, you can change the location of the attachment of the printer or plotter device to the PC. PrintGraph assumes that your printer is attached through the first parallel port on your PC. This is, in fact, how most printers are attached. You can attach the device through a serial port, a second parallel port, or a second serial port, and still have PrintGraph access it. If you are attaching your printer through one of these other interface, you must tell PrintGraph about it.

Saving the Configuration

By selecting Save, you save the configuration to the configuration file. PrintGraph accesses this file every time you run the program. If you have made a permanent change to your configuration, such as changing the printer device or the interface, you should save the configuration. If, however, the change is only temporary (perhaps you borrowed a plotter just to print graphs for this session), don't save the configuration.

The configuration file for PrintGraph is different than the configuration file for 1-2-3, where you also can change printer defaults. If you change the page length for PrintGraph, for example, you are not changing the page length for printing your worksheet.

Resetting the Configuration

If you press Reset, you restore the configuration to a previous version. If you have not saved a configuration in this session, Reset restores the configuration to its state when PrintGraph started. On the other hand, if you have saved a configuration in this session, Reset restores the configuration to the state it was in the last time you saved it, cancelling any changes you may have made after that time. Resetting is a graceful way of having PrintGraph forget configuration changes.

PRINTING YOUR GRAPHS

Once the configuration has been defined—and you must make sure it corresponds to your actual hardware configuration—you are ready to start printing graphs.

Selecting the .PIC Files

If you press Select, you can select any or all of the graph picture files which are in the directory to print. After you have chosen the files, their names and your configuration display in the status area of the screen. You can therefore always see what your current PrintGraph settings are, and you can change them if required.

A nice feature is that, before you select a .PIC file, you can preview it. In that way, if the graph is not to your liking, you can save the time of actually printing it, return to 1-2-3, change the graph settings, save to a new .PIC file, and re-enter PrintGraph. If you press [F10/GRAPH], a preview of how the graph will print displays on your graphics monitor. Of course, if you have a monochrome monitor only, you cannot preview the graph. You'll notice that the previewed graph displays differently from the graph display from 1-2-3. That's because the *printed* graph is of better quality than 1-2-3's *displayed* graph. For example, the PrintGraph can print graph titles using eight fonts—a capability unavailable with 1-2-3's display graphics.

Fancy-Print Options

By selecting Options, you can select from the following options:

```
Color Font Size Pause Eject Quit
```

Using these options intelligently will enhance the printout considerably.

Color

If your printer or plotter permits, you can add colors to your graph by selecting the Color option. PrintGraph figures out, from your device specification, the colors which you can use. You can change the color for the grid (the lines on the graph), and for the A- through F-ranges. Your six ranges can print in six different colors, highlighted by a grid which prints in a seventh color!

Fonts

To print your titles and legends using fonts, select the Font option. You can use Block, Roman, Italic, and Script fonts. Each font can be printed in normal or bold. Thus, you have a choice of eight fonts.

For each graph, you can select a separate font for the main title, called Font 1, and for the other titles and legends, called Font 2. Your current font selections display in the status area.

Graph Size

Based on the page size in the configuration, you can print the graph on the entire page, on half of the page, or on that part of the page that you define.

If you select Size Full, PrintGraph prints the graph horizontally on the full page. If you select Size Half, PrintGraph prints the graph vertically on half of the page. (PrintGraph is installed with Size Half as the default.)

If you want to control placement of the graph, you can select Size Manual.

Specify the height, width, left, and top margins in inches. Since you control these specifications, you can place the graph anywhere on the page. You can place as many graphs as you wish on the page, as well. Since you are controlling the margins, don't expect to get it right the first time. Experiment until the graph prints as you want it to.

In addition to specifying the margins, you can use Size Manual Rotation to specify the rotation of the axes or of the pie, if you are printing a pie chart. Specify the number of degrees to rotate the axes. Zero-degree rotation prints the graph vertically; ninety-degree rotation prints the graph horizontally.

Pausing Between Printing Graphs

By selecting Options Pause, you can control whether or not PrintGraph pauses between printing graphs. You may need to change paper, switch settings on a printer, or change pens on a plotter, between each graph. Initially, PrintGraph assumes you do not want to pause between printing each graph. If you want PrintGraph to pause, select Options Pause Yes.

Controlling Page Eject Between Graphs

By selecting Options Eject, you can control whether or not PrintGraph automatically advances to the next page after printing a graph. This is useful if your graphs are to print on separate pages, even if they do not occupy an entire page. Selecting Yes causes PrintGraph to advance to the next page after printing a graph; selecting No does not cause PrintGraph to advance to the next page. PrintGraph initially assumes no automatic page eject. Controlling Printer Alignment and Page Eject

The Align and Page options operate like /Print Printer Align and /Print Printer Page in 1-2-3. Align causes PrintGraph and your printer to agree on the position of the top of the page and is used most commonly when you interrupt printing a graph (by pressing [CTRL]-[BREAK]) and want to reestablish true top of page. Page is used to cause the printer to advance to the next page, starting the printing on a new sheet of paper.

Printing the Graphs

After you have configured PrintGraph to agree with your configuration, specified the graphs to print and the options for printing them, you can print the graph(s) by selecting Go. If you have specified printing more than one graph, the graphs will print as a group according to the options specified. If you want to stop the printing, press [CTRL]-[BREAK].

You now should be able to display bar graphs, stacked-bar charts, line graphs, pie charts, and XY graphs in 1-2-3. After you have displayed them, you should be able to save the graphs using /Graph Save, and to use PrintGraph to print the graphs. Experiment with 1-2-3 graphics. You'll find them quite versatile and powerful.

PART VI

Database Management

WHAT IS A DATABASE?

Like graphics, 1-2-3 databases are derived from the worksheet. A database is contained in a cell range of multiple rows and columns.

What can you store in a database? Almost any information which you are keeping track of with pencil and paper can probably be stored in a database. You might, for example, keep a list of frequently called customer names, addresses, and telephone numbers in a file of index cards or a Rolodex; or, you might record checks as you write them in your checkbook ledger. In fact, any information for which you are keeping a list with pencil and paper is a candidate for a 1-2-3 database.

Let's see how you might store your checks in a 1-2-3 database. The idea behind database management in 1-2-3 is simple yet powerful. A database is stored in a cell range (a group of rows and columns) in the worksheet. As with 1-2-3 graphics, 1-2-3 database information is stored directly in the spreadsheet.

Why is this simple? Below is a database of checks:

	A	B	C	D	E
4	NUMBER	TO	AMOUNT	DATE WRITTEN	ACCOUNT
5	101	New England Bell	$22.79	25-Apr-83	Telephone
6	102	Northwest Electric	$51.67	26-Apr-83	Electric
7	103	IBM PC Expo	$105.23	01-May-83	Travel and Seminar
8	104	Universal Airways	$305.86	03-May-83	Travel and Seminar
9	105	Compu Software	$500.00	05-May-83	Computer Software
10	106	New England Bell	$23.81	25-May-83	Telephone
11	107	Northwest Electric	$61.99	26-May-83	Electric

Figure VI.1

The database of checks is in the range A4..E11. For each check, you keep track of certain items: the check number, to whom you wrote the check, the amount, the date written, and the account. In 1-2-3, you would store this information in individual *columns*. You would give each column a meaningful label such as NUMBER, TO, AMOUNT, DATE WRITTEN, and ACCOUNT. Each label is called a *field*. The field names are stored in the first row of the database, Row 4.

Information about each particular check would be stored in a particular *row*. The entry for check number 101, written to New England Bell, for $22.79, on April 25, 1983, for the telephone bill, would occupy Row 5. The entry for check number 102, the next check written, would occupy Row 6. Each additional check would occupy the row beneath the last check entry. Each row contains information for a *record* of the database.

The cell range which contains the column definitions on the top row and all the entries for the checks in their individual rows, would constitute the database of checks.

Why go to all this trouble? Once you have organized your checks into a database, you can answer all kinds of questions related to them. These questions are difficult, if not impossible to answer, if the information is entered on index cards or ledger sheets. Examples of questions one could ask are:

- Can I rearrange (sort) all the checks according to who they were written to?
- Can I total all checks written in July, 1983?
- How much did I pay to New England Bell in 1983?
- How many checks did I write in May?

Virtually any type of rearrangement or question (query) can be answered once the information is stored in a 1-2-3 database.

CHANGING DATABASE INFORMATION

If you understand how to change the worksheet, you know how to change information in the database. The following are the most common changes:

Adding a record. If you want to add a record (you have written another check) and want to record this information in the database, add the data in the empty row immediately below the last entry. If you are not adding a record at the end of the database but want to make room for it in the middle of the database, use /Worksheet Insert Row to create an empty row, and add the information there.

Changing a record. To change a record, go to the row containing the information and change it. You are simply changing the data in a cell; the same rules apply.

Deleting a record. To delete a record, use /Worksheet Delete Row. The row is deleted from the database range, and the range shrinks by one row.

Adding a field. To add a field, use /Worksheet Insert Column. A column will be inserted, and the database range will expand. Then, add the field heading and the values for each record. For example, if you want to store ACCOUNT NAME as a field, insert the column, add the label ACCOUNT NAME to the top cell of the column, and add the account names to the individual checks.

Deleting a field. To delete a field, use /Worksheet Delete Column. This will get rid of a field and shrink the database range. For example, if you decided later that you didn't want to store the ACCOUNT NAME field for each check, delete the column, and the database range will automatically shrink.

Database Commands

Once you have organized the information in the database, you can use the /Data Sort and /Data Query commands to rearrange and ask questions of the database; and you can use the database statistical functions to produce statistical summaries based on the database. Chapter 22 will cover /Data Sort; Chapter 23 will cover /Data Query and the database statistical functions. You will discover that, simple as it is to construct, you can ask virtually any question you can conceive of and construct a worksheet to get the right answer from 1-2-3.

CHAPTER 22

Sorting the Database

WHAT SORTING IS

Sorting is another name for rearranging the records. Below is a database of names and addresses of employees of Acme Widget.

	A	B	C	D	E	F
1			ACME WIDGET, INC.			
2			SALES EMPLOYEES			
3						
4	EMPLOYEE	SALARY	STATE	SALES	DATE-HIRED	
5	Smith	$25,000	MA	$95,000	05-Aug-82	
6	Brown	$30,000	MA	$150,000	05-Jan-83	
7	Warren	$35,000	MA	$210,000	01-Jun-83	
8	Wheatley	$15,000	NH	$125,000	05-Nov-82	
9	White	$40,000	NH	$237,100	03-Mar-83	
10						

Figure 22.1

Use /Data Sort to rearrange the database records in A5..E9. Suppose you wanted to rearrange the database in order by state: all the employees in Massachusetts before all the employees in New Hampshire. You would perform the following steps:

Step 1. Use /Data Sort. /Data Sort invokes a menu which contains the following options:

```
Data-range Primary-key Secondary-key Reset Go Quit
```

Since sorting involves specifying more than one option, the /Data Sort menu is another sticky menu.

Step 2. Specify the sort data range.Use Data-range. The data range for sorting *excludes* the top row (the field definitions). 1-2-3 sorts *only* the records, not the field definitions. The sort data range is illustrated below:

	A	B	C	D	E	F
1			ACME WIDGET, INC.			
2			SALES EMPLOYEES			
3						
4	EMPLOYEE	SALARY	STATE	SALES	DATE-HIRED	
5	Smith	$25,000	MA	$95,000	05-Aug-82	
6	Brown	$30,000	MA	$150,000	05-Jan-83	
7	Warren	$35,000	MA	$210,000	01-Jun-83	
8	Wheatley	$15,000	NH	$125,000	05-Nov-82	
9	White	$40,000	NH	$237,100	03-Mar-83	
10						

Figure 22.2 The Sort Data Range

In addition to excluding the top row of field definitions, specify *only* the records to be sorted. Do not include any blank rows because they will be sorted along with the rows containing actual records.

Step 3. Specify a primary key column, and whether to sort in ascending or descending order. Use **Primary-key**. The primary key identifies a column, Column C, which contains the entries for STATE, on which to sort the records. You can rearrange the records based on ascending (increasing) or descending (decreasing) values in the column. Any cell within the column will do—1-2-3 ignores the row reference, using the column reference as the primary key.

Step 4. Do the sort. Use **Go**. The records will be rearranged in increasing order by state. You'll find that the sort is extremely quick, since it's done in RAM.

BEWARE *The Sort Order May Not Be What You Intended*

The rules for the order of sorting are somewhat complicated and may not correspond to how the records display. Keep in mind these rules:

All labels are sorted before all values. The *label* "123 (which starts with a right-aligned label-prefix character) sorts before the *value* 123, even though both display as if they were the same.

Labels are sorted from left to right, one character at a time, according to the ASCII collating sequence. The ordering is as follows:

1. a blank
2. special characters (such as # or !)
3. a number
4. an uppercase letter
5. a lowercase letter

Thus " SALES" sorts before "SALES" (because the first character, a blank, sorts before the S). Consider the following example:

"123"	(a number in a label)
"SALES"	(a label)
123	(a value)

Since all labels sort before all values, "123" and "SALES" sort before 123. Within the sorting of labels, "123" sorts before "SALES" because 1 (a number) sorts before S (an uppercase letter). If the data-range contains blank rows, they sort before everything else, since blanks sort before everything else. If the column contains only values, the sort will be performed in the order of the values. This is the easiest case. If the sort order wasn't what you expected, look for either blanks, or cells which display as values but which in fact are labels, to be the culprits.

Since 1-2-3 stores dates as values, dates entered using @DATE will sort correctly. You can sort this database by DATE-HIRED, for example.

BEWARE *Cells Containing Formulas Outside the Sort Range May Not Adjust Properly*

If the sort range contains formula cells which reference cells outside the range, the sorting will adjust the formula references. If those references are relative references, be prepared for surprises! The formulas will be adjusted relative to their new position in the database. If the references are absolute, however, the formulas do not adjust and the sort will probably proceed as you intended.

BEWARE *The Original Order Cannot Be Recovered*

Because of these BEWAREs, it's likely that the records did not sort as you intended, and the original order cannot be recovered. If you saved the file before you did the sort, you can use /File Retrieve to restore the original database.

Here is a HOW TO that can help avoid this problem.

HOW TO: Construct a Database That Can Be Restored

Before you sort the database, you can add a column called RECORD NO. (use /Worksheet Insert Column) which contains the record number. Use /Data Fill to fill in this number. The database would display as shown in Figure 22.3.

After you use /Data Sort, expanding the data range to include the RECORD NO. column and sorting in descending order of sales, the database displays with the RECORD NO. column displaying the order, as shown in Figure 22.4. If the sort turned out incorrect, you could restore the database to its original order simply by sorting on the RECORD NO. column, in ascending order.

	A	B	C	D	E	F
1			ACME WIDGET, INC.			
2			SALES EMPLOYEES			
3						
4	EMPLOYEE	SALARY	STATE	SALES	DATE-HIRED	RECORD NO.
5	Smith	$25,000	MA	$95,000	05-Aug-82	1
6	Brown	$30,000	MA	$150,000	05-Jan-83	2
7	Warren	$35,000	MA	$210,000	01-Jun-83	3
8	Wheatley	$15,000	NH	$125,000	05-Nov-82	4
9	White	$40,000	NH	$237,100	03-Mar-83	5
10						

Figure 22.3

	A	B	C	D	E	F
1			ACME WIDGET, INC.			
2			SALES EMPLOYEES			
3						
4	EMPLOYEE	SALARY	STATE	SALES	DATE-HIRED	RECORD NO.
5	White	$40,000	NH	$237,100	03-Mar-83	5
6	Warren	$35,000	MA	$210,000	01-Jun-83	3
7	Brown	$30,000	MA	$150,000	05-Jan-83	2
8	Wheatley	$15,000	NH	$125,000	05-Nov-82	4
9	Smith	$25,000	MA	$95,000	05-Aug-82	1
10						

Figure 22.4

Perhaps the salespeople are competing for a bonus for high producers. You could *rank* the salespeople by their sales performance. After you have sorted the records, use /Data Fill to fill the RECORD NO. column with consecutive numbers, starting at 1. RECORD NO. would then record the salespeople's rank.

DEFINING A SECONDARY KEY IN CASE OF TIES

If you select Secondary-key, you tell 1-2-3 what to do in case of ties. For example, you could sort the database by STATE, and for all employees within the state, sort in increasing order by DATE-HIRED, by specifying the DATE-HIRED column as the *secondary key*. Type the following:

/DSDA5..E9[ENTER]	Specify the sort data range
PC5[ENTER]A[ENTER]	Primary key of state (ascending)
SE5[ENTER]A[ENTER]	Secondary key date hired (ascending)
G	Do the sort

The database would sort as follows:

	A	B	C	D	E	F
1			ACME WIDGET, INC.			
2			SALES EMPLOYEES			
3						
4	EMPLOYEE	SALARY	STATE	SALES	DATE-HIRED	
5	Smith	$25,000	MA	$95,000	05-Aug-82	
6	Brown	$30,000	MA	$150,000	05-Jan-83	
7	Warren	$35,000	MA	$210,000	01-Jun-83	
8	Wheatley	$15,000	NH	$125,000	05-Nov-82	
9	White	$40,000	NH	$237,100	03-Mar-83	
10						

Figure 22.5

REMEMBERING AND FORGETTING SORT SPECIFICATIONS

If you save the file, 1-2-3 will remember the sort specifications: data-range, primary key, and secondary key. After you retrieve the file, simply use /Data Sort Go to re-do the sort.

On the other hand, if you want 1-2-3 to forget all sort specifications, use /Data Sort Reset.

Practice a bit with /Data Sort. Find a list that you have always been meaning to organize, enter the list in a 1-2-3 database, and sort the records by columns which are meaningful to you. Try sorting labels and values until you feel comfortable with 1-2-3 sorting rules. Once you are comfortable with them, you're ready to proceed to the next chapter, where you'll learn all about /Data Query.

CHAPTER 23

Asking Questions of the Database

In addition to sorting database records, you can ask questions of the database. This chapter deals with the /Data Query commands, which let you ask questions of the 1-2-3 database.

THE /DATA QUERY MENU

The /Data Query menu gives you the following options.

```
Input Criterion Output Find Extract Unique Delete Reset
Quit
```

The first three options (`Input`, `Criterion`, and `Output`) are separate parts of the worksheet which are needed by the other /Data Query operations. To take full advantage of /Data Query, you must define all three ranges.

The next five options (`Find`, `Extract`, `Unique`, `Delete`, and `Reset`) define the types of database operations you can do. The options are as follows:

`Find` Highlight records in the input range, based on the criteria specified in the criterion range.

`Extract` Copy records from the input range, based on the criteria specified in the criterion range, to the output range.

`Unique` As Extract, except that duplicate records in the input range are not copied to the output range.

`Delete` Removes records from the input range, based on the criteria specified in the criterion range.

`Reset` Causes 1-2-3 to forget all /Data Query ranges.

Finally, since /Data Query is another sticky menu, in which several options must be specified. There is a Quit option, to end database query functions.

An understanding of the three ranges is necessary before discussing the query functions.

THE THREE RANGES

The three ranges (input, criterion, and output) are defined in separate parts of the worksheet. As with the other 1-2-3 cell ranges, they must fit into the active worksheet, the size of which is determined by your computer's memory.

The Input Range

The database itself is stored in the input range. From the menu, you specify the input range using Input. The input range contains both the headings, one column for each field, and the database records, one row for each record. The input range is the database illustrated in Figure 23.1, in the range A4..E9.

	A	B	C	D	E	F
1			ACME WIDGET, INC.			
2			SALES EMPLOYEES			
3						
4	EMPLOYEE	SALARY	STATE	SALES	DATE-HIRED	
5	Smith	$25,000	MA	$95,000	05-Aug-82	
6	Brown	$30,000	MA	$150,000	05-Jan-83	
7	Warren	$35,000	MA	$210,000	01-Jun-83	
8	Wheatley	$15,000	NH	$125,000	05-Nov-82	
9	White	$40,000	NH	$237,100	03-Mar-83	
10						

Figure 23.1. The Input Range.

The Criterion Range

The criterion range defines the criteria by which records in the input ranges are to be processed. The criterion range must be separate from the input range. From the menu, you specify the criterion range using Criterion.

The first row of the criterion range contains headings, which are copies of the headings in the first row of the input range. Up to 32 headings can be defined in the criterion range. Depending on the type of query, the criterion range can contain many rows. The minimum number of rows in a criterion range is 2. Figure 23.2 shows the criterion range, which is set up to select all employees who live in New Hampshire (STATE=NH).

Criteria can become very complicated, as you will see later in this chapter.

The Output Range

The output range is yet another range, separate from the input and criterion ranges. The output range is the area into which records are copied from the input range, if you use Extract or Unique.

Like the criterion range, the first row of the output range consists of labels which are copied from the input range. Unlike the criterion range, you can include as many labels as exist in the input range. To define the output range, select Output from the menu.

To extract the name and date-hired for all employees who live in New Hampshire, set up the output range as shown in Figure 23.3.

	A	B	C	D	E	F
1			ACME WIDGET, INC.			
2			SALES EMPLOYEES			
3						
4	EMPLOYEE	SALARY	STATE	SALES	DATE-HIRED	
5	Smith	$25,000	MA	$95,000	05-Aug-82	
6	Brown	$30,000	MA	$150,000	05-Jan-83	
7	Warren	$35,000	MA	$210,000	01-Jun-83	
8	Wheatley	$15,000	NH	$125,000	05-Nov-82	
9	White	$40,000	NH	$237,100	03-Mar-83	
10						
11	STATE					
12	NH					

Figure 23.2. The Criterion Range.

	A	B	C	D	E	F
1			ACME WIDGET, INC.			
2			SALES EMPLOYEES			
3						
4	EMPLOYEE	SALARY	STATE	SALES	DATE-HIRED	
5	Smith	$25,000	MA	$95,000	05-Aug-82	
6	Brown	$30,000	MA	$150,000	05-Jan-83	
7	Warren	$35,000	MA	$210,000	01-Jun-83	
8	Wheatley	$15,000	NH	$125,000	05-Nov-82	
9	White	$40,000	NH	$237,100	03-Mar-83	
10						
11	STATE					
12	NH					
13						
14	EMPLOYEE	DATE-HIRED				

Figure 23.3. The Output Range.

You can specify the output range by either (a) specifying the first row of the range; or (b) specifying all the rows of the range. When you see how Extract and Unique work, later in this chapter, you will see the subtle difference between these two methods.

BEWARE ***The Headings Occupy Only One Row and Must Be Unique***

You cannot define multi-row headings for any of the ranges. Every heading must differ from every other heading.

BEWARE ***Numeric Headings Are Not Allowed***

The headings must be labels—you cannot define numbers, such as the 1984 to stand for a year, as headings. If you do, the /Data Query operations will not work as advertised. If you want 1984 as a heading, it must be entered as the *label* '1984. Of course, this could lead to trouble if this cell is referenced in any formulas.

BEWARE ***The Ranges Should Not Intersect***

The three ranges should occupy different parts of the worksheet. If, for example, the criterion range shares the same part of the worksheet as the output range, you could easily destroy your database criteria as a result of /Data Query command and thus render the /Data Query commands inoperative.

HOW LARGE CAN THE DATABASE BE?

The database is actually the input range. The other ranges are required only when you are doing the database operations. As you have seen, these ranges must be separate from each other.

The 1-2-3 worksheet contains 2,048 rows. Does that mean that you can have 2,047 records, not counting the first row for the headings, in the database? Not really. If your database contained 2,047 records, assuming you had enough memory in your computer to store the information in them, you might not be able to use any of the database operations because there would be no rows left in the database. You could possibly use other columns in the same row, but the likelihood would be that you would not have enough RAM to accommodate all three ranges.

Normally, the criterion range can be small—10 to 20 rows at maximum. You could theoretically use the Find operation, which uses just the input and criterion ranges, on a database of 2,000 records, but none of the other operations would work. You could also use Delete to get rid of records in the input range.

The problem lies in the size of the *output range*. The output range holds all records which satisfy the criterion. And what if all of the records satisfy the criterion? The output range must be as large as the input range. Since you never can be sure of the number of records which satisfy database criteria, to be safe you should make the output range as large as the input range.

If the worksheet contains at most 2,048 rows, and the input range and the output range must be the same size, and you must allow some room for the criterion range, our limit for database records is about 1,000. Even here, you may not have enough memory to accommodate the information in the database! In my experience, a more realistic limit is 500 records—quite enough for most lists you might have in your office, though not realistic for corporate databases, such as inventory or billing records.

THE DATABASE OPERATIONS

Find

After you have specified the input and criterion ranges, you can use Find to highlight records in the input range which match the criteria. Figure 23.3 illustrates the result of Find finding the first record which matches: the first employee who lives in New Hampshire.

While you are finding records, you stay in FIND mode. You can use [DOWN] to find the next matching record, [UP] to find the previous matching record, [LEFT] and [RIGHT] to move the cursor to the left and right within the highlighted record, [HOME] to highlight the first record (which is highlighted even if the record does not match the criteria), and [END] to highlight the last record (which is highlighted even if it does not match the criteria). If you press [ESC], you return to the /Data Query menu.

If no records match the criteria, or if you go too far [UP] or [DOWN], 1-2-3 beeps, indicating an error.

Complex Criteria

The criteria can be very fancy indeed. When you specify label matches, you enter the label under the heading of the criterion range. If you are entering a value, you must reference the first cell of the record under the heading of the database. For example, if to find all salespeople with SALES over $150,000, enter the criteria as follows:

```
              A
11        SALES
12  +D5>150000
```

Figure 23.4

The formula +D5>150000 references the cell containing SALES for the first record (Cell D5). To get the formula in Cell A12 to display, you must format the cell to Text format. The column width must be large enough to accommodate the entire formula. If not, only the part of the formula which can fit in the column will display.

If you want to specify "AND" criteria, where more than one criterion must be met for the record to pass, expand the criterion range. For example, to find all salespeople with SALES over $150,000 and who live in New Hampshire, enter the criteria as follows:

	A	B
11	SALES	STATE
12	+D5>150000	NH

Figure 23.5

This expands the criterion range to two columns, instead of one. Since the criterion range can have up to 32 columns, you can potentially define up to 32 "AND" conditions.

"OR" conditions, where either criterion must be met for the record to pass, are entered in separate rows. For example, to find all salespeople with SALES over $150,000 or who live in New Hampshire, enter the criteria as follows:

	A	B
11	SALES	STATE
12	+D5>150000	
13		NH

Figure 23.6

Note that the criterion range expanded to three rows.

"AND" and "OR" criteria can be combined. To find all salespeople with SALES over $150,000 who live in Massachusetts, OR all salespeople with SALES over $200,000 who live in New Hampshire, enter the criteria as follows:

	A	B
11	SALES	STATE
12	+D5>150000	MA
13	+D5>200000	NH

Figure 23.7

The formulas in criterion ranges can be as complex as you want. You can even use date arithmetic in criterion ranges. To find all employees hired in January, 1983, enter the criteria as follows:

```
        A
11 | DATE-HIRED
12 |+E5>@DATE(83,1,1)
```

Figure 23.8

For label matches, use the following symbols as wildcards:

* matches any character after the label. The criteria illustrated in Figure 23.11 would find all employees beginning with the letter W.

```
        A
11 | EMPLOYEE
12 | W*
```

Figure 23.9

For criterion ranges, label matches must be exact. Uppercase and lowercase matches matter. The above criterion would not find any employee whose name began with the lowercase letter w.

? matches a single character in a label. The following would find employees such as *Brown* and *Braun*, but not *Boniface*.

```
        A
11 | EMPLOYEE
12 | Br??n
```

Figure 23.10

~ (the tilde) means negation in a criterion range. (In the next chapter, you will see another meaning of the tilde.) The criteria illustrated in Figure 23.11 would find all employees whose names do *not* begin with the letter W.

All of these criterion definitions can be combined to ask virtually any imaginable question you choose from the database. Compare that with sorting through 500 index cards, trying to find all employees beginning with the letter

```
          A
11   EMPLOYEE
12   ~W*
```

Figure 23.11

W, who live in New Hampshire, had sales greater than $150,000, and were hired between August 31, 1983 and December 31, 1983!

The [F7/QUERY] Key

1-2-3 remembers the last /Data Query operation. You can redo it by simply pressing [F7/QUERY]. This is excellent for "what-if" database queries. You can do a /Data Query Find, Quit and change the label, and press [F7/QUERY]to find the records which match the criteria. In this respect, using [F7/QUERY] is similar to [F8/TABLE], which repeats the last /Data Table command, and [F10/GRAPH], which repeats the last /Graph command.

HOW TO: Use /Range Name Labels Down in Defining Formulas

If you use /Range Name Labels Down, specifying the database headers, you will be able to enter the formulas using range names, rather than using cell references. Use the command, specifying the range shown in Figure 23.12.
If you do this, you can then specify the criterion match as +SALES>150000, rather than +D5>150000. This makes the formulas easier to understand.

Extract

Once you understand criterion ranges, everything else about /Data Query is easy! Extract, copies database records which satisfy the criteria from the input range to the output range. Figure 23.13 shows how the output ranges displays after extracting all employees who live in New Hampshire.

BEWARE ***The Output Range is Cleared First***

Before Extract does its thing, it clears the output range. *This is done even if no records match the criteria.* What is cleared depends on how you defined the output range. If you defined it simply as the top row, *all cells to the end of the worksheet in those columns, below the headers, are cleared.* If you defined the output range with multiple rows, *only cells in the output range, below the headers, are cleared.* 1-2-3 does this so that if you ask several questions of the database, records which passed the first time don't stick around the second time.

```
E4: "DATE-HIRED                                                        POINT
Enter label range: A4..E4

          A             B             C             D           E           F
  1                                   ACME WIDGET, INC.
  2                                   SALES EMPLOYEES
  3
  4  EMPLOYEE          SALARY        STATE          SALES DATE-HIRED
  5  Smith            $25,000          MA        $95,000   05-Aug-82
  6  Brown            $30,000          MA       $150,000   05-Jan-83
  7  Warren           $35,000          MA       $210,000   01-Jun-83
  8  Wheatley         $15,000          NH       $125,000   05-Nov-82
  9  White            $40,000          NH       $237,100   03-Mar-83
 10
 11  EMPLOYEE
 12  ~W*
 13
 14  EMPLOYEE      DATE-HIRED
 15
 16
 17
 18
 19
```

Figure 23.12 Use of /Range Name Labels Down

This is what you would want. Unfortunately, in return for clearing the range, you can lose valuable data. So be careful.

HOW TO: Print Extracted Records

You cannot print records from the input range, based on the criterion range. You *must* do /Data Query Extract, extracting the records, and then use /Print to define the print range as the /Data Query output range.

Unique

Unique operates similarly to Extract. However, Unique does not copy duplicates to the output range.

An interesting application of Unique is to obtain unique values in a column, such as the names of all your customers. If your database contains orders, it's likely several orders are from the same customer. To find the names of your customers, define the input range as consisting only of that column,

```
A14: 'EMPLOYEE                                                    READY

          A          B          C          D          E          F
 1                           ACME WIDGET, INC.
 2                            SALES EMPLOYEES
 3
 4  EMPLOYEE        SALARY      STATE        SALES  DATE-HIRED
 5  Smith          $25,000         MA      $95,000   05-Aug-82
 6  Brown          $30,000         MA     $150,000   05-Jan-83
 7  Warren         $35,000         MA     $210,000   01-Jun-83
 8  Wheatley       $15,000         NH     $125,000   05-Nov-82
 9  White          $40,000         NH     $237,100   03-Mar-83
10
11  STATE
12  NH
13
14  EMPLOYEE    DATE-HIRED      STATE
15  Wheatley     05-Nov-82         NH
16  White        03-Mar-83         NH
17
18
19
```

Figure 23.13 Extracting Employees Who Live in New Hampshire

the criterion range as blank (to match all records), and use Unique to copy only unique entries to the output range.

Delete

With Delete, you delete records in the input range which match the criteria in the criterion range. Delete is good for eliminating inactive customers from your database, or for deleting records of personnel who have left the company.

BEWARE ***You Cannot Restore the Deleted Records***

Before you do the Delete, make sure you really mean it. You could do a /File Save before deleting the records, so that you have a way of restoring the database to its former state. Or, you could do an Extract first, look at the output range, which contains the records to be deleted, and decide whether or not you want to delete the records.

1-2-3 realizes the seriousness of Delete. Before it does the delete, 1-2-3 asks you to confirm the operation. Before you confirm, make sure it's what you want to do.

Reset

Reset makes 1-2-3 forget about all /Data Query specifications—the input range, the criterion range, the output range, and the last operation. Reset is useful if you have more than one database in your spreadsheet, but is used rarely.

THE DATABASE STATISTICAL FUNCTIONS

The database statistical functions @DSUM, @DAVG, @DMIN, @DMAX, @DSTD, and @DVAR, let you do statistics on databases. The syntax is as follows:

```
@Dfunction(input-range,column-offset,criterion-range)
```

The column-offset is the column number (starting from 0, as the first column) on which the database statistics are to be computed. These functions resemble the statistical functions, such as @SUM, that you have seen before. The difference is that the database statistical functions produce statistics for databases, rather than for cell ranges. The input range and the criterion range are set up exactly as with /Data Query.

For example, instead of producing statistics for all employees, you can produce statistics for all employees who pass a criterion (such as living in New Hampshire). Figure 23.14 shows the result of using the @D functions to do this.

Now you are a 1-2-3 database expert. In fact, you should now understand all the 1-2-3 commands, as well as the Lotus-supplied programs which support 1-2-3. You've eaten your 1-2-3 meal. This would be a good time to do the Lotus tutorial disk program lessons. They should be much clearer!

But wait! Dessert's yet to come! You can automate all of this, using macros. This is the subject of the last chapter.

```
D14: (C0) @DSUM($A$4..$E$9,3,$,  1..$A$12)                READY
_
```

	A	B	C	D	E	F
1			ACME WIDGET, INC.			
2			SALES EMPLOYEES			
3						
4	EMPLOYEE	SALARY	STATE	SALES	DATE-HIRED	
5	Smith	$25,000	MA	$95,000	05-Aug-82	
6	Brown	$30,000	MA	$150,000	05-Jan-83	
7	Warren	$35,000	MA	$210,000	01-Jun-83	
8	Wheatley	$15,000	NH	$125,000	05-Nov-82	
9	White	$40,000	NH	$237,100	03-Mar-83	
10						
11	STATE					
12	NH					
13						
14	Total Sales:	$362,100				
15	Average Sales:	$181,050				
16	Maximum Sales:	$237,100				
17	Minimum Sales:	$95,000				
18						
19						
20						

Figure 23.14 Using Database Statistical Functions

PART VII

An Introduction to Macros

WHAT ARE MACROS FOR?

Now that you understand the 1-2-3 commands, you can automate 1-2-3 use with keyboard macros to make 1-2-3 remember what you want it to do. Then, instead of having to remember which 1-2-3 commands to use, you simply press two keys, the [ALT] key combined with a letter, and 1-2-3 can do tens, hundreds, even thousands of keystrokes. These keystrokes could be 1-2-3 commands. They could be data that you would enter in the worksheet. They could be function keys. You can make 1-2-3 behave like a genie, your wish becoming its command.

There are three major uses for macros:

1. To save keystrokes, as an alternative to typing. The simplest macros are those in which you tell 1-2-3 which keystrokes you want entered. You can set up a macro so that, rather than entering the keystrokes, 1-2-3 will do the typing. That's why Lotus Development Corporation called keyboard macros the *typing alternative*
2. To create your own menus. You can create menus which behave like 1-2-3 menus. Your menus present a list of choices in the control panel, with a longer explanation of the highlighted choice in the row below it. You select from the menu in the same way as you would from a regular 1-2-3 menu. You can either type the first letter of the option, or use [LEFT], [RIGHT], [HOME], or [END] to highlight your choice, and then press [ENTER] to confirm it. The difference, of course, is that, they're your choices, rather than 1-2-3s.
3. To create programs. The macro language contains commands (called /X commands) which can be used to write simple programs. The commands contain the basic elements of a programming language—an if statement, a goto statement, a pause statement to get input from the user, two assignment statements to ask the user to enter a label or a value, and a method of invoking a subroutine. These are not, by any stretch of the imagination, a full programming language, such as BASIC or PASCAL. However, it is possible to write sophisticated applications using macros.

Chapter 24 introduces you to these capabilities. At the end of the chapter, you should feel comfortable creating macros to make 1-2-3 remember your keystrokes, and creating menus. You should also understand the capabilities of the /X programming commands. However, unless you have previous programming experience, you will need a lot of practice and guidance before you master programming techniques. Since this book is about 1-2-3, rather than how to write a computer program, this is beyond the scope of this book.

CHAPTER 24

Using Keyboard Macros to Automate 1-2-3 Operations

WHAT ARE MACROS?

Macros are, like almost everything else in 1-2-3, part of the worksheet. Macros are stored as keystroke entries in cells, down a column, by using special macro notation in cells. The entries are stored as labels.

After you have entered the keys in macro notation, you tell 1-2-3 where at what cell to start reading the entries. 1-2-3 will keep reading the keystrokes stored in the cells, downwards, until it finds an erased cell. At that point, the macro ends.

You start a macro by pressing two keys, the [ALT] key, combined with a letter of the alphabet. You're, in effect, creating your own function keys. 1-2-3 then does whatever you told it to do.

Since macros are labels, it's easy to change them. Simply use [F2/EDIT] and change the label! If you start the macro, the changed macro will execute.

BEWARE ***Enter the Macro in Cells Away from the Data in the Worksheet***

Since the cells in the macro are part of the worksheet, they can be affected by commands inside the macro. As an extreme example, if you tell 1-2-3 to do a /File Retrieve, 1-2-3 will retrieve the new worksheet file into RAM—and erase the macro! Other commands, such as /Move, /Copy, and /Worksheet Insert, can also change the contents of cells in a macro. So put the macro commands in a part of the worksheet that you know will not be changed by the commands in the macro.

I like to place cells containing macro commands in a column starting to the right of the last column of worksheet data. This would be a separate area of the worksheet (independent of the worksheet data, database ranges, table ranges, and so on). I also like to use /Range Name Create, creating a cell range called MACROS, so that at any time I can use [F5/GOTO] to go to the macro area. Of course, since macros are part of the worksheet, they must fit in the active worksheet. The longer your macros, the less memory you can use for your worksheet data, or for any other parts of the worksheet you may have defined.

CREATING A SIMPLE MACRO

Any of the HOW TOs can be automated using macros. For example, let's create a macro which creates column headings in month-year format (Jan-84,

Feb-84, and so on), in the cell range B3..K3, as you did in Chapter 19. You used **/Data Fill**, starting the fill range with @DATE(84,1,1) (for January 1, 1984). You used 31 as the step value (to make sure the month changed in the next cell) and 99999 as the stop value (to make sure you filled the range). Finally, to display the cell range with dates, the cell range was formatted to (D3) format.

This is quite a bit to remember. By creating a macro, rather than having to remember all this, you press two keys simultaneously ([ALT], combined with a letter), and 1-2-3 would do the rest. The process is simple.

Do the keystrokes yourself, recording them as you go. Make sure the sequence of keystrokes works as you want. In the beginning, you might want to write the sequence on a piece of paper. As you become more skilled in writing macros, you'll probably find that you won't need to do this. Until that time, however, it's good to jot the keystrokes down as you press them.

In our example, the keystrokes are:

`/DFB3..K3[ENTER]`	Use /Data Fill, specifying fill range
`@DATE(84,1,1)[ENTER]`	Start value is January 1, 1984
`31[ENTER]`	Increment is 31
`99999[ENTER]`	Stop value is 99999 (to fill range)
`/RFD3B3..K3[ENTER]`	Format the range to (D3) format

Find an empty columnar cell range to store the labels. Find an empty columnar cell range. Suppose you are not using Column N to store worksheet information. You can use Column N to enter this macro. Starting at N1, enter these keystrokes in *macro language*, using the keystrokes as 1-2-3 expects them. These are labels, entered as follows:

`'/DFB3..K3~`	(in Cell N1)
`'@DATE(84,1,1)~`	(in Cell N2)
`'31~`	(in Cell N3)
`'99999~`	(in Cell N4)
`'/RFD3B3..K3~`	(in Cell N5)

Be sure Cell N6 is erased!

The worksheet displays as follows:

```
         N                 O
  1  /DFB3..K3~
  2  @DATE(84,1,1)~
  3  31~
  4  99999~
  5  /RFD3B3..K3~
```

Figure 24.1

Note the use of the tilde character (~) to indcate pressing [ENTER] in a macro.

Note the use of the label prefix. For Cells N1 and N5, start with a label prefix because you must store the keystrokes as labels. If you enter the slash (/) first, 1-2-3 would actually start doing the keystrokes, rather than storing them in the cell. For Cells N2, N3, and N4, enter the tilde (~) to indicate pressing [ENTER]. Cell N6 must be empty to tell 1-2-3 to stop reading keystrokes. If Cell N6 was not empty the macro would continue. Forgetting to specify an end to a macro is one of the most common BEWAREs in coding macros.

Create a range name to designate the area containing the macro keystrokes. Use /Range Name Create, creating a range name consisting of a backslash (\) followed by a letter. Since you'll use [ALT]A to invoke the macro, the range name must be **\A**. Type the following:

/RNC\A[ENTER]	Create the range name \A
N1..N5[ENTER]	The keystrokes are stored at N1..N5

That's it! To run the macro, and create the headings, simply press the following keys at the same time:

[ALT]A	Press [ALT] and A simultaneously

Now wasn't that simpler than remembering all those commands?

To save the macro for future use, save the worksheet file. Macros are simply labels entered into a worksheet, with special range names which point to the labels. 1-2-3 remembers labels and range names when it saves the worksheet file. Since macros are labels, using /File Save will save the macro commands, along with the rest of the worksheet.

REFERENCING KEYS IN A MACRO

Keys used in macros, such as the function keys and the pointer-movement keys, are enclosed in braces { }. Upper and lower case can be used interchangeably within key names (i.e., {pgup} is the same same as {PgUp}). The following keys can be used in macros.

Control and Editing Keys

Key Name	How Referenced in Macro
[ENTER]	~
[ESC]	{Esc}
[BACKSPACE]	{BS}
[DEL]	{Del}
Pointer-Movement Keys	
[UP]	{Up}
[DOWN]	{Down}

[LEFT]	{Left}
[RIGHT]	{Right}
[HOME]	{Home}
[END]	{End}
[PGUP]	{PgUp}
[PGDN]	{PgDn}
Function Keys	
[F2/EDIT]	{Edit}
[F3/NAME]	{Name}
[F4/ABS]	{Abs}
[F5/GOTO]	{GoTo}
[F6/WINDOW]	{Window}
[F7/QUERY]	{Query}
[F8/TABLE]	{Table}
[F9/CALC]	{Calc}
[F10/GRAPH]	{Graph}

The following keys cannot be used in macros.

[CTRL]
[ALT]
[NUM LOCK]
[SCROLL LOCK]
[CAPS LOCK]
[SHIFT]
[PRTSC]
[TAB]
[F1/HELP]

In addition, you cannot code the brace characters { } as part of a label, i.e. you cannot code a macro to create a macro. You cannot code the tilde (~) in a macro, because 1-2-3 will interpret the tilde as meaning [ENTER].

SOME BEWARES

Writing macros is easy, once you get in the swing of things. However, at first, you may find some problems. Here are the most common problems I have seen in writing macros:

Too many (or too few) tildes. You code a tilde (~) to mean [ENTER] in a macro. It's easy to code either too many or too few of them! 1-2-3 is not always consistent on when [ENTER] is required and when [ENTER] is assumed. Even in the same command, for certain options, [ENTER] is required; for others, it is not. For example, /Range Format Currency assumes a default of 2 decimal positions, but requires you to press [ENTER] to confirm. /Range Format Date, on the other hand, makes no assumption about which of the 3 date formats you need, and does not require you to press [ENTER] to confirm. You need a tilde for the first; you don't need it for the second. Coding the incorrect number of tildes can produce some confusing results. So, as you are writing the keystrokes, make sure you include all the times you press [ENTER] and use a tilde in the macro.

Starting a cell entry with a slash (/). You cannot start a label entry with a slash, because this will invoke the 1-2-3 command menu. You must start this entry with a label-prefix.

Entering spaces in a macro. Spaces are legitimate characters in a macro. Otherwise, you couldn't create a column heading such as "1984 SALES" in a macro. If you inadvertently press [SPACE] while you are entering a macro, the space will be interpreted. This is fine if that's your intention; it's not so fine if it isn't.

Entering a quoted label. If the first character in a cell is a label-prefix such as a double quote, when the macro is executed that character is ignored. To enter a label which *starts* with a label-prefix (for example, if you wanted to label your worksheet "1984 SALES", and to include the double quotes), you must enter a label prefix as the *first* character, and the double-quote as the *second* character, as follows:

```
'"1984 SALES"
```

You must enter the label prefix first. The label prefix is ignored. The second character, the double quote, is interpreted as the first character of the label.

HOW TO: Troubleshoot Problems in a Macro

If the macro is not executing as you would like, you can "single step" through it, keystroke by keystroke. Normal macro processing is so fast that you cannot see the keystrokes in the control panel as they are being executed. However, you can slow 1-2-3 down by pressing [ALT]-[F1/HELP] before you invoke the macro.

If you do this, instead of processing the entire set of keystrokes, the macro processes one keystroke at a time. You make the macro process the next keystroke by pressing [SPACE], or any key on the typewriter keyboard. You are running the macro in slow motion so that you can see the problem. When the problem occurs (it's probably one of the problems I discussed), press [CTRL]-[BREAK] to stop the macro, and edit the cell containing the erroneous label. Then, run the macro again. This process is called *stepping*; if it is active, the STEP indicator appears at the top-right. Once the macro is correct, press [ALT]-[F1/HELP] again to return to normal, fast-paced, macro processing.

WRITING YOUR OWN MENUS WITH MACROS

You use menus to tie worksheets together; for example, if you want (or you want someone else) to choose a worksheet from a list of worksheets. Perhaps you have personnel, inventory, and cash flow worksheets, and you want to display a menu of choices. For this purpose, a menu is ideal.

A menu is defined in a cell range of 2 rows by (at most) 8 columns. The first row is a list of choices; the second row is an explanation. Here's an example of a simple menu, where different types of information are stored in different worksheets.

Option	Explanation
Personnel	Enter personnel information
Inventory	Update inventory worksheet
Cash-flow	Update cash flow projections
Exit	Exit from 1-2-3

You should include an option to exit from the menu because the user will eventually be finished using the options on the menu.

Start with a blank worksheet and define the menu options in the cell range A3..D4. Type the four options in Row 3, as follows:

`Personnel`	In Cell A3
`Inventory`	In Cell B3
`Cash-flow`	In Cell C3
`Exit`	In Cell D3

and the explanations in Row 4, as follows:

`Enter personnel information`	In Cell A4
`Update inventory worksheet`	In Cell B4
`Update cash flow projections`	In Cell C4
`Exit from 1-2-3`	In Cell D4

Your worksheet should display as follows:

```
          A          B          C          D          E
 3 | PersonnelInventoryCash-flowExit
 4 | Enter perUpdate inUpdate caExit from 1-2-3ions
```

Figure 24.2

Don't worry about the labels running into each other. The information is all there; the confusing display is just due to the way 1-2-3 displays long labels. The cell range A3..D4 now contains the menu. It now remains for us to tell 1-2-3 where the menu starts.

The **/XM** (process menu) command is a special macro command to create a menu. Since the menu is in Cell A3, create a range name, telling 1-2-3 (and ourselves) where the menu begins. Type the following:

/RNCMENU[ENTER]A3[ENTER]	Define range name called MENU at A3

In an unused cell, use **/XM** to start menu processing. In Cell A10, type the following:

'/XMMENU~	Process the menu called MENU

Now, create the *macro*, which points to the /XM command, which in turn instructs 1-2-3 to process the menu. Call the macro \A. Type the following:

/RNC\A[ENTER]A10[ENTER]	Create macro called \A at A10

You have now coded a 1-2-3 menu. Press **[ALT]A** to see it.

This menu operates like all 1-2-3 menus, with some minor variations. Since one way of specifying a menu option is to type the first character of the option, you should make each option start with a different character. This is, by the way, true for all 1-2-3 menus.

At this point, you have defined a menu in a macro, but you haven't specified what will happen after the choice is made. Read on and find out.

Processing a Menu Option

Think of a menu as a series of macros in different columns. A menu used by **/XM** can contain up to 8 options. You cannot, by the way, reproduce the 1-2-3 main menu using **/XM** since the 1-2-3 main menu has *nine* options. By selecting an option, you tell 1-2-3 which column to look at for further macro processing. Enter the macro keystrokes in the column corresponding to the menu choice. The macro starts at the third row, relative to the beginning of the menu, in that column. In our example, this is Row 5. To retrieve the file PERSONNEL.WKS when selecting Personnel, INVENTORY.WKS when selecting Inventory, CASHFLOW.WKS when selecting Cash-flow, and to quit 1-2-3 when selecting Exit, type the following:

'/FRpersonnel~	(In Cell A5)
'/FRinventory~	(In Cell B5)
'/FRcashflow~	(In Cell C5)
'/QY~	(In Cell D5)

If you press **[ALT]A** to display the menu and then **P** to select the Personnel option, the PERSONNEL.WKS file is retrieved. PERSONNEL option is in Column A; therefore, 1-2-3 starts processing the macro at A5 and attempts to retrieve the PERSONNEL.WKS worksheet using /File Retrieve. (Remember the BEWARE. This macro will be erased when PERSONNEL.WKS is retrieved.) If you had pressed **I**, you would have retrieved the INVENTORY.WKS worksheet; **C** would have retrieved the CASHFLOW.WKS worksheet. And finally, if you had pressed **E**, you would have quit 1-2-3.

Before processing this menu, you should save the file. Use /File Save, and your menu will be stored, along with the rest of your worksheet information.

If your menu range is invalid (/XM points to a cell range which contains more than 8 entries on the top row, or to an erased cell), the Illegal menu error message displays.

HOW TO: Link Menus Together

The actual syntax of /XM is as follows:

```
/XMstart-of-menu-range~what-to-do-if-[ESC]-pressed~
```

Normally, pressing [ESC] returns you to a previous menu, or back to READY mode. With /XM you can specify what should happen if the user presses [ESC]. For example, suppose you wanted to link menus together because you could not fit all the options on one menu. Define MENU2 as another menu, which is linked from MENU.

If the /XM command to process MENU2 is as follows:

```
/XMMENU2~MENU1~
```

you are telling 1-2-3 to process MENU2. However, if the user presses [ESC], process MENU1. You can define an entire series of menus (MENU, MENU2, MENU3, and so on), and the user can press [ESC] to get to the previous menu—just like in 1-2-3 menus!

PROGRAMMING WITH MACROS

In addition to the /XM command to process a menu, you can do some programming using /XI, {?}, /XG, /XQ, /XL, /XN, /XC, and /XR. These commands will be discussed in this section. If you have used programming languages such as BASIC, PASCAL, or COBOL, these commands should be familiar. If you have not programmed before, you'll probably need some practice before the commands become familiar to you.

Decision Processing

With /XI, the if test command, can change the way the macro executes based on a condition. The syntax of /XI is:

```
/XIexpression~what-to-do-if-expression-is-TRUE~
```

/XI is frequently used with {?}. {?} pauses the macro and allows the user to enter information. After the information is tested as long as it can be evaluated to a value, the macro can use /XI to make a decision.

To show how **/XI** works, create the following macro, which will pause. If the user enters the number 1, the macro will list worksheet files in the directory, using **/File List Worksheet**. If the user enters anything else, the macro ends. Type the following:

```
'{GoTo}A30~             In Cell B20
'{?}~                   In Cell B21
'/XIA30=1~/FLW~         In Cell B22
```

To create the macro, create a range name called \B at Cell B20, as follows:

```
/RNC\B[ENTER]B20[ENTER]          Create range name \B at B20
```

If you press **[ALT]B** the macro will first, go to Cell A30, the effect of using **[F5/GOTO]** in the first label in the macro. Then, the macro will pause, the effect of the {?} in the second label. Finally, the macro will test whether the value in Cell A30 is a 1, the **/XI** condition. If it is, the macro will list the worksheet files; if it isn't, the macro ends.

Press **[ALT]B**, enter a 1 when the macro pauses, and the worksheet file names will list. Press any key to clear the worksheet files. Then press **[ALT]B** again and enter a number other than 1. This time, the worksheet files will not list, showing that the **/XI** condition was not satisfied.

BEWARE ***/XI Cannot Test for Labels in an Expression***

You cannot code the following:

```
/XIA30="LIST"~/FLW~
```

/XI can only test for *values* in an expression. All labels evaluate to 0.

Branching and Quitting

/XG (branch to a cell containing macro commands) lets you control where the next cell containing macro commands is to be found. **/XQ** lets you end a macro before 1-2-3 encounters a blank cell.

The syntax of **/XG** is as follows:

```
/XGcell-address~
```

Within a macro, you can go to another cell containing macro commands. The macro below simply branches to cell A73, which lists worksheet files. Try this with the following macro:

```
'/XGA80~        (In Cell A73)
'/FLW           (In Cell A80)
```

Then create a range name called \C, pointing to Cell A73, by typing the following:

/RNC\C[ENTER]A73[ENTER] \C starts at A73

Now press [ALT]C. The worksheet files display. This occurred because the macro started in A73, but *branched* to A80 to read additional keystrokes, in this case /File List Worksheet.

/XQ is used to end a macro even if the macro has not finished. Enter the following labels:

'/XQ	(In Cell A90)
'/FLW	(In Cell A91)

Create a range name called \D, starting at A90, as follows:

/RNC\D[ENTER]A90[ENTER] \D starts at A90

Press [ALT]D. The files do not list because the /XQ command halted macro processing. The macro never processed the command in Cell A91; it quit at Cell A90.

BEWARE ***You Should Use Range Names with /X Macros***

As often as possible, you should use range names with /X macros. Macros are stored as labels; if the cell which you reference is relocated, the reference to it in the /X command is not adjusted. You shouldn't expect this adjustment to occur: 1-2-3 cannot tell whether a label is part of a macro or not. Would you really want a label like "JANUARY 1984 SALES" adjusted? If you use /Range Name Create to name a cell location for /XG, however, the range names are adjusted if a cell is moved or copied. Therefore, instead of coding /XGB8~ to go to a location, use /Range Name Create, to create a named range called SALES. If you want the macro to go to Cell B8, code /XGSALES~. Since 1-2-3 does adjust range names, SALES will point to the new location if the Cell B8 is relocated.

Coding Subroutines

/XC (call subroutine) and /XR (return from subroutine) provide a method for coding primitive subroutine calls. A subroutine is a set of programming statements done repeatedly. Subroutines are a standard part of a programming language. You usually *call* a subroutine. The subroutine then processes; when it finishes, it *returns* to the point from which it was called. A subroutine call is like a branch in a program, except that the program remembers the return address.

The syntax of /XC is as follows:

```
/XCcell-address~
```

The syntax of **/XR** is simply **/XR** to return to the cell immediately below the cell containing the /XC command.

Enter the following macro to illustrate **/XC** and **/XR** subroutine calls.

```
'/XCA119~          (In Cell A110)
'/FLP              (In Cell A111)
```

The subroutine is in A119..A120. Type the following in these cells:

```
'/FLW              (In Cell A119)
'/XR               (In Cell A120)
```

Now create a range name \E, pointing to A110 for starting macro execution, as follows:

```
/RNC\E[ENTER]A110[ENTER]      \E starts at A110
```

Press **[ALT]E**. The macro starts in A110, calls the subroutine in A119, which does the **/File List Worksheet**. After you press any key to clear the display, the macro returns (the /XR in A120 does that), and processing resumes at A111, to execute the **/File List Printer**, listing print files.

Subroutines are useful for executing parts of macro commands which are used by more than one macro.

Requesting Labels or Values

/XL and **/XN** are used to request labels or values from the user. You can create a macro to cause 1-2-3 to pause, place a message of up to 39 characters in the control panel, and wait for the user to enter either a label for **/XL**, or a number for **/XN**. The syntax of **/XL** is as follows:

```
/XLmessage~cell-address~
```

The format of **/XN** is as follows:

```
/XNmessage~cell-address~
```

/XL and **/XN** are almost identical in operation. The only difference is that whereas **/XL** will store a label into the cell-address, **/XN** will store a value. With **/XN**, *you cannot enter a label into the cell*. If you try, 1-2-3 beeps.

Try the following macro to see how **/XL** and **/XN** work. Type the following:

```
'/XLlabel please~B134~       (In Cell A130)
'/XNnumber please~B135~      (In Cell A131)
```

Enter the following to create a range name called \F, at A130, to indicate where the macro is to begin processing.

/RNC\F[ENTER]A130[ENTER] \F starts at Cell A130

Press **ALT]F**. The macro will pause with the prompt label please, waiting for you to enter a label. The response will be stored as a label in Cell B134.

After you enter the label, the macro pauses with the prompt number please. Your response is stored in B135 as a value. If you do not enter a valid number, 1-2-3 beeps.

The messages for /XL and /XN should be meaningful, so you can get the correct type of information. For example, if you want the user to enter sales for January, a good /XN message would be Enter January sales:

HOW TO: Automatically Execute a Macro

In addition to the 26 macros (\A to \Z), you can define a special macro (\0) which is invoked *automatically* when a worksheet is loaded (using **/File Retrieve**. In this way, rather than being required to press **[ALT]** and a letter, our menu would automatically display when the file was retrieved. You would then simply select from the menu and go.

HOW TO: Automatically Retrieve a File When You Enter 1-2-3

In addition to the \0 macro, you can automate 1-2-3 one step further. When you enter 1-2-3, 1-2-3 looks in your directory for a worksheet file called AUTO123.WKS. If 1-2-3 finds this worksheet, it automatically retrieves it, as if you had used **/File Retrieve**.

Why is this powerful? If your menu macro was saved in the AUTO123.WKS file, with the range name of \0, *the menu would display as soon as you entered 1-2-3!* You need not retrieve any files—the menu is staring at you. This technique is especially useful if people with limited 1-2-3 knowledge are going to use your worksheets. In this way, they don't have to become 1-2-3 experts (as you are by now) in order to use the worksheets.

CONCLUSION: YOU'RE READY TO BE CREATIVE WITH 1-2-3

You've gone all the way from a basic description of the PC and PC-DOS, to the basic 1-2-3 worksheet commands, to the advanced commands, and finally, to keyboard macros. 1-2-3 is such a powerful program that you can be creative at whatever level you are comfortable. If you want to create simple worksheets only, you can be creative at that level. If you want to write sophisticated models, you can add to your base of knowledge. If you want to become a power user of 1-2-3, you can customize the applications with macros.

One final note. I have worked extensively with Lotus' Symphony program, and I am excited by what I have seen. Many of the BEWAREs of 1-2-3 have been corrected in Symphony. My next book will be a guide to Symphony directed to 1-2-3 users, to be published by Brady. Not only does Symphony improve on 1-2-3's spreadsheet capabilities, Symphony also provides word processing, form-oriented database management, and telecommunications capabilities not available in 1-2-3.

It's now up to you. I hope I've lit up the path for you. Good luck, and happy problem solving!

Appendix

Documentation for the Optional Accompanying Diskette

Description

The optional accompanying diskette for *Lotus 1-2-3 Self-Taught* is available as a supplement to this book. It contains a series of 1-2-3 worksheets, 33 in all, tied together by menus which show, step by step, examples of many 1-2-3 commands. Two graph picture files, which you can use to experiment with PrintGraph, are also included and described.

The worksheets are intended to reinforce the concepts introduced in this book, providing you with step-by-step examples of many of the 1-2-3 commands. In addition to the commonly used commands, several powerful but infrequently used commands, such as /Data Table, /Data Distribution, and /Range Justify, are illustrated. For advanced users (or those who want to become advanced users) the section on macros should get you comfortable with the power of the macro language.

How You Can Use These Worksheets

Since these worksheets are intended as a tutorial, you can use then to strengthen your understanding of 1-2-3. If you train others in 1-2-3 use, you can customize the examples to meet the learning requirements of your students.

Since these worksheets are ordinary 1-2-3 .WKS files, you can incorporate them without alteration into your own applications. If your applications don't quite fit, you can customize the worksheets to your liking.

I included common applications, such as consolidation of worksheets and use of the financial functions for investment analysis. If you need to do these applications, the worksheets should help you get started.

You may find the techniques I used in developing the tutorial useful. If you understand macros they are there for you to read. I used macros to tie the worksheets together by menus. I used, additionally, a \0 macro in an AUTO123.WKS worksheet file. This causes the initial menu to display automatically when you enter 1-2-3 (if you are using Version 1A of 1-2-3). As a further convenience, you can restart any worksheet demonstration by pressing [ALT]A.

Installing the Tutorial Worksheets

The tutorial worksheets are supplied on one 5 1/4" double-sided, double-density diskette, formatted with PC-DOS Version 1.1. The diskette is readable on an IBM PC or PC/XT running either PC-DOS Versions 1.1, 2.0, or 2.1. Since the diskette contains only data files, it should be readable on virtually all IBM PC compatible machines. The operating rule is: if your PC compatible can read data files written by PC-DOS, it can read the diskette.

The installation process is as follows:

1. Use PC-DOS to boot your PC. If you do not know how to do this, refer to Chapter 3.
2. Be sure your copy of 1-2-3 has been properly configured for your hardware. If you do not know how to do this, refer to Chapter 4.
3. If you are storing 1-2-3 data files on diskette, insert the tutorial diskette in the diskette drive used for these files, and close the drive door.

If you are storing 1-2-3 data files on a hard disk using PC-DOS Version 2, you must copy the files on the diskette to 1-2-3's default directory. Insert the diskette into the A-drive and close the drive door. If your data files are stored in a directory called \LOTUS type the following:

`A>C:[ENTER]`	Switch to the C-drive
`C>CD \LOTUS[ENTER]`	Change directory to \LOTUS
`C>COPY A:*.*[ENTER]`	Copy the files to \LOTUS

These commands will cause the files on the diskette to be copied into the \LOTUS directory.

You might consider setting up a separate directory for the tutorial worksheet. In this way, the tutorial worksheet files will be kept separate from your business-related worksheets. If you are using PC-DOS Version 2 and wish to store the files in a directory called \TUTOR, type the following:

`C>MKDIR \TUTOR[ENTER]`	Create a directory called \TUTOR
`C>CD \TUTOR[ENTER]`	Make \TUTOR the current directory
`C>COPY A:*.*[ENTER]`	Copy the files to \TUTOR

Running the Tutorial Worksheets

If you are using Version 1A of 1-2-3, and the tutorial worksheet files have been installed in 1-2-3's default disk directory, the initial menu should display. The diskette contains an AUTO123.WKS file with a \0 macro, causing the menu to display automatically. From there, select from the menu options.

If the the initial menu does not display, one of the following is probably the cause:

1. You are using Version 1 of 1-2-3. Version 1 of 1-2-3 does not support automatic macro execution. You can still run the tutorial, however. After entering 1-2-3, issue the following commands:

/FRauto123[ENTER]	retrieve the AUTO123.WKS file
[ALT]A	press [ALT]A to start the menu

From there, you can select a menu choice. However, to start the demonstration of a particular function, you must press [ALT]A after you have retrieved the file. All the examples, with the exception of the illustration of the /XL and /XN macros, will run in Version 1.

2. 1-2-3 cannot locate the directory containing the tutorial worksheet files. Use /File Directory to display the directory in which 1-2-3 thinks the files are stored. If this is not the directory where your files are stored, use /Worksheet Global Default Directory to change the directory to point to the files. Then, use /Worksheet Global Default Update to update 1-2-3's configuration file so that the next time you run 1-2-3, the menu will display.

While you are using the worksheets, make sure that the SCROLL, NUM, and CAPS indicators, on the last row of the display, are off. Refer to Chapter 7 if you are not sure of the meaning of these indicators.

The Menu Options

The examples are organized in groups, accessible from the initial menu. These groups are: elementary worksheet skills, advanced worksheet skills, graphics, information management, and an introduction to the macro language. The examples are grouped as follows:

ELEMENTARY WORKSHEET SKILLS

- Moving around the worksheet
- Entering labels
- Making changes to cells
- Entering values
- Saving and retrieving disk files
- Using cell ranges in formulas
- Numeric formats
- Controlling the worksheet display
- Copying cell ranges
- Inserting and deleting rows
- Printing the worksheet

ADVANCED WORKSHEET SKILLS

- Statistical functions
- Financial functions

- Table lookup functions
- Sharing other 1-2-3 worksheet data files
- Creating "what if" tables
- Using /Data Distribution
- Creating memos with /Range Justify

GRAPHICS

- Specifying line, bar, stacked-bar, pie, and XY graphs
- Creating graph picture files for PrintGraph
- Specifying titles
- Specifying horizontal and vertical grid lines
- Formatting the graph scales

INFORMATION MANAGEMENT

- Defining the input, criterion, and output ranges
- Sorting records in a 1-2-3 database
- The /Data Query functions

AN INTRODUCTION TO THE MACRO LANGUAGE

- Using macros to save keystrokes
- Creating a menu using /XM
- The /X programming functions
- Coding If Tests in Macros
- Coding Branch Statements
- Requesting User Input
- Requesting Label or Value Input

Index

Special Characters and Commands

A

B

I

J

K

L

M

N

O

P

About the Author

A computer consultant, Ira Krakow has had over 10 years of professional experience in a variety of computer software disciplines—programming, database management systems design, user training and seminar development, and technical writing. He has worked with all types of users, from computer novices to seasoned systems designers, on all types of computer systems, from microcomputers such as the IBM PC to large mainframe systems.

Before starting his consulting company, Ira was National Technical Manager for EPS, Inc., the vendor of a series of powerful decision support software products. He also was a database designer, technical writer, and manager of software quality assurance for Wang Laboratories.

Ira has done extensive work with the IBM PC. He has taught seminars on Lotus 1-2-3, dBASEII, Multiplan, and PC-DOS. He reviews software monthly for *Business Computer Systems* magazine. And, in addition to this book, he has written *Managing Projects Using the IBM PC*, also published by Brady Communications Company, Inc.

Ira prides himself on never having taken a computer course. He learned about computers by working with them. He graduated Columbia College with a major in European history. He holds a masters degree in European history from Washington University in St. Louis, and a masters degree in mathematics education from Northeastern University.

Ira lives in Stoneham, Massachusetts with his wife, Sandra, and their two children, Laura and Sam.